# Whatever Happened to Class?

Class explains much in the differentiation of life chances and political dynamics in South Asia; scholarship from the region have contributed much to class analysis. Yet class has lost its previous centrality as a way of understanding the world and how it changes. This outcome is puzzling; new configurations of global economic forces and policy have widened gaps between classes and across sectors and regions, altered people's relations to production, and produced new state-citizen relations. Does market triumphalism or increased salience of identity politics render class irrelevant? Has rapid growth in aggregate wealth obviated long-standing questions of inequality and poverty? Explanations for what happened to class vary, from intellectual fads to global transformations of interests. The authors of articles in this book ask what is lost in the move away from class, and what South Asian experiences tell us about the limits of class analysis. Empirical chapters examine formal and informal-sector labor, social movements against genetic engineering, and politics of the "new middle class." A unifying analytical concern is specifying conditions under which interests of those disadvantaged by class systems are immobilized, diffused, coopted — or autonomously recognized and acted upon politically: the problematic transition of classes in themselves to classes for themselves.

Articles in this book were published in a thematic issue of *Critical Asian Studies* (vol. 38, number 4, 2006) and in the March 2007 issue of *Critical Asian Studies* (vol. 39, number 1).

**Rina Agarwala** is an Assistant Professor in the Department of Sociology at Johns Hopkins University. She holds a Doctor in Philosophy (Ph.D.) in sociology and demography from Princeton University, a Masters in Public Policy (M.P.P.) in political and economic development from Harvard University, and a Bachelor of Arts (B.A.) in economics and government from Cornell University. Agarwala has also worked at the United Nations Development Program (UNDP) in China, the Self-Employed Women's Association (SEWA) in India, and Women's World Banking (WWB) in New York.

**Ronald J. Herring** teaches political economy and political ecology at Cornell University, where he has held the John S. Knight Chair of International Relations and served as director of the Mario Einaudi Center for International Studies, chair of the Department of Government, and acting director of the Title VI National Resource Center for South Asia. His earliest academic interests were with land relations: *Land to the Tiller: The Political Economy of Agrarian Reform in South Asia* (Yale and Oxford University, 1983). Current work includes state property in nature, politics of genetically engineered organisms, and connections between economic development and ethnicity. See, for example, *Carrots, Sticks and Ethnic Conflict: Rethinking Development Assistance*, edited with Milton Esman (University of Michigan Press, 2001).

# WHATEVER HAPPENED TO CLASS?

## Reflections from South Asia

Edited with an introduction by
Ronald J. Herring and Rina Agarwala

Routledge
Taylor & Francis Group
LONDON AND NEW YORK

First published 2008 by Routledge
2 Park Square, Milton Park, Abingdon, Oxfordshire OX14 4RN

Simultaneously published in the USA and Canada
by Routledge
711 Third Avenue, New York, NY 10017

First issued in paperback 2016

*Routledge is an imprint of the Taylor and Francis Group, an informa business*



Typeset in the USA by BCAS, Inc.



British Library Cataloguing in Publication Data
A catalogue record for this book is available from the British Library

ISBN 13: 978-1-138-98706-7 (pbk)
ISBN 13: 978-0-415-45468-1 (hbk)

# Contents

*Abstracts* v

Introduction — Restoring Agency to Class: Puzzles from South Asia 1
*Ronald J. Herring and Rina Agarwala, guest editors*

1. On the Decline of Class Analysis in South Asian Studies 24
*Vivek Chibber*

2. Was the Indian Labor Movement Ever Co-opted? Evaluating Standard Accounts 50
*Emmanuel Teitelbaum*

3. Workers' Organizations in Pakistan: Why No Role in Formal Politics? 73
*Christopher Candland*

4. From Work to Welfare: A New Class Movement in India 91
*Rina Agarwala*

5. Middle-Class Activism and the Politics of the Informal Working Class: A Perspective on Class Relations and Civil Society in Indian Cities 109
*John Harriss*

6. Why Did "Operation Cremate Monsanto" Fail? Science and Class in India's Great Terminator-Technology Hoax 127
*Ronald J. Herring*

7. Hegemonic Aspirations: New Middle Class Politics and India's Democracy in Comparative Perspective 146
*Leela Fernandes and Patrick Heller*

*Notes* 166
*References* 185
*Contributors* 206
*Index* 208

# Abstracts

Introduction — Restoring Agency to Class: Puzzles from South Asia

*Ronald J. Herring and Rina Agarwala*

Class explains much in the differentiation of life chances and political dynamics in South Asia. Yet in the subcontinent class has lost its centrality as a way of understanding the world and how it changes. Indian intellectuals have been a major force in the eclipsing of class through discursive strategies of constructivist idealism. Formalism in social sciences finds class relations elusive and difficult to measure. Market triumphalism eclipsed concern with rehabilitation of "weaker sectors" and redressing of exploitation as measures of national success. Class analytics, however, continues to serve two critical functions: disaggregating development and explaining challenges to rules of the game. Restoring agency to class requires attention first to relations that structure choice in restricted or expansive ways. Global forces have altered people's relations to production and to one another, as have changes in the political opportunity structure, with significant effects on tactics and outcomes. Knowing how to aggregate or disaggregate classes is more complicated than ever. Nevertheless, alternative understandings of class structure are more than academic: they reflect the strategies of political actors. The difficulty for class analysis is to illuminate the conditions under which interests of those disabled by particular class systems may be inter-subjectively recognized and acted upon politically at the local and/or international levels. Appropriate and robust sociopolitical theory for this purpose is illusive, but no more so for class than for other bases of difference — caste, community, identity, gender — that likewise seek to explain transformation of locations in social structures to effective collective agency.

1. On the Decline of Class Analysis in South Asian Studies

*Vivek Chibber*

The decline of class analysis has been pervasive across the intellectual landscape in recent years. But South Asian studies stands out in the severity with which it has been hit by this phenomenon. It also is the field where the influence of post-structuralism has been most pronounced in the wake of Marxism's decline. This essay offers an explanation for both the decline of class analysis and the ascendance of post-structuralism in South Asian studies as practiced in the United States. I suggest that the decline of class theorizing was a predictable and natural result of the decline of working-class politics in the United States. But the severity of its decline in South Asian studies in particular was a symptom of its never having made much of a dent on the field in the first place. This left unchallenged the traditional, Indological approach, which was heavily oriented toward culturalism. This in turn made the field a hospitable ground for the entrance of post-structuralism, which, like mainstream Indology, not only eschews materialist analysis, but is largely hostile to class. South Asian studies is thus one of the few fields in which traditional scholars and younger ones are both able to agree on their hostility to class analysis. Finally, I argue that the decline of class is now visible in Indian universities too, and this is largely caused by the overwhelming influence that U.S. universities have come to exercise over Indian elite academic culture.

2. Was the Indian Labor Movement Ever Co-opted? Evaluating Standard Accounts

*Emmanuel Teitelbaum*

Despite its central importance to India's political and economic development, the organizational capacity of India's working class is poorly understood. Standard social scientific accounts portray the Indian working class as weakened by continual fragmentation and wholly dominated by political parties and the state. Social scientists therefore assume that the Indian working class is economically and politically inconsequential. This essay challenges these prominent misconceptions. Drawing on original survey data, government statistics, and a discussion of Indian industrial and labor law, the author shows that the Indian labor movement has been much more unified, much more contentious in the collective bargaining arena, and much more politically influential than previously assumed. The author speculates that the key reason social scientists have misjudged the strength of organized labor in India is that their assessments have relied too heavily on "key source" interviews with business, political and trade union elites, all of whom have incentives to portray workers as divided and weak.

3. Workers' Organizations in Pakistan: Why No Role in Formal Politics?

*Christopher Candland*

Why have Pakistani workers failed to transform their evident street power into sustained influence in formal politics? Throughout South Asia, worker' organizations formed alliances with political parties, political parties formed workers' organizations, and governments incorporated worker' organizations into state consultation machinery. With the exception of Pakistan, in each of the countries of South Asia, representatives at these workers organizations have become members of parliament and cabinet ministers. In India, a workers' representatives even became president. Why have workers' representatives been almost completely absent in Pakistani governments? This essay argues that Pakistan's traumatic creation — one of the twentieth century's greatest humanitarian disasters — unleashed ruling class insecurities that were unfavorable to workers' organizations. The managers of the new state demanded centralized power. Authoritarian colonial institutions were ready at hand. Pakistan's international alliance with U.S.–anticommunist alliances led to the suppression of workers' organizations and precluded their influence in formal politics. The ruling classes targeted workers' organizations. Pakistani governments ensured that workers' organizations were excluded from formal politics. Before concluding, the essay considers whether military governments are necessarily inimical to workers' organizations.

4. From Work to Welfare: A New Class Movement in India

*Rina Agarwala*

The rigidity of early class analysis and the recent demise of any type of class analytics have turned attention away from examining the growing population of informally employed workers as a class. By not examining informal workers as a class "*in* themselves," we are losing insights into how they are translating their positions into a class "*for* themselves." As a consequence, the recent literature on globalization and liberalization is increasingly concluding that the decreasing proportion of formally employed workers (and the subsequent rise in informal employment) the world over signifies a decline in all class-based organization. Such arguments have obscured our understanding of the current social dynamics of exploitation and resistance. In an attempt to begin filling this gap, this article recovers class as an important analytical tool with which to examine (1) the current relations of power between the state, employers, and the majority of India's workers, and (2) how the structures of production within which informal workers operate affect their collective action strategies. A reformulated labor movement model is offered to expose the underlying mechanisms through which informal workers translate their location in the class structure as a class "in itself" into a political group as a class "for itself." Insights into how informal workers organize can have profound implications for our understanding of changing state-labor relations as national governments attempt to liberalize their economies and simultaneously rein in their welfare functions.

5. Middle-Class Activism and the Politics of the Informal Working Class: A Perspective on Class Relations and Civil Society in Indian Cities

*John Harriss*

This article, drawing on the results of both survey research and of ethnography in Delhi, Bangalore, and Chennai, concerns the relationships between the middle class and the informal working class in Indian cities in the sphere of civil society. These relationships are shown to be very significant in the definition of the "middle class" and a critical dimension of the reproduction of class relationships. They also demonstrate that civil society should not be abstracted from the field of class relations, in the way that characterizes some contemporary arguments about the potentials of civil organization. Civil society is shown to be distinctly stratified. On the whole it is a sphere of middle class activism, and such activism is one of the defining features of the middle class. Members of the informal working class, on the other hand, are largely excluded from active participation in civil society organizations, so that increasing opportunities for political participation through civil organization may be associated with increased political inequality. The exceptions to this general rule are sometimes interlinked movements for women's rights, for the rights of informal workers, and for rights to housing — in which women from the informal working class are notably active. The issues of housing and of rights to livelihood, however, frequently bring the middle class and the informal working class into contention. Politics is often the only resource available to informal workers and their valuation of electoral democracy is to be understood in this context.

6. Why Did "Operation Cremate Monsanto" Fail? Science and Class in India's Great Terminator-Technology Hoax

*Ronald J. Herring*

Though promoted by the Government of India, and endorsed by dominant international organizations concerned with agriculture, biotechnology has produced fierce resistance and divisions. "Operation Cremate Monsanto" combined nationalist appeals, opposition to multinational capital, and rejection of genetic engineering in one integrated critique. The movement failed; Monsanto's technology spread rapidly and widely in India. The movement illustrated a larger problematic of understanding interests under conditions of rapid and complex technological change. Science continually presents new challenges to the way interests are understood by citizens and political classes that control states; the sea change in redefinitions of interests — of both individuals and states — introduced by, for example, the atmospheric science of ozone holes and climate change is archetypal, as are the internationally contentious battles in trade and property of "genetically modified organisms." Interests in biotechnology are screened by science, understandings of which are unevenly distributed. Asymmetries of knowledge and skill repertory necessary for participation in global networks of contestation create new class positions within India, and corresponding contradictions in social movements. Cultural capital matters fundamentally in differentiating classes and class interests; authenticity rents become available to some class positions but not others. Divisions matter because movements seeking environmental integrity and social justice may ultimately be weakened by egregious inaccuracies of framing, however effective the short-terms gains in dramaturgy may be.

## 7. Hegemonic Aspirations: New Middle Class Politics and India's Democracy in Comparative Perspective

*Leela Fernandes and Patrick Heller*

This article uses an analysis of the rise of India's New Middle Class (NMC) to develop a class analytics of democratic politics in India. The article locates the politics of India's democracy within the framework of comparative class analytics and integrates class analysis with the politics of caste, religion, and language. The article develops two central arguments. The first is that the dominant fraction of the middle class plays a central role in the politics of hegemony. These hegemonic politics are played out both as attempts to coordinate the interests of the dominant classes and to forge internal unity within the highly diverse fragments of the middle class. But rather than producing the classical pattern of liberal hegemony (in which the ruling bloc actively elicits the consent of subordinate classes) in India these projects have been marked by middle-class illiberalism, and most notably a distancing from lower classes. Second, we argue that the contours of the NMC can be grasped as a *class-in-practice,* that is, as a class defined by its politics and the everyday practices through which it reproduces its privileged position. Sociocultural inequalities such as caste and language are an integral part of the process of middle-class formation. We argue that the NMC is a tangible and significant phenomenon, but one whose boundaries are constantly being defined and tested. The hegemonic aspirations of the NMC have taken the form of a politics of reaction, blending market liberalism and political and social illiberalism.

❑

# Introduction

## Restoring Agency to Class: Puzzles from South Asia

Ronald J. Herring and Rina Agarwala

CLASS ANALYTICS WAS ONCE CENTRAL TO SOUTH ASIAN STUDIES, and South Asian contributions to global discourse around class were prominent. The decline of class is difficult to measure, but beyond dispute. Why has class lost, in the subcontinent and elsewhere, its importance as a way of understanding the world? Can it be that class now explains much less in the differentiation of life chances and political dynamics than previously? Has class analysis been sidelined by competing intellectual fads and political interests?

This puzzle is more pronounced when we consider that class differences across the subcontinent are changing form and magnitude, and they are becoming more politically charged with rapid growth and structural change of economies. A growing middle class is celebrated as evidence of increased opportunities. Yet since the Indian government began implementing economic reforms in 1991, per capita income differentials across states have risen, along with inequality within states. These trends have moderated the effects of economic growth on poverty reduction.[1] The postindependence ideal of a secure, protected labor force in India has been supplanted by the more typical phenomenon of capital's pursuit of cheap, flexible informal workers without state protection; the percentage of workers in the formal sector has dropped by 2 percent since 1990.[2] India's agrarian sector offers evidence of crisis and armed conflict. In April 2006, India's prime minister, Manmohan Singh, addressed chief ministers of six states affected by violent agrarian insurgency: "It would not be exaggeration to say that the problem of Naxalism is the single biggest internal security challenge ever faced by our country."[3] Ranjit Kumar Gupta, former police commissioner of Calcutta, estimated that the Naxalite movement has spread to 20 percent of India's districts (159 districts in 14 states) since it began in 1967.[4] In neighboring Nepal, Maoist rebels exercised total sovereignty over vast areas with de facto freedom to operate in virtually all rural areas by 2005.[5] Agrarian radicals in armed conflict with police and military claim to be fighting a class war, a war for a classless society.

Class analytics itself can and does evoke theological permutations among pure theorists, but the essential perspective is both straightforward and commonsensical. Though much has been made of distinguishing Marxian from Weberian class analysis, for example, both emphasize the primacy of economic assets as differentiating people across classes. Class analysis always takes the material world seriously, and empirically: it is never simply a construction or an imaginary. Class structures relations among people; these relations are critical for understanding not only life chances, but also political behavior. Authors in this collection hold to no orthodoxy. But we all agree on the asymmetric and consequential elements of class location, and thus the essentially structural embedding of class analysis. Jon Elster writes: "A class is a group of people who by virtue of what they possess are compelled to engage in the same activities if they want to make the best use of their endowments (i.e., tangible property, intangible skills, and cultural traits)."[6]

Class location for Elster predicts and explains "endowment necessitated behavior."[7] Class determines what people must do, what they have the freedom to do, what they cannot do. It structures the realm of choice. Though "choice" — whether "rational" or otherwise — dominates much of contemporary social science, a structural understanding of class illustrates why there is no choice independent of some matrix of constraints and payoffs external to the individual decision maker. Defining that choice matrix reveals a structure of freedoms, capacities, and compulsions: i.e., the class structure.

One of the many hundreds of new, chic cafes and bars that have emerged in Bombay, India, to cater to the city's growing wealthy population. (Rina Agarwala)

This structure defines relations of power; exploitation becomes a possibility missing from a choice frame of neoclassical economics. Not everything is a choice. Eric Olin Wright concisely defines exploitation as the antagonistic interdependence of material interests among actors within a set of economic relations.[8] Exploitation of a commodity — labor power — is inextricably linked to exploitation of a person possessing — and forced to sell — that commodity. The purchaser of that commodity must somehow realize more from its use than has been paid for it; this is the systemic imperative facing capital. Class theory then deflects policy from Gandhi to Ambedkar: justice is not a question of reforming the hearts and minds of propertied people, but rather a question of reducing the dependency and destitution that subject those without property to abject subordination, including the rich tapestry of humiliation and degradation implied by "caste." Obscuring class analysis contributes to thought and policy harmful to those least capable of pursuing their interests via either state or market.

Has class analysis declined because of some inherent weakness in explaining either differentiation of life chances under economic change or political responses to inequality? If so, what is class analysis missing? In our effort to recover class, we ask two central questions. First, what is lost in the move away from class? Second, if the move had to do with weaknesses of class analytics to address reality on the ground, what does experience in the subcontinent tell us about needed *refinements* and *limits* of class theory? What would it take to recover class?

A typical early morning scene in a slum in Chennai, India, where women line up at 5 A.M. to receive their daily water supply of two buckets. "Since the Indian government began implementing economic reforms in 1991, per capita income differentials across states have risen, along with inequalities within states." (Rina Agarwala)

## Whatever Happened to Class?

It seems especially odd that so obvious a tool for explaining differentiation of life chances, as well as political dynamics that have so often historically developed from moral outrage at inequality, should wither in contemporary South Asia. Some obfuscation is transparently instrumental: it is in the interest of winners in booming economies — and regimes seeking credit for growth — to emphasize aggregate gains, not class divisions. During the 2004 elections in the United States, the incumbent administration of George W. Bush strategically branded any critique of redistribution of income to the already wealthy as "inciting class war."[9] During the 2004 elections in India, the incumbent ruling party, Bharatiya Janata Party (BJP) claimed success for an aggregate "India Shining"; opposition parties tried to disaggregate the picture into winners and losers in globalization. In the dominant legitimation of global market integration, functionalist accounts held suppression of labor to be necessary for competitiveness. Class divisions were viewed as dysfunctional for national success.

Market triumphalism itself was reinforced by the demise of Soviet-style dictatorships; in a rather bizarre non sequitur, Marx was somehow rendered quaint thereby, and, with Marx, the question of class. Claims of rigid autocracies to be "state socialist," though empty by any Marxian criterion, had married repressive politics and economic disaster to nominally Marxian analysis, tainting the essentially critical nature of the latter with the oppression and inefficiency of the former. Yet, writing on Eastern Europe, David Ost concludes that in the demise of centrally planned economies, class analysis is ironically rejuvenated: "retiring class with communism...just will not do." With the transition to market society, familiar class cleavages take center stage in Eastern Europe.[10] In India, a neoliberal consensus rejected much of the aspirational Nehruvian project of a "socialistic pattern of society," and with it the centrality of redressing class dominance.[11] Over time, public discourse turned to empty aggregates without relational content: "the weaker sections," "poverty," and other obfuscations replaced the acute class analysis of early nation-building.[12] The competitive pressures of an increasingly globalized economy joined the normative calls of a diminished neoliberal state to naturalize as inevitable a perceived decline in class-based organization. National production enters a "post-fordist" era, where the producers of goods and services are not among the intended consumers. Corporations are forced to lower their costs by hiring workers informally; states turn a blind eye as employers avoid legislation designed to protect workers' rights.[13] Yet, in India, Rina Agarwala finds that class-based organizations are reincarnated in new forms by informal workers, who, despite these pressures, are finding ways to advance their humanity by organizing around their class interests.[14]

In the realm of ideas, global intellectual dispensations have militated against class analysis. At one end, idealist constructivism abandoned the very gritty empirical work that class analytics demands. In constructivist accounts, epistemological relativism challenges — or denigrates as simplistic — empirical science. Empirical inquiry becomes reified as "Western science" or "imperialist science." Science itself has become "an enemy of the people" in critiques of some activist intellectuals. Vivek Chibber calls this aggregate dispensation "post-structuralist/postcolonialist," but it is hard to pin down; part of the dispensation is precisely the denial of an operational definition.[15] Discursive moves to more micro levels (the body as site of contestation, the subject, the individual) or more macro (globalization, modernity) both exclude precise specification of class actors and the problematic of collective action: under what conditions do individuals with similar interests unite to promote common goals?

At the other end of the intellectual spectrum, positivist and formal-theoretic turns in the social sciences have obscured class. First, the most extreme forms of positivism privilege the measurable over the real, even if available measurements poorly tap the concept one requires and data are acknowledged to be deficient. Second, the implantation of U.S.-style positivism has emphasized measurable stratification over less easily measured relational variables. Social relations, central to class analytics, give way to easier-to-measure proxies, such as income and education, which emphasize static comparison among status groups, not class interaction. Finally, the aggregationist language of developmentalism has privileged wholes over parts. "Strengthening civil society" replaces improvement in income distribution or agrarian reform. Gross Domestic Product (GDP) or Gross National Product (GNP) and change therein become operative measures of success, whatever the distributive consequences.[16] Place and context became less important to explanatory models in neoliberal prescriptions of the "Washington consensus," where one medicine famously treats all diseases, regardless of cause.[17]

The move away from class analytically seems validated by apparent failures of class-based organizations and political parties.[18] Even if true, failures would be no indictment of class analysis, any more than any particular recession indicts macroeconomics. Instead, class analytics points to the obvious comparative question: why do class-based parties and organizations succeed electorally in West Bengal to a remarkable extent, but fail in Gujarat — or Pakistan? Why did social democracy succeed in Europe but there is famously "no socialism in the United States?"[19]

Theorists of social movements have found, not surprisingly, that strategy, success, and failure depend a great deal on the political opportunity structure faced by movements.[20] What niches are available for mobilization? How open is the system to new actors? What allies are available, and what resources do they have? How likely and effective is repression? Historically, expressing left politics in Pakistan could get one killed;[21] the same behavior in Kerala or Bengal could lead to a comfortable career. Political party *systems* then determine what interests can be mobilized, with what effect. With the decline of the "Congress system" in India, the left in Sri Lanka, and the absence of a competitive party system in Pakistan, the rise of nonprogrammatic parties characterized the subcontinent. Nonprogrammatic parties have great latitude in adopting symbols to mobilize support, deploying social identities rather than class-relevant programs. Within India, disintegration of the Congress system made for a politics of opportunistic alliances that rendered all political parties less programmatic and simultaneously less relevant to redistributive politics. Under these systemic conditions, the possibilities for obfuscation of interests via alternative identities ramify: nation, region, caste, community.

Indeed, the mass political energy of the past two decades in the subcontinent has seemed to be more accurately represented by "identity politics" (struggles of women, *adivasis* ["tribals"], and *dalits* [members of the lowest castes]).[22] Gruesome communal conflict suggested the extreme salience of an identity politics that overwhelmed all interest-based accounts of political action. Though sophisticated analysts recognized the interpenetration of class and identity, class was largely submerged in favor of identity. This was an odd outcome; class locations have always been inhabited by people with multiple identities, and must necessarily remain so. Moreover, as identity politics was sweeping academic treatments in the 1980s, a strong leftist coalition led by the Communist Party of India-Marxist (CPI-M) was consolidating what has turned out to be the longest running democratic government in India — and one of the longest in the world: in West Bengal, a state of 82 million people, now twenty-eight years and counting.

No one denies the significance of identity politics, but privileging identity over class raises three analytical problems. First, attributing political behavior to identity too often takes constructions of political entrepreneurs at face value, thus obscuring material interests behind a claim of ascriptive solidarity.[23] Second, identities exhibit the same explanatory ambiguity in relation to politics and collective action as do classes. Which of the competing identities do individuals choose as a basis for collective action? For this very reason, constructivist idealism is attractive as academic practice and not very useful as social science. Finally, the either-or formulation of identity vs. class deflects attention from the additive dimensions of inequality. Class produces divisions in ascriptive identities that reduce potential for collective action (rich women and poor women, for example), just as ascriptive identities may divide — or in rare cases — activate potential solidarities of class (for example, anti-brahmin movements in South India historically united disparate castes horizontally against privilege). No robust theory answers these questions, in part because of the necessarily overlapping and additive effects of hierarchy in social systems.

Class mobilization is also increasingly in competition with civil society organizations. Nongovernmental organizations (NGOs) claim to represent single-issue topics (such as the environment or poverty) or constituencies defined by scriptive characteristics (women, tribals, children). Hindu, Christian, and Mus-
n fundamentalist organizations the world over provide support for the NGO
ıere, as do development institutions. Class-based organizations receive little
ling and media attention relative to the exploding array of "grassroots orga-
ions" and stake-holders. Women's micro-finance organizations based in
ms of Bombay, Bogotá, or New York City use fashionable policy prescrip-
individual behavior and self-sufficiency to complement neoliberal cuts
welfare support. This template is sufficiently attractive that Citibank,
Sachs, HSBC, Standard Chartered, ABN Amro, Deutsche Bank, and
anley have all begun to join the micro-finance effort. Building "social

capital" is more attractive to capital — which can influence these flows — than organizing workers for enforcement of health and safety standards or minimum wage statutes. As John Harriss shows, multiple sources of material support for NGOs are augmented by a tendency of middle-class Indians with concerns for activism and social change to think of all politics as a "dirty river," reinforcing the ranks of "grassroots" organizations with talent and energy.[24]

Though the NGO phenomenon has blunted and complicated class organization, class analysis may aid in understanding new developments. Harriss shows that different classes participate in activist organizations in different ways. Moreover, he finds that part of "being middle class" in India now often includes social activism. Being middle class facilitates activism both through the cultural capital of that class and the freedom from the dull compulsion of economic necessity that hems in other classes.[25] Ronald Herring finds the same to be true of mobilization against new technology in agriculture; Vandana Shiva can afford to label Bt cotton seeds "suicidal," then "homicidal," and finally in 2006 "genocidal" because she is free from dependence on cotton production for her livelihood. Cotton farmers, who lack this freedom, but face compelling economic pressure, experiment with Bt seeds, and in the aggregate adopt them rapidly. "Operation Cremate Monsanto" failed in part because activists misunderstood class interests in biotechnology, its property configuration and relations: particularly the capacity of farmers to appropriate the technology under the radar screen of both Monsanto and Delhi. An approach that analyzed this movement without reference to class, property, and the cognitive screen of science would lose explanatory power; as important, the failure of movement leaders to take a class perspective hindered their ability to represent the class they claimed.[26]

Class analytics has also been sidelined by the rise of alternative intellectual models. Gary Becker won the Nobel Prize for his *Economic Approach to Human Behavior* in 1992; the recognition was indicative of the pervasive spread of rational-choice theory into social science disciplines to explain a wide range of behavior and relations, including marriage, education, immigration, families, crime, and elections.[27] The promise of methodological individualism to provide robust and parsimonious explanations for long-debated and perennially muddled phenomena held great attraction. As Jon Elster eloquently demonstrates, rational choice theory and class-based analysis are not mutually exclusive.[28] There can after all be no choice outside some structure of constraints and payoffs. Though rational-choice theory and class analytics are often pitted against one another, synergies abound. The healthy contribution of rational-choice theory to South Asian studies is its rejection of Orientalist assumptions about difference; the imprinted cultural other becomes instead an agent making decisions within (often binding, and certainly class-differentiated) constraints.[29] Methodological individualism in turn becomes robust only through specification of structures that bind, guide, and differentially reward choice.

Methodological positivism, unless tempered by a realist philosophy of science, has a difficult time with relations as opposed to discrete values of a variable. There are few good proxies for relational constructs. In practice, the enumerated takes precedence over the theoretically important or empirically significant: class is but one example. Moreover, a purely positivist dispensation — precisely because it takes the world as presented by existing indicators and has no method to probe deeper — often fails to recognize that data are themselves products of social interaction, their relation to reality varying with conditions of their production.[30] For want of precise indicators of class, proxies are deployed as both independent and dependent variables: income, education, and skill level. Stratification studies operationalize hierarchy by means of easily measurable, independent categories with no attention to interaction among status groups. Stratification theory treats a relation of comparison, not interaction.[31]

Postmodernist theory from the humanities undermined class analysis through rejection of both causal theory based on demonstrable mechanisms — the core of class analytics — and empirical referents as a measure of the truth value of statements of fact — the core of positivism. This literature resisted attempts to distinguish and define specific social categories according to transparent and consistent criteria. Instead, scholars turned attention to examining how, by whom, and under what conditions social categories were created. Positivism and class analytics can share a platform, though it is understood that there will be arguments about appropriate proxy measures, about valid indicators, about the priority of naked data over multidimensional confirmation of empirical statements.[32] This is a nonantagonistic contradiction. The same meeting grounds of ontology and epistemology are less readily apparent between constructivist idealism and class analytics, with arguably deleterious effects on progressive scholarship.[33]

## What Explanatory Work Do We Ask Class To Do?

Too much has been expected of class theory. The hubris of mono-causal grand theory is not limited to class; social science feeds on and from long cycles of master narratives. Nevertheless, bold claims to a universalist framework making strong predictions rendered class theory uniquely vulnerable. Overreaching political prediction from class theory especially undermined the scientific aspirations of the enterprise: why are there no revolutions among workers? Why is voting only imperfectly correlated with class?

Dueling orthodoxies and partisan theoretical product differentiation have exacerbated these critiques. The authors in this collection agree fundamentally with Eric Olin Wright's observation: "Class analysis is based on a conviction that class is a pervasive social cause, and it is worth exploring its ramifications for many social phenomena. This also involves understanding the limits of what class can explain."[34] If we expect the framework to explain a broad range of phenomena, four discrete components are essential: class structure (class-in-itself for Marx), class consciousness (understanding by individual actors of their class interests), class formation (collectively organized actors of similar structural position, constituting a class-for-itself in Marx), and class struggle (collective practices of actors for the realization of class interests against interests of other classes).[35]

Specifying how class structure interacts with societal development is now a more complicated task than in the time of Karl Marx, or even Max Weber. Few doubt that ownership and control of property explain changing forms and degrees of inequality and common political responses over historical time: there would be no social democracy in Western Europe otherwise. It is one thing — and a valuable, too often slighted, thing — to take class into account in explaining different life chances during economic change. It is much more demanding to expect class — or any notion of social structure — to predict or explain politics that drive policy. Class structure defines positions for individuals, based on their relationship to economic assets; these class positions in turn differentiate objective material interests: landlords and tenants, workers and owners. Under certain conditions, these interests may be recognized, mobilized, and acted upon — thus ultimately explaining collective action in which people attempt to improve their life chances through politics and policy: land reform, minimum wages, welfare transfers, income redistribution.

Though it is true that ownership of the means of production cleaves a fundamental division in society, it seems equally clear that two giant classes — bourgeois and proletarian — are inadequate for understanding politics of contemporary class systems, especially in semi-agrarian nations. In India, for example, a "new middle class" evokes intensive interest. However much or little physical capital members of this class may control, they bring important forms of cultural capital to the marketplace. Yet most work for bosses, many have servants, some face extreme insecurity and financial pressure; others not only aspire to, but live, a globally cosmopolitan life. How finely does one divide such a stratum? Or should we think of it, as Leela Fernandes and Patrick Heller argue, a genuine class in the making, a class tentatively, unevenly *for itself?*[36]

This multi-jointed path from class structure to class consciousness to class formation to politically efficacious class politics immediately suggests limits and contingencies of class theory.[37] Interests are not always transparent, to individuals or observers. The paternalistic attribution of "false consciousness" is currently out of favor, but it is hard to accept the romanticization that subordinates always see through the ideologies of superordinates — i.e., are not mystified.[38] All interests are necessarily filtered through cognitive screens. What is the workers' interest in monetary policy and exchange rates, World Trade Organization (WTO) rulings, and Trade-Related Intellectual Property Rights (TRIPs)? Does the answer vary by sector? Over what time period? Cognitive screens process "interests" such that they can be recognized, evaluated, given meaning, ordered, and thus rendered actionable by individuals. These screens necessitate modesty in reading claims of interests off structures, as much classical class theory did. Some workers believe party-affiliated unions to be an appropriate vehicle for guarding their interests, others in the same structural location think not — for many reasons.[39] Informal laborers, who are increasingly doing the same work as formally employed laborers, are often willing to accept insecure jobs for wages that are far below the hard-fought minimum wages in return for relatively small welfare benefits from the state.[40] A deep irony of "farmers' movements" for higher agricultural prices is that very poor farmers and landless workers often join in, though the net effect of higher prices is a heavier burden on food-deficit households — i.e., virtually all of the rural poor. Thomas Frank puzzles over U.S. working-class support for economic policies that are not in their interest: ***What's the Matter With Kansas?***[41] His answer is that their attention has been effectively shifted to "moral" issues that create validation and solidarity, but distract from the reality of income redistribution to the very rich at the expense of the average worker. Through the lens of filth on television, burning flags, abortion rights, and gay marriage, political entrepreneurs of the right have been able to change the subject in U.S. politics. Political strategy and framing thus confound any direct deduction of class interests; good rational choice theorists understand the problem, as did Marx.[42]

With technical and economic integration characteristic of globalization, scientific knowledge becomes asymmetrically distributed, both globally and within social movements, between leaders and those represented. Different cognitive screens cause divergent perception of interests in such critical science-embedded problematics as climate change or genetic engineering. Biotechnology offers a particularly contentious case, as many NGOs present the interests of farmers as threatened even as farmers themselves find the technology to be so much in their interest that an underground market in transgenic seeds develops.[43] Cognitive screens are not given by class position, but are conditioned in important ways: activists are free to use junk science for dramaturgical effect, and indeed agitational politics creates selection pressures for junk science.[44] More generally, political ecology produces interest complexities unfamiliar to long-established class routines, from landscapes to genomes.[45] Nature presents special problems for analysis of interests: interests of many primary producers are embedded in local nature, yet are contingent on dynamics of larger biophysical systems nowhere fully understood.[46] Moreover, state property in nature dominates private property in nature; Nancy Peluso calls the results "secret wars and silent insurgency" inimical to conservation.[47] As in the case of informal sector workers, demands are often targeted on the state rather than capital, yet property is still the crux of conflict.[48] Variable class structures also affect political ecology outcomes. Ramchandra Guha notes that the relative absence of class inequality was a necessary condition for both conservation and collective protest in Uttarakhand forest mobilization.[49]

Some objective interests are then both difficult to understand and subject to alternative cognitive screens, or framings. Not all who are objectively members of a class may recognize that position; not all who recognize their location in a class structure will find that particular dimension of inequality most salient, or most amenable to change; not all who seek to alter the terms of their class position will find sufficient colleagues to make collective action feasible; and not all class-based collective action will be effective: much will be suppressed, bought off, tactically flawed, or ignored by political actors with alternative support bases.

Empirical evidence of unrecognized or mis-recognized interests leads logically to cultural, psychological, and situational variables that intercede between class location and behavior. James Scott's great accomplishment in ***Weapons of the Weak*** was to work through empirically and theoretically the limitations on class collective action in a particular village in Malaysia at a particular point in

time. Class anger and envy remained offstage, deflected to alternative channels, few of which enhanced interests of the poor materially.[50] Yet Scott's celebration of Malaysian farmers' ability to penetrate hegemonic ideologies does not resonate with patterns of self-defeating behavior in many other settings — such as Kansas.

## Indian Exceptionalism: Isn't Class Irrelevant Because of Caste?

In Indian studies, informed by an Orientalist focus on the exotic nature of otherness, religio-cultural overlays on class stratification have understandably loomed large. Moreover, economic class has always seemed too simplistic and materialist a concept for the richly stratified layers and dimensions of privilege and deprivation in Indic society. Rather than class, every student learned, "caste" dominated.

On reflection, we find this a puzzling construction. First, economic compulsion and social subordination in the caste system tended to correlate: low or "untouchable" (*avarna*) status almost always meant property-less existence and degrading labor. All class systems valorize behaviors and characteristics of super-ordinates, denigrate the language, dress, manners, living conditions, and mores of subordinates. All class systems, to greater or lesser extent, structure interaction among classes: whom one lives among, eats with, goes to school with, marries.[51] In India, distinctions are explicitly codified in caste-based norms — though the reification and timelessness of caste were certainly influenced by colonial rule.[52] The word "caste" itself is from the Portuguese *casta* suggesting "race, lineage, breed" — among animals as well as people; it connoted "pure or unmixed (stock or breed)." Pure or unmixed derives from the word's origins in Latin: *castus* meaning pure or unpolluted, from which English also derives *chaste*. Darwin used the term for classes among social insects, such as ants. Before 1800, the spelling in English was "cast," illustrating more clearly its derivation from the verb: i.e., "a throw or stroke of fortune; *hence*, fortune, chance, opportunity; lot, fate."[53]

From the beginning, English-language usage and colonial practice reinforced Hindu ideology's focus on fate, purity, heredity: one is cast into a class position, from which movement is sanctioned. Members of the avarna or "untouchable" castes in South India were defined by their lack of land and their denigrating work as serfs or slaves even into the twentieth century; socially, they were forbidden to cover some parts of their body with clothing, to use certain forms of address and grammar, to travel public roads, to enter temples.[54] Class disabilities and distinctions were mapped onto social clusters glossed ideologically as caste: i.e., a class location for which there is a reason.

Indology makes much of the rich particularity of caste's extra-economic distinctions, yet an argument for uniqueness is hard to sustain. Shakespeare was by law forbidden to wear the fine clothes reserved for gentry when he left his own stage, where he had portrayed characters of higher classes than his own — to which he aspired by pursuing his father's failed dream of acquiring a coat of arms. His caste was hereditary, but accident of birth could be corrected with cash — suggesting how little purity of birth line had to do with it in the first place. Shakespeare was told that his family was so cast that it fell below the gentleman class, but he knew there were ways to turn resources into mobility, despite accident of birth.[55] Where race differs from hereditary caste is the difficulty of passing, or erasing, evidence of birth. Increasingly, South Asians flock to cities where losing heredity is much easier, easier to shed in fact than the disabilities of class. One can disguise village origins, but cannot pass as capitalist without capital.

Indian exceptionalism in social science has often used caste as exhibit one; but the dichotomy is false. The challenge for Indian class analytics is to demonstrate how extra-economic aspects of class location — e.g., caste — aid in understanding political responses. Dimensions of class subordination are elaborately codified — how many steps must the "untouchable" stay from "clean" castes? What body parts may be covered? These dimensions of subordination affect the freedom and dignity of particular class locations, as well as efficiency of labor markets and educational capital. Deprivation of freedom and dignity in turn may well fuel moral outrage more than mere economic deprivation. Moreover, the sociological reality of caste groupings may affect potential for collective action. Common deprivations and common interests generated by stratification are conjoined with a social basis of organization: caste (*jati*) is ultimately a local phenomenon, with propinquity of members, marriage connections, and authority. Castes thus may exhibit more potential for political solidarity than do classes of the potatoes-in-a-sack variety. On the other hand, subtle caste distinctions and competition among subordinates in similar class positions also generate obstacles to horizontal solidarity, much as race or ethnicity divides subordinate classes in many societies. Finally, the ideological underpinnings of caste almost perfectly explain away exploitation: one's station in life is justified by one's previous conformity with *dharmic* law, which enjoins adherence to *dharmic* law, which means accepting subordination as both inevitable and justifiable.

Assuming for a moment that caste is more than the "euphemization of class," the common assumption that caste is the bedrock of political behavior is seldom tested and increasingly problematic. Anirudh Krishna concludes from his surveys in North Indian villages: "Caste continues to be a primary source of social identity in these villages, people live in caste-specific neighborhoods, and the clothes that they wear reveal their caste identity. Yet insofar as political organization is concerned, caste no longer has primary importance." Krishna finds that primordial loyalties are very much still in place, but that patronage and material advantage figure prominently in political connections, as Kanchan Chandra's work on castes in Uttar Pradesh likewise illustrates.[56]

Class analysis sensitive to caste social embeddings has proved an indispensable conceptual tool in explaining differences in redistributive policy in India, as indicated by such measures as poverty reduction or agrarian reform, and resultant differentials in life chances at the bottom across Indian States.[57] Barrington Moore Jr., in his classic *Social Origins of Dictatorship and Democracy,* posed a challenge to Indologists: given the extensive misery at the bottom of Indic society, why have there been so few effective radical challenges to the social order — particularly in comparison to China? The answer is complicated, but must in part ride on politically critical variations in caste-class relations of dominance.[58] Moral outrage at the injustice of hierarchy in some cases drove ameliorative politics; in the long development of left movements and parties in Kerala — class analytics provide an explanation for exceptional enhancements in quality of life and protection of the weakest classes through public policy.[59] More commonly, dominance prevented or co-opted lower-order mobilization. Variations in political opportunity structure and party systems have mattered fundamentally. Atul Kohli's early work contrasted Karnataka with West Bengal to illustrate how a committed and disciplined left-of-center party could effect poverty alleviation in ways not possible in states lacking this political resource.[60] John Harriss complements Kohli: as important as electoral politics is a decisive break of "caste-class dominance."[61] Successful redistributive parties nurture and reinforce this decisive break, spurring and building on horizontal mobilization in civil society. Such mobilization then energizes reforms: uncovering malfeasance, pressing for timely action, intimidating colluding bureaucrats. The conclusion is that successful redistribution requires a break in caste-class dominance. Kerala's early success in poverty reduction unambiguously developed from successful political mobilization of subordinate classes. Congress hegemony was replaced by a distributive anti-elite populism in Tamil Nadu, and by aggressive left coalitions in Kerala (first) and West Bengal (more enduringly). As importantly, in Kerala the Congress and its permutations responded to electoral competition with left forces, particularly on land policy, making the party less conservative than most Congress state units in India.[62] An alternative pattern was produced in States with middling-caste/class-dominated regimes — such as Maharashtra, Karnataka, and Gujarat — where Congress was effectively challenged but did not collapse. In these states, the politics of accommodation vis-à-vis lower-class interests has worked effectively, especially in Maharashtra and Karnataka, and less so in Gujarat. There has been no decisive rejection of caste-class dominance of the old social order through politics and public policy, and redistributive policies have not been robust. In states where caste-class dominance has survived unchallenged, poverty alleviation has been correspondingly weak.[63]

What do we learn from these divergent patterns of subnational societal development? First, successful class mobilization in India deviated from European orthodoxy in favor of organic class theory: grown up from the ground, based on political experience. The move was from urban proletarians of received theory to coalitions of the despised, insecure, and less-privileged. Any Marxian notion of bimodal classes was replaced in practice by extensive differentiation of targets of mobilization, building on locally understood forms of exploitation. And finally, multiple dimensions of humiliation and oppression embedded in caste dimensions of class mattered politically. Piling on multiple dimensions of inequality — and not simply terms of the commodity exchange — fueled challenges to the class-caste system.[64]

Caste theory provides a useful reminder for materialists: good class analysis is inherently multidimensional. Living bearers of a commodity — labor power

— are subjected to the impersonal forces of market capitalism that treats them as the commodity — which may or may not be in sufficient demand to earn a decent living, or provide dignity and security to individuals.[65] Exploitation of a commodity — labor power — is inextricably linked to exploitation of a person possessing that commodity. Exploitation between classes then describes and enables a system of power, not just one of privilege, rooted in unequal access to economic assets.[66] "Moral outrage" is more explainable in the multidimensional world of oppression and dominance than in the discrete step world of stratification. Theories that reduce inequality to mere stratification miss this relational component; by doing so, they de-emphasize dynamics of domination, power, and exploitation.

## Lumpers and Splitters of Classes

How many classes are there? Where are the boundaries? As often, there are lumpers and splitters. Karl Marx boldly lumped layers of stratification together into two classes: bourgeois and proletarian. Dividing society into two megagroups (the exploiter and the exploited) creates "classes" of great heterogeneity but periodic subjective reality — *nosotros los pobres; hum garib log*. If giant classes are to act politically, coalitions across subgroups must be hammered out. Modern stratification theory tends to produce dimensions that can be represented by a continuous variable — e.g., income, education — creating an infinite number of classes, or none at all. Some literature divides the population into a very large number of fine-graded categories based on occupation, in the name of "class."

The analytical problem is real. David Grusky and Jesper Sorensen raised the question starkly with their 1998 article, "Can Class Analysis Be Salvaged?"[67] The "big class assumption" — that there are a small number of big classes, generated by the forces of industrialism — is one held primarily by academics and rarely by class members themselves. Instead, Grusky and Sorensen argue that structure at the site of production is comprised of much smaller classes defined by functional positions in the division of labor. Grusky and Sorensen argue that these institutionalized occupation groups have greater explanatory power than the "big classes" in terms of collective action, as well as group identification, interests, and culture. This perspective mirrors common perceptions of caste: an exceptionally finely graded hierarchy of occupation and ritual ranking. But if identities and occupational interests become infinitely divisible, why not speak merely of occupations, dropping altogether the term "class"?[68]

At the other end of the spectrum, Pranab Bardhan argued that India was controlled by three "dominant proprietary classes," in an "uneasy alliance" that maintained power by sharing out spoils of patronage and subsidies through log-rolling across issue areas. Two of Bardhan's classes were familiar to students of both class analysis and of India: landlords and industrial capitalists. But the third — the "professional class" — was more problematic. In one sense Bardhan's professional class owned the state, and the incalculable rents appropriable from command of office. Bardhan attributed the power of this class to "the scarcity value of education" — a value reproduced over time by the state's failure to democratize schooling.[69] Yet it would seem today that the "scarcity value of education" is too narrow for all the advantages of that messy but real category of a "new middle class" in India.[70] Pierre Bourdieu popularized the use of a concept of cultural capital that is broader than education, though certainly congruent with command of knowledge and intellectual skills: slippery assets such as attitudes, status, expectations.[71] We would add connections. Likewise, it is clear that command over people and resources now has a broader ambit than ownership of positions in the license-permit-quota raj (rule) of India's pre-liberalization era. One new set of class positions is generated by the intersection of the international politics of globalization and the cultural capital of sectors of the metropolitan middle class: the NGOs, consultants, and global activists who are disproportionately important in driving media and public policy in India.

Lumping and splitting stratification systems in India offers almost infinite possibilities. For Bardhan, the proof of the theory revolves around power in shaping development policy and state discretion: who gets what and how? This is the core developmental question. As the developmental state assumed central importance in driving economic change and mitigating consequences, Bardhan argued that it was necessary to separate those who essentially owned the state from those without access to the state. Is the middle-class activism in civil society emphasized by Harriss, and the retreat of middle classes from politics, predicated on the declining importance of the state in a neoliberal political economy?

An illustration of the power of this insight comes through the work of Aseema Sinha.[72] Sinha asks the profound question: if economic interventionist policies from Delhi were so bad for growth, as mainstream economists, international financial institutions, and many citizens of India have concluded, why is there so much variance among subnational states within India? The national average growth rate was low over the period 1947–1985, but some states grew rapidly and experienced significant structural transformation; others stagnated or experienced structural retrogression. One conclusion is that the developmental state literature is right, but at the wrong level. In a large federal nation, developmental state dynamics happen below the level of Delhi (and scholars working at that level). Gujarat does what much of the developmental-state literature suggests is important for promoting growth, and it works. One common reading of the original developmental-state theory based on Japan (Chalmers Johnson's original work) was that the special genius of the Japanese state was to ascertain what capital needed to grow and then to do it.[73] This is the structural power of capital: every state must promote "business confidence," whether or not particular capitalists are politically active or not. India's "license-permit-quota raj" had done quite the opposite: discouraged capital in general while treating well-connected capitalists with boons through embedded particularism.[74] This system was condemned for stifling growth, but without consideration of relations between particularities of the capital-state relationship, where the state resides in Gandhinagar, not Delhi. Capitalists must matter; it would be puzzling indeed if so powerful a class were helpless before mere bureaucrats or did not know what it needed, or how to get it. That relations between provincial-level states and a partially formed national capitalist class differ in so diverse a country as India is not surprising; that much mainstream literature misses this critical determinant of economic growth is.[75]

## The Agrarian Question: Classes and Politics[76]

Rural India illustrates themes developed above: the nature of the class system was theoretically disputed and politically contested; lumpers and splitters found evidence for divergent interpretations; and multiple dimensions of degradation and privilege defined rural power relations. Moreover, these differences mattered to politics. Theorists, political entrepreneurs and activists have variously assumed identity, class, regional, and sectoral dimensions to be the key to rural mobilization.

Debate around rural class relations in independent India grew from intimations of agrarian unrest: might the "green revolution turn red"? This possibility seemed pressing in the wake of the Maoist-influenced Naxalite movement, and of widespread "agrarian tension" — as officially described in a report of the Ministry of Home Affairs in 1969. Might agrarian tensions be aggravated by the development of agrarian capitalism, spurred by the Government's support of technological change and "building on the best" in rural areas? The great puzzle of the twentieth century for Marxists was that agrarian upheavals brought down governments and overturned societies, not working-class revolutions.[77] India became the center of a global debate around models of peasant economies and what becomes of them under capitalism. One line of theorizing, derived from Lenin's work *The Development of Capitalism in Russia* projected differentiation of peasant producers into distinct classes.[78] In theory, the development of capitalism would eventually create a rural society of largely dichotomous and antagonistic classes: agricultural capitalists and an agrarian proletariat. Proletarianization would plausibly lead to labor-capital conflict, perhaps revolution, in rural areas.

In direct opposition to the class polarization model was that of a "peasant economy," derived largely from the work of the Russian economist A.V. Chayanov. In this model, household production has its own very specific economic characteristics, with economic drivers quite different from maximization of profit at the margin. Rather than being exploited by superior classes, peasant families engaged in "self-exploitation" — using family labor intensively at submarket rates of return. Self-exploitation in theory allowed the peasant household to survive in circumstances that would be irrational for a capitalist farm. Chayanovian logic suggested that rural household production could continue indefinitely despite the development of agrarian capitalism. Small farmers could reproduce themselves by exploiting their family labor, propped up unevenly by government aids in extremis (loan *melas*, debt cancellations, input subsidies, public works, etc). Ironically, stagnation and relatively stable agrarian structure were also implied by a largely Marxian perspective on "semi-feudal" agrarian structure. Semi-feudal landlordism could survive indefinitely, enabled by abject dependence of labor on landlords, and hence great opportunities for exploitation. Landlords would not necessarily follow the incentives of market capitalism for investment and technical change in agriculture, because they could reap more surplus through domination of the peasantry by usury, unpaid labor (*begar*), extortionate rents, and starvation wages.[79] Another alternative to development of thoroughly capitalist relations in agriculture was posed by Lloyd and Susanne Rudolph, who projected the emergence of powerful "bullock capitalists" rather than full-scale development of capitalist relations in agriculture.[80]

In retrospect, rural capitalism has generated no radically polarized class structure. There has generally been what Byres referred to as "partial proletarianisation"; small and marginal peasant producers have continued to reproduce themselves.[81] Chayanovian self-exploitation is now joined by migration (both rural-rural and rural-urban, both short-term and long-term), associated remittances, and diversification of employment in rural areas outside agriculture to sustain small-scale farming.[82] Marginal farmers have been partially sustained by subsidized institutional credit, as in most countries, though market criteria are now increasingly important in agricultural credit via neoliberal logic. Constantly shifting development "schemes" contribute as well — for example, micro-finance programs, rural public works — and by state welfare provision.[83]

Broader processes of economic change, much accelerated since liberalization in 1991, have altered the relationship between land ownership, power, and poverty. Diversification of rural livelihoods and the increased importance of nonagricultural employment among rural people, both locally and in distant places, have altered relations between agrarian capital and rural labor. Though the "patron-client relationship" has been much romanticized in academic work, face-to-face contact over time between families is waning with differentiation of the rural economy and market-rational behavior. Where the incidence of rural poverty has declined, it has been because of purposive public policy or the tightening of labor markets, both of which may reduce abject dependence of labor on capital. Land ownership may still mean considerable wealth, and remains an asset for local status and power. But economic rationality drives much investment out of agriculture, toward education and activities with higher rates of return. Along with declining profitability declining status has moved some landowners out of agriculture.[84] As ascriptive status converts less easily to political power, one finds emergence of a new generation of local leaders from among educated but often unemployed younger men.[85] For all these reasons, the class power of "rich farmers" of higher ranked castes appears to have declined significantly. Collective action of farmers reached a high point in the 1980s, built on multi-class, sometimes caste-based, mobilization around costs of production and prices of outputs.[86] Farmers' movements have been less significant since the early 1990s.[87] Ironically, some of the largest collective actions in recent years have come in protest against Delhi's banning of genetically engineered (Bt) cotton in 2001.[88] Here the issue was, for a significant farmers' movement, autonomy from the corrupt and costly interference of the state in agriculture, exemplified by the denial of access to knowledge farmers wanted — biotechnology — that Delhi sought to "bottle up in the cities."[89]

Ties of dependency of the rural poor in class relations have loosened, but their interests are only weakly articulated politically — except in regional pockets and in the leftist states of Kerala and West Bengal. There is abundant evidence for what Frankel and Rao described as "the decline of dominance" — referring to "the exercise of authority in society by groups who achieved socio-economic superiority and claimed legitimacy for their commands in terms of superior ritual status."[90] Democratic deepening has enabled much greater assertiveness among subordinate rural people. There are large regional differences; uprisings against Brahminical power in the South preceded by decades mobilizations of "backward-caste" groups in Bihar and Uttar Pradesh, now joined by and in competition with dalits.

Globalization and accompanying neoliberal policies have increased pressures on the agricultural sector, but means of class formation remain illusive. One formulation has been a politically imagined super and inclusive class — i.e., agriculture as a sector, Bharat as a place. The Bharat-vs.-India formulation attempted cultural and economic synthesis of rural India as a class for itself, focused on rolling back "urban bias" in development policy. The framing of farmer movements — and the Bharat against India construction in general — failed not so much for reasons of primordial loyalties, as Ashutosh Varshney suggested, but for reasons of intra-sectoral differences of interest, conflicting economic ideologies, and factionalism.[91] After the 1980s, the ability of this imagined aggregate rural class to influence prices and subsidies was diminished by the failure of political organization. Moreover, globalization produced a new focus of mobilization, to which farmer organizations responded in divergent ways, partly for difference in interests, partly for differences in ideology. For example, the Shetkari Sanghatana — one of the largest farmer organizations in India — took a pro-liberalization, pro-technology, anti-state program even to small farmers and landless laborers; other farmer organizations (e.g., Nanjundaswamy's KRRS) prominently joined the anti-globalization and anti-technology forces. Despite divergent programs, most farmer organizations have been dominated by commercial and larger farmers.

The aggregative class strategy — a rural class for itself, coalitional agrarianism for sectoral advantage — largely failed, as did efforts to organize "classes within the peasantry" — again with a partial exception of India's "red belt." Kerala's Left organized agricultural workers as a class, not as a subset of an organization of farmers who pay their wages. West Bengal's Left preferred the national ***kisan sabha*** construction that assumes interests in agriculture to be complementary, not antagonistic. Bengali communists papered over the class contradiction between labor-hiring farmers and labor-selling workers; Kerala communists accepted the reality of conflict and built organizations accordingly. The Bengal model of rural class cooperation worked better politically than Kerala's confrontationist model.[92]

In official understandings of rural India, the cycle has returned to the 1969 report of the Home Ministry on "agrarian tension." Naxalism again threatens law and order — and thereby investment and growth. The grievances of rural "Maoists" build upon additive dimensions of subordination developed above:

landless workers of "tribal" or outcaste standing suffer from social oppression, political exclusion, and economic exploitation. Reciprocally, the state faces a rising tide of mobilization against its integration with the global economy generated by middle-class activists with great skills and connections. Anti-globalization campaigns portray severe and generalized agrarian crisis, as indicated by what is held to be a rising tide of suicides.[93] As a sector, agriculture continues to account for a smaller percentage of the workforce each year, as in all industrializing societies. But the class structure of agriculture is not static. In the first systematic data of Independent India, in 1951, 82.7 percent of the population was rural; 71.9 percent of rural people were cultivators, 28.1 percent were agricultural laborers. The ratio is that of a peasant society: dominated by farmers, with a significant rural proletariat. By 2001, only 72.2 percent of the population was "rural," but farmers were a bare majority: 54.4 percent of the rural population. Agricultural workers — now much more diversified in employment — constituted 45.6 percent of the rural population. This is the truly awkward class: largely unattached to anyone's land, selling labor power as a commodity in an unpredictable market, often uprooted by pushes and pulls of market forces, and largely without representation.[94]

## Recovering Class: Contributions and Puzzles

What do we lose from the marginalization of class analysis? At the aggregate level, representation of whole societies by summary compressions such as GDP per capita loses variance. Class analytics depends on disaggregation, of moving beneath aggregate presentations of economic well-being to the level where people live, where life chances are still, perhaps more than before, unequally distributed. It is not surprising that a rising and prosperous middle class, along with rapid technical change and explosion of consumption opportunities should overwhelm seemingly quaint Nehruvian concerns with "weaker sections" and inequality. Yet class itself certainly does not go away with wealth. Most bluntly, how long one can expect to live, and how well, even in the richest countries, depends on the lottery of class.[95] The loss of class analysis to fads of developmentalist or constructivist aggregations obscures deprivations of those who have little power to defend themselves in either markets or politics. "Development" shorn of class is a lazy and ideological distortion.

The more ambitious explanatory project is to explain how class structure influences political behavior and thus social change. As with identity — and other broad characterizations of groups — class enables explanation of collective action that may change the rules of the game at a societal level. Class analysis has given us appreciation of historical junctures and path dependency in explaining contemporary variation; of the agency of subordinate classes in the face of binding constraints on action; of the impact of new production relations on new strategies of workers. Our historical understanding of the subcontinent would be impoverished without studies of class forces in challenging colonial rule, establishing independent states, devising development strategies.[96] Understanding new state-society relations under conditions of globalization will depend on better class analytics, encompassing strategic choice as a fundamental element, with attention to variable political opportunity structures created by party systems and states and new modes of integration with the global economy.[97]

Neoliberal reforms deregulate the workplace as a matter of policy, and simultaneously rein in welfare functions of government. Recent literature concludes that with globalizing neoliberalism informal workers are replacing formal-sector workers; contract labor that operates outside the protection of labor laws increases in train. The decreasing proportion of formally employed workers the world over is held to signify a decline in class-based organization, undermining labor-union power and membership at the global level.[98] Rina Agarwala, however, finds that as capitalists become less recognizable in a world of subcontracting and informalization of work, informal sector workers seek to translate their collective position as a fragmented class-in-itself to a politically effective class-for-itself.[99]

The informal economy illustrates the necessity of original class analysis and possibilities for rethinking theory. It is not that informal-sector workers fail to organize for class interests, but rather that new structures of production alter their strategies. Because capital takes the form of constantly changing employers, who may even be unknown at the point of production, worker organizations take their demands to the state, rather than to capital. Demands for expansion of citizenship rights focus on welfare benefits (such as health and education), rather than workers' rights (such as minimum wage and job security). Because neither employers nor workplaces remain constant, informal workers organize around the neighborhood, rather than on the shop floor. These strategic changes have an impact on class identification: a unique class identity that simultaneously asserts workers' informality *and* their position within the working class. Informal workers employ a rhetoric of "citizenship" and mobilize votes to institutionalize rights.[100] Without understanding the changing structure of class under globalization, and its relational nature, and without a focus on the strategic aims of labor within a particular political opportunity structure, our understanding of outcomes in this growing sector would be much impoverished.

Workers must interpret their interests to make a strategic choice under altered conditions about the most promising collective action; aggressive and disruptive union tactics may be attractive to some workers, but depress investments when compared to unions that buy in to institutional labor compacts.[101] Objectively there is an argument for abandoning class confrontation; that many workers see the world differently illustrates the critical nature of cognitive screens in mediating between interest and action. That these differences exist reduces the ability of a class for itself to form. Formal-sector workers have been much studied — though misread, as Emmanuel Teitelbaum demonstrates — but most workers are relegated to the informal sector. Changes in structures of production — informalization, outsourcing — have facilitated, often necessitated, new strategies as discussed above.

The "middle class" — or classes — have especially multiplex interests; their allegiances have been historically opportunistic.[102] Evidence from South Asia suggests a significant leavening of celebration of the middle class as the bedrock of democracy and economic dynamism. Governments present an expanded middle class to foreign capital as reason for investment.[103] In turn, the new middle class deploys a range of strategies to protect their privileges in the face of political empowerment and growing assertiveness of the poor. Democratic deepening strengthens ties between the poor and political parties. The empirical work of John Harriss and colleagues suggests that middles classes increasingly cede the public sphere to the poor and their "dirty-river" politics. Agarwala's findings on informal workers' movements holding the state responsible reinforce Harriss's findings that Indian politics is increasingly becoming the realm of the poor. The affluent defect to private provisioning as the state declines in authority and capacity.[104] Participation in NGOs is important for the middle class, as it is for many of the poor, but participation itself takes on forms differentiated by class.[105] For example, Ronald Herring's findings on the movement to "cremate Monsanto" reinforces Harriss's findings on the "activist" nature of middle-class identity and class-differentiated interests in collective action.[106] The failure of that movement in part reflects the radical freedom of those with cultural capital and connections based on middle-class brokerage positions to ignore the compelling facts of material production: what farmers face in their fields. Activists are free to adopt discourses tuned to global coalitions that offer authenticity rents but are divorced culturally and materially from those they claim to represent. The brute facts of biological processes confront direct producers: farmers are constrained by their role in production to skepticism about claims of "suicide seeds" — or "genocidal" seeds — and forced into a grounded empiricism that cannot afford junk science. As systems of production and distribution ramify globally and technically, these cognitive screens are of increasing importance to understanding interests. Framing has the power attributed to it by social movement theorists, but within limits, many of which are mediated by class structure.

In recovering class, we find a useful rethinking of the deductivist and macrohistorical logic of dominant versions of European class analytics. Uncovering mechanisms takes priority, and the uncovering must be an empirical process. How do things actually work? Mechanisms focus attention on behavior of historical actors, recovering in the process human agency, both from its obscurantist obliteration in ideational constructivism and its a-contextual incarnation in certain brands of rational-choice theory. We find that complexities of class structures, and their interpretations from specific class positions, necessitate a less determinative intellectual architecture than *The Communist Manifesto*.

Historically, class analysis has tended to focus on explicit moments of the articulation of class interest (elections, insurrections, repression, etc.). These moments are of course important: indeed, as Christopher Candland finds in Pakistan, institutions for expression of class interests are so feeble and discontinuous that working-class power has been expressed primarily in convulsions that brought down political systems, but could not maintain a continuous presence in struggles for class interests.[107] To assume that these convulsions were the only relevant aspect of class in Pakistan would be naïve. At the micro level, where all of us live, are the day-to-day practices through which classes define and reproduce themselves. Old class analysis was not so interested in these struggles in civil society. Marx himself was convinced that the point of production was decisive as a determinant of class formation and collective action. Yet class struggles also take place in communities and local institutions. Where aggregate developmentalism posits civil society as an organic entity, class analytics provides more finely grained understandings of the divisions, tensions, and conflicts in civil society. Examples would include efforts to claim and horde education/science/culture, to secure legal sanction (reservations, definitions of formal vs. informal sector, labor regulation) or to secure institutional support (conflicts over space, or government policies). These struggles have important material effects; emphasis on the material forms of property alone deflects attention from the importance of cultural capital and the role of the developmental state in distributing life chances.[108] In pursuing these ends, individuals are strategic, and objects of larger strategies; struggles often take highly euphemized forms, as in struggles over caste, identity, and culture, that are then often interpreted as evidence for Indian exceptionalism.

For reasons that this essay has explored, the decline or rise of political organizations on the left has little to do with the validity of class analytics; indeed, a full understanding of how class works politically and socially aids in understanding why subordinate classes typically remain subordinate. The complexity and overdetermination of electoral and organizational outcomes creates puzzles for analysis, not refutation of an approach. There are many slips from perception of interests to mobilizational strategies to coalitional tactics that result in political success or failure. Moreover, assessment of political success or failure is highly time-dependent. After decades of decline, the resurgence of the Left in Latin America through new coalitions along horizontal lines, largely defined by winners and losers in neoliberal policies, underscores this point.[109] Left parties in India had been largely written off before the national elections of 2004, when the communists had their best-ever national showing. Simultaneously, Delhi rediscovered a sporadic agrarian class war that had become more widespread and deadly. The spectrum in the subcontinent moves from Pakistan to regional social democracies in India to effective insurgency in Nepal. In Pakistan, working class power has been episodic in expression, but unable to institutionalize itself. In Kerala and West Bengal, class formation is advanced and politically competent. But there is also Bihar, as the conventional wisdom goes. Amid the general assertion of nations as operative political identities, the regional isolation of Left parties in West Bengal and Kerala reminds us of the need to disaggregate to the level where political action can be effective.[110] This is why one does comparative research: under what conditions does Bihar become more like Kerala, or vice versa?

Unfortunately, neither class theorists nor anyone else has robust political theory. Were economics judged by outcomes, at least half the profession would be disbarred. Political outcomes are messier still. This is true because of the complexity of cognitive mediation in decisions of individual actors concerning class identification, class interests, and likely political outcomes of class formation and class struggle. It may not be rational for the individual to fight a landlord over crop shares or an employer over wages if the outcome is to lose access to the means of production. That tenants accept illegal and extortionate production relations is a common finding; the finding itself is explained by both power asymmetries of the class structure and the choice set facing the landless.[111] Knowing the class structure in agriculture cautions against mistaking acquiescence for legitimacy, or being surprised by agrarian insurgencies. Likewise, the larger political opportunity structure affects the rationality of expressing class interests collectively: there may be no point in voting for a party that cannot win, nor going to the streets if the army shoots protesters. The working classes of Pakistan, suppressed and divided though they have often been by ideology and primordial loyalties, were critical in convulsions that ousted very powerful military dictators, though they ironically failed to benefit from democracy.[112] For such low-probability events, no one has good predictive theory.

These indeterminacies are not overcome by a claim that identity politics has replaced class politics: we are equally unable to provide compelling theory on the conditions under which some identities will be chosen over others, or why answers vary over time. Nor do we know how some identities produce successful politics when others do not. We do know that such choices are embedded in structures of constraints and opportunities. However one's identity gets constructed, economic dependency matters fundamentally. Probing class structures and the choice sets of rational — or at least reasonable — actors recovers individuals from the cultural dopes of Orientalism or stomachs attached to calculating machines of economism. The really difficult tasks concern specification of the conditions under which interests of those disabled by the class system can be inter-subjectively recognized and acted upon politically. These conditions cover a wide range: from basic political rights to cognitive mediation of interests to structural power of capital. The transition first noted by Marx — from a class-in-itself to a class-for-itself — is not particularly predictable, but, as with many unpredictable outcomes, the consequences for the subcontinent are profound.

❑

# 1. On the Decline of Class Analysis in South Asian Studies

**Vivek Chibber**

THERE IS NO DENYING THAT CLASS ANALYSIS HAS BEEN IN DECLINE in South Asian studies over the past two decades, at an accelerating pace. This is not in itself surprising, since it is symptomatic of Marxism's decline as an intellectual and political force more broadly, and the Marxist tradition has historically been the main source of class theory. What gives added urgency to the issue is the nature of the theories — and politics — that have gained prominence in its stead. On the Right, it is of course the revival of free-market ideology and, more broadly, neoliberalism as a political project. On the Left, it is the rise of post-structuralism and, in area studies particularly, postcolonial theory (the tandem is hereafter referred to as PSPC). Indeed, the proponents of PSPC have rather boldly laid claim to the mantle of radical theory in the wake of Marxism's retreat.[1] Nowhere is this more apparent than in South Asian studies.

This essay takes three components of this transformation as its focus. First, what explains the retreat of class analysis in the field? If the retreat had been only in the United States, it would not be particularly surprising, and hence of little analytical interest. But as just noted, it is a phenomenon that has swept across the continental divide, into Great Britain, and India too, where class had been the language of scholarship for decades. Second, it seeks to examine why South Asian studies has been hit especially hard by the PSPC phenomenon, as compared to some other branches of area studies — especially scholarship on Latin America and Africa. This is not to imply that these fields have been left untouched by PSPC, for they have not. But they have retained a greater space for political economy and class analysis than has the study of India. PSPC has had to coexist with political economy, whereas in South Asia scholarship — as practiced in the U.S. setting — the former has largely displaced the latter. Lastly, I examine the basis for the extraordinary influence of the Subaltern studies series in the United States since the 1990s. This phenomenon is interesting for a couple of reasons. First, the Subalterns have been pivotal in shepherding the transition into PSPC among scholars of India. Second, they have done so, in part, because of the fact that they are an intellectual current based on the Indian subcontinent. They provide to the PSPC trend a patina of authenticity, where otherwise its overwhelming focus on culture and symbols might raise hackles among scholars of a critical bent.

The focus on PSPC requires some explanation. It certainly is not the only influential intellectual current these days. Neoliberalism, or what is sometimes referred to as "free market fundamentalism," could justifiably lay claim to real dominance in the field. I do not by any means deny that neoliberalism exercises tremendous influence among South Asianists. But I have chosen to largely ignore it in this essay for two reasons. First, its influence is largely confined to one discipline — economics — though it certainly exercises some weight in parts of political science. In terms of sheer numbers, this means that it forms part of the working assumptions of a very large proportion of practitioners in the field, simply because of the size of the discipline itself. But with regard to the disciplinary map of South Asian studies, neoliberalism has been less successful. It remains marginal in the other key disciplines that comprise the field: history, anthropology, and cultural studies.

Second, and even more to the point, it is not very puzzling, as a matter of analysis, why neoliberalism should be influential today, and why, in particular, in economics. A doctrine that is hostile to state regulation of markets, typically regards labor unions as infringements on market freedoms, downplays the social character of wealth, and hence is opposed to redistribution — such a doctrine has great resonance in a period when labor is weak and capital strong. Further, the doctrine has been assiduously propagated by corporate-sponsored think tanks for over a quarter century now, and has constituted the lodestone for mainstream politics in the United States, across both major parties. It is no surprise at all that it should exercise some influence in academic life as well. Even less so that it becomes prominent in the economics profession, which orbits more tightly than any other discipline around the business community and the halls of political power.

That PSPC should become so prominent, however, is not nearly as obvious. The decline of class analysis, in itself, could have given rise to a variety of new fashions. Everything else being equal, one might have expected that academic culture would settle into a kind of revived and more humane liberalism, which would have been in closer approximation to the culture outside the academy. Or perhaps there might have been a revanchist turn to more conservative views, in reaction to the advances the Left had made in the 1970s. This did not happen, however. Instead, the erstwhile Marxist intelligentsia transmuted into various species of post-structuralist theory. This merits attention. What makes the slide into PSPC politically interesting, and important, is that this is a theoretical current that, while holding on to the mantle of radical critique, has evinced not only a suspicion of class theory and the Marxist tradition, but an outright hostility to it. It is perhaps the first time that a major radical current in the Western intellectual firmament has been so hostile to the entire tradition of class analysis, and by extension, class politics. So while Marxists came to expect criticisms from the Right over the past century, they have now had to contend with a well-armored phalanx attacking from the Left. Hence, it is not that the retreat from class has heralded a fading of left-wing scholarship. It is, rather, that the very meaning of Left critique is changing. Class is just being pushed out of the progressive milieu.

What is more, the displacement of class analysis will most likely deepen over time. For one thing, the very fact that the turn to PSPC theory is strongest in elite universities gives it a privileged position in the production of future scholarship — via job placement, control over journals, influence over allocation of research funds, etc. But even more important is a mundane fact about demography. In both countries, a spectacular generational bubble is working its way through the intellectual community. Most of the scholars committed to class analysis belong to the generation that came of maturity in the 1960s and '70s, and are now fairly advanced in their careers. Conversely, class is much less a concern among scholars who finished graduate studies in the 1990s and after. Hence, the number of Marxists among the younger scholars in South Asian studies is already fleetingly small. Thus, even though things are bad, we haven't yet seen the worst. Within the next decade, as scholars who were radicalized in the 1960s wind down their careers and the baton is passed to the next generation, there is likely to be an even further drop-off in the visibility of class analysis.

### *Some Provisos*

It may be useful to declare some provisos at the outset of the argument. First, the most obvious explanation for the rise of PSPC, and one that many in South Asian studies no doubt subscribe to, is that it is just the best theory around — it displaced class analysis and political economy because of their obvious shortcomings. I shall not try to counter this notion. In other words, this article will examine the social conditions that explain the rise of PSPC; it will not attempt a substantive assessment. It will be obvious enough that I do not subscribe to this view. I will assume that the reader will be willing to entertain the notion that the causes of PSPC prominence are at least in part institutional and social.

Second, it should be stressed that an argument dealing with trends in intellectual fashion cannot avoid relying on "stylized facts" — somewhat general descriptions that capture basic trends. Hence, for every characterization that I make about South Asian studies over the past three decades or so, it will no doubt be possible to adduce the exception, the example that seems to undermine the argument. But such strategies would undermine the very idea of cultural analysis. I will ask the reader to use some discretion in her use of counterexamples, keeping in mind the distinction between representative works and outliers.

Lastly, our main interest is in the scholarship coming out of the United States, and then from India, with an occasional glance at the British scene. The focus on the United States, as against England, would have been a highly questionable strategy for a paper on South Asian studies even a decade ago. But with every passing year, the center for India scholarship in the Atlantic world is increasingly shifting away from England — its traditional base — and into U.S. universities. This is hardly surprising, given that the phenomenal growth of the U.S. universities in the postwar era has propelled them to dominance in a large number of fields. South Asian studies is no exception. Another reason to focus on the United States is that, in addition to its sheer weight in the production of scholarship, it is where the postmodernist turn has been strongest and the retreat from class analysis the most complete.

## 1. Class Analysis Enters the U.S. Academy

The advance and retreat of class analysis in South Asia scholarship has been tied to the fate of class more generally in the intellectual culture. In this section, I will offer an account of the conditions that allowed for the remarkable resurgence of Marxist theory during the 1960s and '70s in the United States. These were, in some ways, the same as those operative during previous episodes of radical resurgence; but they were also, in other ways, quite unique. In particular, the central place of the university as the site for class theorizing is the crucial fact about both the rise of Marxist theorizing in our time, as well as its demise. In what follows, I will examine how and why the university came to occupy such a central place for the development of radical theory after the 1950s. Within that, we will see how this process, while generalized across the disciplinary divide, was nonetheless uneven in its effects. In particular, while the study of the South was deeply affected by the wave of radicalization, India scholarship underwent a process quite distinct from that of other area specializations. This was to have lasting effect on its subsequent evolution.

Marxism's decline in U.S. academic discourse is unmistakable. But even more remarkable is that it should ever have had any such influence at all. In the twentieth century, there were two periods of massive radicalization and mass mobilizing in the Western world — the decade and a half after World War I and the mythologized "sixties." Each one gave rise to a commensurably deep radicalization in intellectual life, leading to foundational work in Marxist theory, and in radical analysis more generally. What differentiates the two, however, is that much of the theorizing that was done in the earlier period took place in sites outside the university — Lenin, Gramsci, Trotsky, Luxemburg, and the legions of theorists associated with the artistic and cultural movement in the 1920s were all located in Party circles. Even if they had academic jobs, the momentum behind their work came, directly or indirectly, from organized politics. In the United States, even though some inroads were made into the university during the Popular Front period, they were limited.[2] Left theorizing still got most of its energy from sources close to organized politics. One only has to peruse the main academic journals of various disciplines from the time to see that Marxist theory remained quite marginal to mainstream academic life.

The reason for this is not hard to fathom. Universities were, through the interwar period, steadfastly elite institutions. In 1920, around 0.5 percent of the U.S. population attended college, a figure that increased rapidly, but only to reach a miniscule 1.19 percent in 1946, one year after World War II.[3] While the number of colleges and universities grew fairly steadily through the interwar years, the increase basically kept pace with population growth, there being no great explosion in institution-building till a few decades later. In the entire period of the Second and Third Internationals — the highpoint of the socialist movement in the advanced capitalist countries — higher education in the United States remained largely closed to working people. A second reason, the importance of which would become clearer later, was that political organizations of the Left in these years were still viable and a source of attraction to intellectuals, even in the United States. The Communist Party in the 1920s and '30s was not only growing, but became something of a center of gravity for intellectuals, especially during the Popular Front years.[4] So too with smaller Far Left groupings like the Socialist Party and, later, the Socialist Workers Party, which, though small, produced a vibrant internal culture of debate.[5] Hence, while academia remained remote and distant from radical currents, the traditional sites for left-wing theorizing were still a viable option, and exerted great force in setting the agenda for intellectual work.

By the end of World War II, things were already beginning to change. As Perry Anderson has argued, the development of Marxist theory in the postwar world was different from that of the interwar years, in that the site for theorizing was already shifting from Left organizations to the university.[6] Two points ought to be made in this regard. First, even while it is true that Marxists were folded into the university, it is also the case that within this setting they remained a quite marginal force until the middle of the 1960s. With a very few notable exceptions, Marxists were relegated to the margins of debate. They were productive and active, no doubt, but their circle of influence remained quite small. Second, while Marxists did find a haven in academic settings, they were more successful in doing so in Europe than in the United States. In the United States, the 1950s were a historic low point in the visibility of Marxism. It is said, famously, that in that decade, when Paul Baran landed an appointment in the Stanford economics department, he was the only Marxist economist in a major U.S. university. While this may not be technically true, it captures the sense of the times, in the aftermath of McCarthyism, when a whole stratum of Left intellectuals was either pushed out of academic jobs, denied entry, or cowed into silence. The turn to academia after the war was thus real, but it did not by any means insert class analysis as an influential current in Western academic life.

The upsurge of the 1960s turned things around. The mass movements around imperialism, gender, civil rights, and the brief but quite massive labor upsurge, all served to revitalize the Left. But this revival of fortunes did not repeat the experience of the earlier episode around World War I. For one thing, as is well known, the turn to the Left came in large measure from outside the official Communist movement — indeed, it was because of its critiques of the politics of the established parties, and in particular of Stalinism, that this generation came to be known as the New Left. There was some revival in the fortunes of the official Communist parties, no doubt, but by and large, these organizations were as bewildered by the mass mobilizations as were more elite groups. But while the New Left criticized and rejected the conservatism of the official Communist parties, this did not lead to the formation of a new generation of revolutionary organizations, as it had after World War I. Small groupings, largely on the fringe of political life, did spring up for a short period, but few survived the 1970s and fewer still secured any kind of mass base.

The sheer scale and duration of the new movements could not but affect the broader culture. Establishing the lifespan of a mass movement is always difficult, but we can say with confidence that the "sixties" ran into the several years of the following decade. But it was not just the scale of the mobilization that affected intellectual production. Left to its own, this upsurge may have been successfully repelled by the academy much as the one a half-century prior. But this time, the movements coincided with the second salient fact about this episode, which created a distinct identity and trajectory — namely, that these were also the years of the most massive enlargement of higher education in the twentieth century. Between 1945 and 1980, the number of colleges and universities in the country doubled, from 1,650 to more than 3,200, with the bulk of the growth coming after 1960.[7] Furthermore, the university itself became a site of struggle — indirectly, as students swarmed to social movements that were sweeping the nation, but also directly, once the military draft was instituted and hit the student population in particular. University campuses, which had always remained relatively insulated, were now sucked into the vortex.

The coincidence of these two factors made for an intellectual environment radically different from the one fostered by the upsurge of the 1920s. Whereas the burst of theoretical and artistic energy in the 1920s had occurred outside the university, and in the orbit of the organized Left, this time the radicalization of the intelligentsia occurred mainly within the academy. This was especially pronounced in the United States, where the Left political parties were confined to the very margins of national politics — far more than in Europe — and the powerful socialist currents in the labor movement had been purged or driven underground in the 1950s. There were simply very few magnets for the young generation of activists and budding intellectuals outside the boundaries of the campus. On the other hand, through the latter part of the 1970s, the expansion of the higher education system offered an easy and quite safe haven to deepen their analyses and continue some form of radical engagement. The New Left, therefore, not only established a presence in campus life, as the early postwar Marxists had, but because of its numerical weight in the concurrently expanding educational system, actually managed to exert real influence on mainstream academic production.

## 2. The Transformation of Area Studies

This is the context in which we need to approach the advance and retreat of Marxism, or class analysis, within South Asian studies. As academic culture became radicalized and transformed by the tumult, it was to be expected that area studies generally would share in the process. Indeed, if anything, the study of the Third World was at the epicenter of the radicalization. On campuses, the Vietnam War formed something of an axis for many of the movements to come together, and it naturally placed the problem of imperialism at the core of much intellectual work being undertaken at the time. But within this, South Asian studies in the United States stood slightly apart. While it too experienced some growth in class theory and political economy, this was, relative to the experience of other specializations, more limited in scope and depth. As a result, when the New Left went into decline a decade later, South Asia as a field had fewer defenses against the PSPC onslaught. In a very real sense, I will argue, to call the fate of class analysis in South Asian studies a "retreat" is a misnomer — for class as an organizing concept had never advanced very far to begin with.

The most powerful change in analytical frames was probably witnessed in Latin American studies and African studies, though not evenly. This should not be surprising. In the United States, the radicalization brought about by resistance to the Vietnam war naturally led students to begin questioning the nature of U.S. involvement in its own "backyard," and from there, it was but a short step to carry a Marxist framework to the region's internal politics and history. The emergence of powerful revolutionary currents in the region itself gave the radicalization an additional fillip. The Cuban Revolution was of course an electrifying event, but the ongoing radicalization through the 1960s, culminating in the surprising victory of Salvador Allende in Chile and the extraordinary struggles of his regime against internal and external subversion — all this suffused the study of Latin America with debates about the class, class struggle, socialism, etc. This led to the formation of the Union of Radical Latin Americanists in the early 1970s, and its launch of the journal *Latin American Perspectives* some years later under the editorship of Ronald Chilcote.[8]

A similar process was underway with respect to the study of Africa. The 1960s witnessed the onset of decolonization on the continent, a process that continued apace into the 1970s, and again brought U.S. students into direct contact with radical currents from the region that they were studying. As in Latin American studies, it was extremely significant that Africa was not only being swept up into anti-imperialist movements, but that many of these were captained by political organizations committed to some kind of socialist ideology — starting with the Algerian F.L.N and reaching to Frelimo in Mozambique during the 1970s. It would be fair to say that, while African studies in the United States was certainly influenced by the currents, the turn to class was probably more pervasive in the British end of the discipline. Here too, as in Latin American studies, the shift culminated in the establishment of a journal committed to radical and materialist analysis, the remarkable *Review of African Political Economy*.

The range and quality of scholarship generated by these parallel processes is quite extraordinary. For almost two decades, U.S. and British scholars were immersed in an intense series of debates on class dynamics in Latin America and Africa: the structure of capitalism, the nature of the state, the role of imperialism, the composition of the ruling coalitions, the strength and weakness of popular movements, etc. By the middle and end of the 1980s, the bedrock of work on the political economy of both regions was impressive. While internally uneven, the value of this work is not to be underestimated. The deep inroads that Marxist political economy made in these specializations left a lasting impression on their internal culture — which was to become more apparent in the 1990s, in that they were better able to fend off PSPC than was South Asian studies.

## 3. The Peculiarity of South Asian Studies

To an extent, South Asian studies shared in the process of radicalization that overtook other area studies. The founding in 1968 of the Committee of Concerned Asian Scholars and the launch of the *Bulletin of Concerned Asian*

*Scholars* in May 1969 created an opening for Marxist and radical analysis of Asia, in broad parallel with the other left-wing area studies journals. Even though BCAS was initially more focused on East Asia than it was on South Asia, the latter region nonetheless figured prominently in the journal's pages. The subject that experienced the deepest inroads by Marxist analysis was, unsurprisingly, agrarian relations, both in the United States and in Great Britain. Under the steady hand of Terry Byres, the London-based *Journal of Peasant Studies* quickly emerged as the central locus for agrarian studies generally, but with a particular interest in the subcontinent. Byres himself penned some highly influential essays on the Indian rural scene,[9] but the journal became the center of gravity for several U.S. and British names associated with the class analysis of Indian agriculture: John Harriss, Keith Griffin, Barbara Harriss-White, Ronald Herring, Gail Omvedt, and others.[10] To this day, in the English-speaking world, the analysis of Indian rural social structure and history remains class oriented, and in no small measure due to the body of work published by this journal.

Still, if we look beyond the domain of agrarian studies, what stands out about South Asia scholarship in the United States is that Marxism and political economy made little impression on the field in the 1970s. It remained curiously resistant — or perhaps unattractive — to the New Left. Hence, class analysis rarely reached out beyond the confines of rural social structure or movements. With the exception of Francine Frankel's book on post-independence politics, U.S. and British scholars produced little on the class basis of the Indian state;[11] less still on the Indian capitalist class, or on the dynamics of industrialization; virtually nothing on the structure and fortunes of the labor movement, etc. If we compare this with the flood of class analysis focused on other regions, the difference is striking. While the collapse of democratic regimes in South America was the occasion for Guillermo O'Donnell's analysis of bureaucratic authoritarianism, which in turn triggered an immensely rich debate on the dynamics of development in the region, it had no counterpart in South Asia scholarship — even after the Emergency. And while the Tanzanian experiment under Julius Nyerere gave rise to a whole literature on the nature and limits of "African socialism," nothing even remotely comparable analyzed its Nehruvian counterpart; no parallel to the "Kenya debate," which became an opening to study the regional bourgeoisie in Africa; nothing on the internal structure of the Indian ruling class; there still is not a single study of postwar labor in India beyond a few journalistic books. Indeed, it is fair to say that while class analysis was growing by leaps and bounds for other regional specializations social scientific work on India more generally slipped into decline in the 1970s and 1980s. So it not just that class analysis failed to transform the research agenda in these years — it is that materialist analysis as such remained on pretty shaky ground.[12]

There are, I believe, two likely reasons for the discipline's imperviousness to Marxism. The first — and this is somewhat conjectural, though, I believe, reasonable — is simply a matter of timing and geography. Latin American studies and African studies attracted some of the best and brightest of the New Left because those regions were undergoing momentous changes at the time. The 1960s was when British colonialism finally collapsed in Africa, but more importantly, the whole colonial game seemed to be coming to an end — not only exciting times to be studying Africa, but a good reason to *enter* the field. India, on the other hand, had shaken off British rule almost a half-century before — and was thus less attractive to young radicals. In the United States, it was not only that Fidel, Che, and Allende appeared relevant to students, but U.S. citizens also felt a responsibility to involve themselves in the struggle of their counterparts below — after decades of U.S. subversion and terror in the region. India, on the other hand, was pretty remote and rather mysterious in comparison. On both sides of the Atlantic, it was the combination of geographic and historic links, on the one hand, and the explosion in class conflict in those regions, on the other hand, that seems to have attracted activist and radical scholars. India as well had mass mobilizations at this time, and its own radicalization, as I will discuss later, and this did attract some to the Marxist current, but nowhere near on the same scale as in the other two continents.

A second reason for the weaker Marxist impulse, I believe, is that South Asian studies already had a well-consolidated and entrenched internal culture, namely, classical Orientalism. Had a powerful radical current desired to enter the field and take it over, it might perhaps have been able to push back the older approaches and take their place, but given that India's attraction to student radicals was weaker to begin with, old-style Indologists never had to work particularly hard to maintain their dominance. This is crucial, because the traditional approach to Indian studies was as far removed from class analysis as is imaginable. Whereas Marxism was motivated by a bedrock materialism and universalist assumptions about human needs and interests, the Orientalist tradition was resolutely *culturalist* in approach — meaning not just that it focused on the production of culture, but on culture as the *source* of the institutional and structural differences of these areas from the West.

So, because of the weaker attraction of the field to young radicals, and because of the presence of a powerful and consolidated tradition that was markedly uncongenial, not just to Marxism, but even to materialism, South Asian studies was not transformed to anywhere near the same extent as the other two areas I have discussed. And even more ominously, as I noted above, it was not just Marxism, but social science approaches more generally in the field that went into temporary decline.[13] It is easy to forget that in the early-to-mid 1960s social science literature on India was abundant and shared similar basic assumptions with scholarship on other regions. Indeed, the work on India fares pretty well in comparison to what was being produced on the other parts of the world. Books by Stanley Kochanek, Alvin Hansen, Myron Weiner, Paul Brass, and others were certainly not exemplars of radical analysis.[14] But they were entirely in synch with the social science literature on, say, Latin America — and sometimes better. Indeed, the stream of U.S. scholarship on India in the two decades after Independence was noteworthy and it strained mightily against the conventions of Orientalist scholarship. But even this framework suffered a relative decline in the 1970s.

Two consequences of this retreat are worth noting. First, within the social science scholarship on India, there was not much change between the 1960s and the 1980s. Kochanek, Hanson, and others had worked within a basically pluralist framework, which was in keeping with the conventions of the time; two decades later, Lloyd and Suzanne Rudolph published ***In Pursuit of Lakshmi***, the major study of the Indian political economy produced in the 1980s —an exemplar of the same pluralist analysis.[15] It was as if the New Left had never existed. But more importantly, even the social scientific literature — such as it was — did not set the tone for the discipline. Because of the unshaken place of old-fashioned Indology, culturalism retained a very strong hold on the discipline's basic assumptions, and in its mode of training. Religion, language, literature — these were what incoming students encountered when they took a South Asian studies class. They served not as the phenomena to be explained, but as the *sources* of Indian history and its politics.

Here, then, is the answer to the first question that I proposed to take up in this article. Why did PSPC take deeper root in South Asian studies than in other regional concentrations? Because South Asian studies never underwent the kind of transformation that other parts of the area studies field had experienced in the 1970s. By the 1980s, Latin American studies and Africana had been overtaken by the New Left on a scale sufficient to establish a solid political economy tradition. Not so in the case of India scholarship. The New Left largely passed India by. This was particularly important for South Asia scholarship, because the traditional approach of the field was one that gave central importance to discourse and culture. This trajectory made the field especially fertile ground for not only a decline in class analysis — since the latter had never been very widespread in the fist place — but for the rise of PSPC in particular. When the full force of PSPC came to be felt in area studies during the 1980s, it could easily meld with the existing practice of this field in particular. South Asian studies was to provide fertile ground for the growth of PSPC.

## 4. The Social Basis of Nativism

Had the convergence between New Left's trajectory and old-style Indology remained the provenance of U.S. scholars, its influence would have been significant, but limited. It would have been too easily associated with a kind of conservative reflex in the wake of the Left resurgence of the 1970s. But by the late 1980s, this trend was given an additional boost by the emergence of a stratum of Indian intellectuals — some based in the subcontinent, but many located in U.S. universities — who were operating in a methodological framework that also gave culture, symbols, and discourse a central explanatory role. Further, these were intellectuals whose self-identity was openly radical and anti-imperialist, and this only added legitimacy to arguments that progressives at least would have regarded as a continuation of the conservative tradition of old-style Indology. To understand how this strand of theorizing could not only emerge but become so influential, and how Indian intellectuals could play so prominent a role in its dissemination, we must again locate the evolution of

South Asian studies in the wider trajectory of the New Left in the United States after the 1960s.

I argued in the preceding section that the New Left failed to transform the basic assumptions guiding South Asia scholarship in Anglo-American universities. But while the New Left may have failed to have a direct effect on the field, it did exercise an important *indirect* effect, by transforming the academic and cultural environment in which area studies functioned. In particular, it created a ***structural space*** for intellectuals from the Global South to wield real influence. In more propitious times, this probably would have given a significant impetus to Marxist and class-based scholarship on U.S. campuses — indeed, for a while it did, and in some cases, it still does. But the timing was largely detrimental to any such outcome. The internationalization of the fields came at a time when there was a greater space for scholars from the Global South, but when interest in class theory was in rapid decline. Even more, the Left was turning firmly toward a culturalist bent. This placed a filter on the kinds of Third World scholarship that elicited interest in the United States. The arrival of projects like Subaltern studies did not, therefore, signal a continuation of the radical thrust of the 1970s. What it did, ironically, was legitimize and give a radical face to a literature that undermined class analysis.

### *The Sixties Civilizes the United States*

The massive increases in higher education during the 1960s and '70s created an enclave where radicals could find some haven, as described in the preceding section. But another critical consequence of this same phenomenon was that it also changed the social ecology of the university. This not only meant a massive increase in the sheer number of Americans undertaking some form of higher education, but a change in their composition as well — chiefly, much greater numbers of women and students of color. Higher education now became much more of a mass institution than it had been in the interwar years; and while universities did not, by any means, overturn class hierarchies with their "massification," nor could they simply be regarded as the ivory towers of years past. The social composition of student bodies was now more representative of the population at large. This would have had an appreciable effect on intellectual culture under any circumstances: a new stratum of students would never have streamed into colleges and passively abided by the traditional elite canon. Academics would have been under considerable pressure to address, at the very least, matters of racial and gender dynamics.

But what greatly heightened the prospects of such a turn was that this transformation of students' social composition was occurring in the midst of a mass radicalization of students across the country. In more neutral circumstances, there would have been some pressure for changes in curricula and instruction, perhaps to make it less glaringly reflective of the dominant culture. But in the context of the times, the push went further, toward a more profound change of academic culture itself. On one side, entire new programs focusing on ethnicity, gender, African Americans, Latinos, and the like were established. And these focused specifically on the power relations in which these groups were enmeshed, bringing matters of oppression and marginalization to the fore.

Just as important as the changes in curriculum, however, was a powerful momentum for initiating changes in the composition of staff and faculty. Universities now entered an era when it could no longer be taken for granted that patterns of departmental staffing would remain unaffected by the content of the curriculum. Newly formed African American studies or Latino studies departments, for example, could not ignore the need for racial diversity — whether in their faculty, or in the literature they taught. This was one of the most important cultural advances brought about by the movements of the 1970s — the aggregate effect of the anti-imperialist and civil rights movements in the United States, not to mention the global collapse of colonial empires since the 1960s. The scope of what was regarded as acceptable intellectual production exploded to not just include the work of subordinate groups and regions — but to demand it.

As part of this transformation, the content of area studies could not remain dominated by Anglo-U.S. scholarship. And, after a time, nor could hiring patterns continue unchanged. By the 1980s, it was possible to observe a noticeable shift in graduate curricula, as U.S. scholars actively included research coming out of the developing world — not just as ornamentation, but as a valid and essential part of the scholarly universe. A structural space had opened up for some of the extraordinary outpouring of scholarship, literary work, and polemics from the postcolonial world. This was to have a profound effect on the evolution of the field, in two ways. First, scholarship coming out of the Global South was now considered not only a legitimate part of the intellectual universe, but in some respects even central to it. In English departments, for example, it was in the 1980s that the study of colonial and postcolonial literature became a legitimate specialization for Ph.D. students. Second, once this new culture had set in, it would incline area studies departments to consciously seek out scholars from the Global South in their hiring practices, or at least to include the latter in their ambit. Disciplines where area specialization played a central role — history and anthropology, but cultural studies as well — felt the pressure especially strongly.

## *The Limits of Campus Radicalism*

While these advances in the academic culture were real, they were structured by an underlying contradiction, viz., that as matters of social oppression were entering the mainstream of scholarly production, the concern with class and capitalism was beginning to wane. This was to have a tremendous impact on the kind of work from the South that would be promoted in the Atlantic world, so it is worth considering.

In principle, the inclusion of gender, race, etc., as central to radical analysis could have led to a deepening of the class-based agenda of the 1970s — and for a brief spell it did. But the dominant trend was for an abandonment of the latter. This should not be surprising. Intellectuals associated with the New Left were primarily located in universities. They were therefore subject to two sets of influences: their immediate professional surroundings and the wider social integument. It was the latter that had drawn students and academics toward Marxist and socialist currents in the 1970s, through the anti-imperialist movement and the labor mobilizations at the beginning of the decade. By the end of the decade, however, while the movements around nonclass identities had scored impressive gains, there was no comparable advance for the working class. Indeed, the balance of class power shifted powerfully to the right, and by the onset of the Reagan era, a full-scale assault on labor and the Left was underway. As a class movement, the New Left had met with a crushing defeat.

In some respects, this mirrored the defeats of the working class movement worldwide in the 1930s, which was followed by rightward shift in political culture. But the setbacks of the New Left during the 1970s were in many respects deeper. For the upsurges of the first quarter of the twentieth century had left in their wake a panoply of socialist parties and class organizations, which provided the milieu in which radical intellectuals survived for much of the century. They served as conduits — however weak — to the more radical sections of the labor movement, and immersed the intellectuals in an intensely charged culture outside of academic institutions. But in the case of the New Left, even this was not accomplished — its defeat was more complete, leaving no organizational legacy, and hence no political milieu that could sustain its intellectual coherence. The environment that most directly shaped the evolution of New Left intellectuals, therefore, was the academy.

The defeat of the working class upsurge across the advanced capitalist world was critical to the evolution of the New Left. Intellectuals had little or no connection with actual working class organizations — unlike the Left of generations past — and what they saw of the movement was now in tatters. Their world was now confined to the walls of the university, and their social milieu consisted of the professional middle class. This set into train a somewhat natural process of deradicalization. First, and most directly, it triggered a growing sense of disillusionment — first with the prospect of anticapitalist movements, and later, with the very idea of mass organizing.[16] It was during the 1980s that the argument become increasingly popular within radical circles that a major flaw in Marxist theorizing was an overly optimistic, even teleological, take on class formation. Marx was guilty of assuming highly deterministic relations between class structure and class formation — or between class-in-itself and class-for-itself, as the jargon would have it. Such criticisms led to two reactions. One was a gathering pessimism about the salience of class analysis itself, within large sections of the erstwhile Left; the second was a turn to culture and discourse to explain the highly mediated relation between class structure and class formation — a turn that, over time, gave shorter and shorter shrift to the former pole of the dyad.[17] This wing of the New Left became the vanguard of the turn to culturalism over time, and provided the seedbed for the growth of PSPC, both within area studies, and without.

By the middle of the 1980s, the New Left had mostly been domesticated into academic culture. Class analysis was practiced only within a small slice of it, and this was an increasingly marginal component of the academic mainstream. If a pressure for the deepening of class analysis was to come, it would have had to be from below — the students. But here too, there was no reason to expect any such development. For students, a college education is a means of social mobility. Even though their origin may be in the working class, their aspirations are of a more elite nature. For those students who make it into college, the mere fact of social advancement serves to confirm central elements of the dominant ideology, which insists on the fluidity of social hierarchies, and the absence of structural constraints. The mere fact of more working class students entering higher education — as they did after the 1950s — would not generate a mass base for socialist ideas. On the other hand, while students coming to college are escaping from their class constraints, they continue to experience varieties of social discrimination, even in their new environment — around issues of identity. So while college dilutes awareness of class exploitation, it often heightens sensitivity to one's subordination on social lines. The result is to create a mass base for the study, and the critique, of nonclass forms of domination — or at least, to evacuate the class dimensions of social domination.

This institutional environment created a mass base for what we now call "identity politics" on the campus. This meant that even though class analysis was on the decline, there would be no return to the status quo ante — at least on these other issues. Hence, while the retreat of radicals into the university established an "upper limit" on their radicalism — in that class was more or less taken off the table in rapid order — the changes of the 1970s also put in place a "lower limit" on how far toward the past the culture would drift. In other words, the changed composition of the campus, in the context of the shifts in broader culture, meant that the retreat from class politics would not trigger a slide away from radicalism as such. Criticism of class domination would find firm anchor in universities. Hence, forms of radicalism that were indifferent to, or even hostile to, class politics would find fertile ground on U.S. campuses in the 1980s — compared to the 1950s, when any kind of radicalism would have met with great hostility. To anticipate, this created the mass base for a movement like PSPC, which advertised itself as a critique of colonial and postcolonial domination — but with little reference to those elements that Marxists had always focused on: class, exploitation, etc. So as area studies came to include more and more voices from the South in its normal functioning, scholars who found this political shift away from class most appealing were the ones who got the greatest attention.

The forgoing discussion lays the basis for understanding our main concern: how South Asian studies, as practiced in the United States, not only experienced a turn to PSPC, but did so with scholars of Indian origin playing a central role. The discussion in Section 3 explained how South Asian studies was especially vulnerable to the advance of PSPC, because Marxism never made much of a dent on the field, leaving a heavy bias toward cultural analysis. In the present section, I suggested that while the New Left did not directly enter the field, its gains in academia more generally, and the consequent transformation of academic culture, did have a critical *indirect* effect on how South Asia scholarship was practiced: it was now impossible to ignore the rich outpouring of scholarship from the subcontinent. Intellectuals of South Asian descent were seen as peers and as natural leaders in the field, whose work was now actively, even eagerly, promoted.

One effect of the changed university environment, then, was to create a space for the increased prominence of Indian intellectuals. But this still left considerable leeway for choosing between different strands of research — different orientations — among such scholars. And this is where the limits of the New Left, as it entered the 1980s, came into play. By the time that the cultural changes had seeped into the firmament of area studies, class analysis was in deep decline. As Anglo-American scholars looked out into the South and sought out scholarship with which they could relate, which they valued and considered exemplary, there was a natural affinity with approaches that *eschewed* a central focus on class and even materialism altogether. Indeed, there was an inclination to view Marxist work as somewhat quaint, or worse, as simply lacking in sophistication. The selectional pressure *against* class, in other words, was complemented by a selectional bias *toward* work that could be easily assimilated into the dominant trends in the field — an emphasis on cultural or discursive frames within which to analyze.

This was the breach into which stepped Subaltern studies, and this was the environment that shaped its evolution toward exemplifying PSPC.

## 5. The Arrival of Subaltern Studies (and Such)

What is remarkable about the importation of the Subaltern studies series into the United States is how influential it has been beyond South Asian studies, a field that has historically occupied a relatively ghettoized position in U.S. academia. That it could do so is largely because the series melded easily into the intellectual culture of area studies, and of disciplines in which area specializations play an important part — especially history and anthropology. In some respects, the fact that Indian scholars experienced particular success in the new context was institutionally driven First, there was the mundane and quite ordinary fact that, unlike much of the developing world, Indian intellectual production was carried out primarily in English. It was thus readily accessible, not just to specialists in South Asian studies, but to the far reaches of the academic community. This immediately distinguished it from Latin American intellectual circles, which were also producing extremely rich and textured scholarship, but out of reach to anyone lacking the language skills. On top of this was the fact of networks. Indian scholarship was already located in the social milieu of Anglo-American universities, not only by its existing connections with U.S. universities, but also by its long connections with Cambridge, Oxford, and London. This was a circuit that many U.S. scholars knew well, far more so than one that went through Dar es Salaam, Mexico City, or Cairo — all of which were producing tremendous scholarship of their own at the time.

But of course, it wasn't just any Indian scholarship that benefited from these factors. If it were just the institutional factors mentioned above, the importation of scholarship from the subcontinent would have been much more broadly based. There was a flourishing school of Marxist historians and political economists in India who were not given anywhere near the same attention as was Subaltern studies. Indeed, many of the same factors also applied to historical and political research being conducted in South Africa, but which, at the time, was strenuously Marxist in orientation. This latter stream of work, if anything, ought to have resonated more powerfully in the United States, since the middle and late 1980s was the time when campuses across the country were humming with antiapartheid activism. But while the South African Marxists, and their Indian counterparts, did garner some attention (especially the former), this did not even approach the accolades that were showered on the Subaltern series. So, clearly, more was at work here than the mere fact of linguistic affinity or academic networks.

Perhaps the most important element favoring the patronage of work such as that of the Subaltern collective was that it contained streams within it that not only came out of a familiar institutional milieu, but were also moving in a *theoretical* direction that was familiar and attractive — both to the New Left and to the practitioners of South Asian studies. This is an important point to stress, because in the commentaries and reflections that are in circulation, the role played by Gayatri Chakravarty Spivak in promoting the series is given a great deal of attention. It is becoming something of a fixture that Volume Four of the series, in which Spivak's famous essay "Subaltern Studies: Deconstructing Historiography" was appended as the closing chapter, forms something of a watershed. This is often presented as the point when the series made its entrance into the U.S. scene, and which triggered the turn in a more committed post-structuralist direction.[18] Spivak's imprimatur is accorded some significant responsibility for the series' subsequent success, in that it acted as a stamp of approval to the broader post-Marxist currents. When, a few years later, Edward Said did the same by writing the Foreward to a collection of essays from the Subaltern series, it only added to this dynamic.[19]

Spivak's role in legitimizing Subaltern studies to the U.S. academic crowd can't be denied; her influence was enormous. But it should not be exaggerated. The intellectual community would hardly fete unquestioningly everything Gayatri Spivak, and later Edward Said, ordained. . What made their endorsements effective was that, from the start, the series was crafted in a framework attractive to reigning sensibilities in area studies, both its Left variant, and its more traditional one.

The most important component of this framework was the influence of Antonio Gramsci. It was the influence of Gramscian concepts that made Subaltern studies appropriate for consumption in the United States — both in South Asia scholarship and within the New Left. The very title of the series signaled his importance to the project. But most crucially, it was their interpretation of Gramsci's work that made it attractive. This was an interpretation that took him to be a theorist of culture and consciousness. Hence, while the series in its early volumes did contain essays of a recognizable Marxist bent, those of a more consciously Gramscian orientation were concerned with the analysis of discursive formations and the production of consciousness. From the start, the collective accorded a central role not just to peasant consciousness and discourse, but to the discursive basis of elite hegemony over the nationalist movement, and to the qualities of nationalism as a discursive formation. This was most evident in the work of Partha Chatterjee and Ranajit Guha, who also went on to become perhaps the most influential members of the collective.[20] But it was a preoccupation that ran through the whole collective, effectively marginalizing the concern with the material conditions of class domination.

This struck a resonant chord with the prevailing understanding of Gramsci in the West. The middle of the 1980s was probably the time when Gramsci's influence was peaking in Anglo-American scholarship, particularly in the historical profession.[21] But it was a specific interpretation of his work, particularly of his theorization of hegemony, that was gaining currency. By the middle of the 1980s, two interpretations of his argument were making the rounds. One was an ***interest-based***, or objectivist, interpretation, formulated most clearly by Adam Przeworski. For Przeworski, Gramsci based the stability of class domination in the ruling class's successful coordination of its interests with those of subordinate groups. The clearest example of successful hegemonic rule was, on this argument, European social democracy — since it embodied an ongoing negotiated settlement between representatives of labor and capital.[22] Similar approaches were taken by Michael Burawoy, Erik Olin Wright, and Joseph Femia, among others.[23]

A second interpretation took hegemony to be grounded in the ruling class's successful ***ideological or cultural*** indoctrination — "interpellation" — of subordinate groups. In this approach, interests played a secondary role in the process, not least because the very idea of objective interests was frequently denied. ***This*** Gramsci could be traced back to Althusser's followers,[24] as filtered through the influential Birmingham University's Centre for Cultural Studies, Ernesto Laclau and Chantal Mouffe's ***Hegemony and Socialist Strategy,***[25] and others. Hegemony thus came to be taken as grounded in the generation of effective discursive strategies. Hence, whereas the analytical focus of the former group of theorists tended to be class organizations and class strategies, the latter group trained its lens on the instruments of ideological production — literature, television, film, etc. Indeed, for a number of years, before post-structuralism took deep roots in the Anglo-American academy, cultural studies subsisted in a basically Gramscian framework.

Even though both of these interpretations of Gramsci were in circulation, it was the second, cultural take, that was far and away the dominant one, especially in the humanities and anthropology. And this was also the very approach that was (and continues to be) accepted by the Subaltern collective. The Subalterns' Gramsci was, as in much of the New Left at the time, a theorist of ideology and culture — not of the material basis of consent, or of class struggle. Gramsci in Delhi and Calcutta was as much a culture maven as he was in Chicago, New York, or London — not to mention Birmingham.[26] This take on his work thus provided a natural point of convergence between the two streams, and a bridgehead for the series into the circuits of the New Left. It is in this context that Spivak's endorsement ought to be viewed. Her patronage was effective because the Subaltern series was recognizable, and digestible, to the U.S. audience. Now of course, *given* this underlying convergence, her intervention was of enormous importance. Without it, the series would have been read and admired, but probably as one of the several efforts at a "history from below" that were ongoing both in the North and South — important, and innovative enough, but not of particular interest to those beyond the specialist community. With the ongoing interest shown by Spivak, and especially by the influential essays she wrote interpreting and introducing Subaltern studies, the project graduated from a disciplinary initiative to something much more. This was the ingredient that allowed the series to break out of the South Asia ghetto and explode onto the larger academic scene.

From that point on, Subaltern studies marched in lockstep with the New Left's turn away from class analysis and toward a wholesale embrace of post-Marxist theorizing.[27] Indeed, while the Gramscian roots of the project made it digestible to the New Left in the West, and hence eased its entry into the American academy, the project quickly assumed the role of a vanguard in the drive toward post-Marxism. And with every new volley against the putative shortcomings of the Marxist tradition, the leading theorists of the *Subaltern* series vaulted into ever greater prominence as *radical* theorists. As we have seen in the preceding discussion, the broader demise of class analysis among intellectuals was already underway, a more or less direct result of the rightward political shift, the defeat of working class movements, and the domestication of Marxists within the university. But at the same time, the real gains made by nonclass movements, along with the changed composition of the student body, created conditions friendly to critical analysis of a limited kind — indeed, its very hostility to class made it quite appealing to upwardly mobile students and the radical professoriate. What gave the Subalterns special relevance was that this was an intellectual project that came out of the South, and which not only was shedding its Marxist roots, but was blazing the trail in bringing PSPC to area studies. The very fact of the Indian identity of so many of its leading lights gave legitimacy to the theoretical shift.

The culturalism of the series — whether Gramscian or post-structuralist — also made the series palatable to the more traditional wings of South Asia studies, who had been trained to view India through the prism of its culture and ideology. One might have thought that mainstream Indologists would have little interest in an intellectual project inspired by a Marxian perspective, regardless of its particulars. But by the 1980s, the culture of South Asian studies had moved decidedly to the Left in at least this respect, that critical views of colonialism had to be taken seriously, and especially if they were coming out of Indian scholarship. What is more, the Gramscian or culturalist wing of critical scholarship was taken, both within the field and in area studies more generally, as being at the cutting edge. Traditionalist scholars had every reason to join the stream. Here was a field — old-style Indology — that was quite at ease in presenting basically Orientalist constructions of Indian history and politics, explaining economic or political dynamics through the content of religious texts or as expressions of deep cultural facts of a civilization — and it was handed a theory (PSPC) that not only took social reality to be a discursive construction, but stamped it with the moral and intellectual authority of the latest radical fashions. The cache of its moral authority should not be underestimated here. The most venerable of nineteenth century disciplines, long associated with conservative and colonial sympathies, was able to integrate itself with an intellectual trend that carried its anti-imperialism on its very decked-out sleeve.

One consequence of this turn of events was that, in rapid order, well-established traditionalist scholars were able to reinvent themselves as sophisticated practitioners of the new discourse theory. Thus Ronald Inden, who penned a well-known, and thoroughly traditionalist, text on Bengali caste and culture in the 1970s,[28] emerged a decade later as a self-proclaimed scourge of that approach with the publication of *Imagining India* — which, despite its excoriation of Orientalism, never strays far from the relentless preoccupation with ritual, symbols, and caste.[29] Inden gave an explicit nod to Subaltern studies as "the first time, since colonization [sic]" that Indians are "showing sustained signs of re-appropriating the capacity [sic] to represent themselves" — the evidence being, not surprisingly, that the collective's approach converges with Inden's own.[30]

Thus, the strenuously culturalist commitments of the Indian avant-garde gave it a natural resonance within South Asian studies in the United States, where traditionalist approaches had never been dislodged, as well as providing the bridge to the broader New Left. From the Left, the route to treating the social world as an artifact of culture, or of discourse, came through a defanged and denatured Gramsci, and then French philosophy; from the more conservative wing, it came through the Durkheimian framework of a Dumont or through the traditional Orientalist tradition. Now even if class analysis had made serious inroads into the field, there is little doubt that a PSPC turn would have wielded significant influence after the 1980s — its spread occurred throughout area studies, regardless of their association with Marxism in the 1970s. But it is equally plausible to suggest that, if the landscape had not been so barren of class analysis, the slide into PSPC would not have been so severe — as, indeed, it has not been in more radical wings of the area studies universe. South Asian studies turned out to be one of the few fields in which the radical and the not-so-radical wings of the field could converge on their hostility to class theory.

## 6. The Empire Strikes Back: India as Satellite

The decline of class analysis, and its displacement by PSPC, has been especially severe in South Asia scholarship as practiced in the United States. But it would be wrong to imagine that matters in India itself remained unchanged. It is hard to miss the fact that decline in the United States has been mirrored by a similar dynamic in Indian scholarship as well. The culturalism and anti-Marxism of PSPC that have affected South Asian studies in the United States have become tremendously popular in academic settings in India. And here too, we see a generational bubble similar to the one in the West: to the extent that class analysis and Marxism still survives, it does so mainly among intellectuals of the older generation, radicalized in the 1960s and after. Within the younger generation, the far more common orientation — especially in the humanities and anthropology — is firmly set in the direction of PSPC. Class analysis in India, while certainly more visible than in the West, is unmistakably under stress, especially in elite universities.

Now, an immediate caveat is on order. And it is an important one, for it also provides a clue to some of the sources behind Marxism's decline. The turn away from class analysis has not spread across, or even through, most of the forums for intellectual production in the subcontinent. In universities and settings outside the major metropolitan centers, Marxism continues to play a central role in political and cultural debate. Literary production continues to have a deep base in socialist traditions, especially in vernacular languages. Theoretical debates, too, continue to utilize class analysis in settings where the English-speaking intelligentsia have not usurped the available space. Where class *has* made a visible retreat is in the English-speaking elite universities located in Delhi, Calcutta, Hyderabad, and a few other cities. Further, even though Marxism has taken a beating in the elite Indian universities, I do not intend to suggest that it has disappeared. A respectable phalanx of Marxists continues to persevere, not only in the social sciences, but also in cultural studies — the field where, in the United States, there has been the greatest retreat.

The basic causes behind the retreat of class in intellectual discourse in elite universities in India is, I believe, two-fold: first, a fairly deep shift in the social environment of academic production, and second, a much deepened integration of elite academic life into the U.S. orbit since the 1990s. The former weakened the Marxian impulse in Indian academic culture, so that it was, by the late 1980s more hospitable to various flavors of post-Marxist theorizing; the latter functioned to amplify these tendencies by inserting a large number of Indian academics into U.S. academia, either as professors, or as visiting scholars, or as graduate students.

### *Sources of Vitality*

It is a remarkable fact that, for close to four decades, class analysis occupied a prominent place in elite academic production in India, even if it was not the dominant strain. Certainly, some institutional and political facts accounted for this state of affairs.

There is no doubt that an "official" commitment to socialism — even if it was, in reality, state-capitalism — was an enabling factor in the longevity of class analysis. Hence, the very fact of a powerful Planning Commission created a space for structuralist and heterodox economists, making it easier for Marxists to achieve respectability; Indira Gandhi's decision to set up Jawaharlal Nehru University (JNU) in the early 1970s, and to allow it an avowedly progressive mission, provided institutional support to radical scholarship. JNU became an extraordinary space for critical analysis in the two decades that followed; and even the official state discourse of egalitarianism, despite its obvious ideological functions, sustained an attention to class issues.

But this tilt within the state could only create the *space* for radical analysis. It could not determine scholarly quality or vitality. If it were only the state's adoption of socialism that sustained the culture of class analysis, there is no reason to have expected Indian Marxism to be any more creative or vital than the stultifying theoretical work that emanated from the Soviet Union or comes, these days, from China. The remarkable vitality of intellectual production on the Left — not only in specialist circles, but also in the political magazines like the *Economic and Political Weekly*, *Mainstream*, *Frontier*, and others — required fuel from independent sources. The main such source was the two eras of mass radicalization that came with the wave of mobilization before Independence, and then the resurgence of Left struggles in the wake of Naxalbari. Two generations of intellectuals were deeply affected by these movements, each of which had not only a significant class content, but articulated its concerns in the language of class.

The whole arc of politics from the 1960s to the late 1970s is important in this regard. The radicalization of intellectual culture that came in the ea of late colonialism was very significant, no doubt. But left to its own, the impulse would have most likely spent itself within a generation. Naxalbari served to not only renew Left culture, but to unleash a torrent of debate on everything from political strategy to the more abstruse questions regarding the conceptualization of Indian history and culture. In doing so, it opened entirely new vistas in scholarship. India in the 1970s thus joined the global melee that produced a whole new generation of radicals, and in the subcontinent, a new generation of Marxists. Indeed, this was probably the zenith of class analysis in South Asia; if Marxism ever approached dominance in the subcontinent, it was probably in the heady decade of the 1970s, as the generation of '47 was joined by the newer cohort of radicals from the turmoil of '68.

This direct engagement with politics was amplified by more distal factors, chief among which was the tectonic shift occurring in world politics — most importantly, the epochal collapse of colonial empires. If we start at the immediate postwar years, the whole period witnessed an escalating progression of mass struggle and decolonization, most all of which was led by avowedly socialist parties — again, ignoring for the moment the actual content of these "socialisms." Whatever their actual politics may have been once in power (or even before), the combination of their rhetoric, with their very real imbrication in mass movements, added to the resonance that Marxist ideas had for middle class intellectuals. On the other side of this equation, the very vulnerability of colonial powers to these struggles gave great succor to those (like Marxists), whose framework rested on the centrality of class conflict and mass struggle. The whole dynamic reached its crescendo in the mid-'70s with the U.S. withdrawal from Vietnam, on the heels of which came the abrupt and total collapse of Portuguese rule in Africa. This global political dynamic served to amplify the effects of more local political shifts. For two generations, it must have seemed as if capitalism was reeling under the hammer blows of radicalized mass movements.

And yet, a decade later, class analysis in the subcontinent began its decline. In some ways, this is not altogether surprising. By the end of the 1980s, Marxism was in retreat not just in India, but across much of the world. Intellectual discourse was, by that point, being shaped by new forces, that pushed class analysis to the background before marginalizing it altogether. To some extent, it was only natural that South Asia scholarship should be pulled into this slipstream. What is noteworthy is how rapidly the change occurred among Indianists, and the particular intellectual currents that now emerged as dominant. In a country like the United States, where Marxism had never been anything but marginal in intellectual life before the 1970s, it was not unexpected that this kind of radical scholarship would wane over time, as the pull of social movements weakened. But given that South Asia scholarship, particularly coming out of India itself, had been so steeped in the language of class for four decades, its marginalization merits some discussion.

## *Sources of Decline*

While Marxist intellectual culture has undergone a decline across much of the world since the 1980s, the decline has by no means been universal, even in the developing world. Through the end of the 1990s, there remained a visible stream of literature emanating from Brazil, South Korea, and to a lesser extent, South Africa, that was committed to some kind of class-based theorizing. The factors responsible for this are not hard to locate. In each of these countries, the 1980s and after witnessed significant mobilizations of workers and peasants, led by fiercely left-wing union federations and political organizations. On the subcontinent, however, the political winds pushed in the opposite direction. The past two decades have marked something of a watershed in modern India. In contrast to the four decades that preceded it, the period since the mid-1980s has been distinctly unpropitious for radicalizing the intelligentsia.

To begin, liberalization has, at least to this point, been a distinctly conservatizing force on the urban middle class. An expanding private sector, the opening up of consumer credit, the greater presence of multinationals looking for English-trained talent — all of this has ballooned the income of several layers within the middle class. And as elsewhere, the cultural and political effects have rippled far beyond the incidence of actual material changes. Even if urban youth and aspirant professionals do not achieve the full extent of their ambitions, it is the orientation to these career paths, and their cultural accoutrements, that is at issue. One need only look to the extraordinary enthusiasm for liberalization in the English media to get some idea of the hostility that the middle class evinces toward the Left, or toward any whiff of class mobilization.

This broad cultural turn has only been exacerbated by the fate of political movements. The uprisings around the time of Naxalbari, which played such an important role in radicalizing a generation, were only twenty years removed from the mass upheavals that accompanied Independence. It has now been close to forty years — twice as long as the preceding hiatus — since Left movements of anywhere near that scope or longevity have emerged in India. Indeed, the mobilizations that have occurred have tended to further *conservatize* the urban middle class: the emergence of Hindutva as a mass strategy of the Sangh Parivar in the 1990s, and the massive mobilization against the Mandal Commission.[31] Not surprisingly, the political culture within universities tilted visibly in a rightward direction during the decade.[32]

These are not propitious conditions for a renewal of Marxism or class analysis. By the late 1980s, it was already possible to see an increasing prominence of various and sundry post-Marxist strands of theorizing in the academic culture. What gave this movement explosive force, however, was some more narrowly institutional facts about elite academic life in India. Chief among these was a deepened integration of Delhi, Calcutta, and some other cities into U.S. academic life. It is important to stress, again, the specificity of the U.S. connection, so as to avoid characterizing it as an integration into the West as such. Indian intellectuals had been integrated into Western academic life for a very long time — only the main conduit had, for obvious reasons, been the United Kingdom. There were two changes that came in the 1990s.

The first was the basic reorientation, with a relative shift away from England, and toward the United States.[33] This should not be surprising, since, in the wake of Thatcher's assault on higher education in the United Kingdom, U.S. universities had rapidly risen to preeminence in the developed world, especially for graduate instruction. Across the whole of academic life, the entire world was orbiting around the U.S. university system, so much so that there were loud complaints of a British brain drain across the Atlantic. So it is no surprise that Indian intellectual production, too, shifted its frame of reference increasingly to U.S. shores. This was accelerated by the undoubted success of Subaltern studies, and the preeminent positions of personages like Spivak and Homi Bhaba in U.S. academia. Not only was the latter becoming more influential in setting academic fashions, South Asians were experiencing very real success in them. Indeed, they enjoyed some measure of influence in *setting* the fashions.

The second change followed on the first, but was relatively independent of it. This was the apparent increase in numbers of Indians having some experience with the U.S. academic scene. I characterize this as an "apparent" increase, because data on this matter is very hard to obtain. But over the course of the 1990s and after, there seems to have been a noticeable increase of Indian scholars in South Asian studies in American academia. This is an interesting phenomenon. After the end of the cold war, there was a general expectation that area studies as a field would be gradually wound down. This may still happen. But at least with regard to South Asian studies generally — by which I mean not departments that come under the label, but, more broadly, academic positions created for the teaching of, and research on, South Asian culture and history — the trend seems to have been firmly in the opposite direction.[34] In the past decade alone, there have been initiatives to either reinvigorate, or launch entirely new programs of, South Asia centers and departments in Columbia University, Johns Hopkins, the University of Michigan, UCLA, Harvard, and others.

Now, if this had been the 1950s, it is most likely that scholars of Anglo-American origin, practicing traditional lines of research, would have filled these new positions. But because of the changes brought about by the movements of the 1970s — discussed above — there has been a laudable impulse to look first, or at least very seriously, at scholars from South Asia or of such descent. This is not just because of the antecedent success of Subaltern studies — though no doubt the latter has endowed Indian scholars with a certain cachet. The receptivity toward Indian academics has its own — independent — sources, in the changed ecology of U.S. campuses, and the greater cosmopolitanism of intellectual culture. Given these changes, and given the incredible successes of the Subalterns, it is no surprise that the eyes of university hiring committees have turned to Indian elite universities. Over the past few years, a steady stream of anthropologists and historians have settled into permanent positions in the United States. Others cycle through, either as half-time professors or visiting scholars. What is more, their arrival has been mostly at the elite U.S. universities, since this is where South Asia positions have been opened up (though this is now changing and seeping into smaller colleges).

The mere fact of academic integration is neither here nor there. Its impact on scholarly culture depends on the broader political and intellectual environment in which it transpires. Had it happened in happier times, had effort to give greater presence to Indian academics occurred when Marxian analysis was peaking, the result would have been quite different. But given the changes described in the preceding sections, the whole dynamic has had the effect of further weakening class analysis — and strengthening PSPC. The fact that Indian postcolonial theorists have been most successful in elite U.S. universities has given them significant influence over the direction of future research, even in India. Most of the graduate training in South Asian studies in the United States occurs in elite universities, since it is taught only sporadically in smaller colleges or state universities. Indian students coming to the United States, therefore, are trained mainly at these venues. Western trained PhD's in Delhi, or Calcutta, or Bombay are thus, in increasing numbers, the next generation of PSPC theorists.

The result of this process of integration is that a circuit has been created, linking centers of South Asia scholarship in the United States with elite universities in India. In the past, such circuits had mainly functioned as means of graduate training, funneling Indian graduate students into Western (mainly British) universities, and then back to India for academic employment once they had completed their PhD's. This is still very much the case today, only with two changes: the center of gravity has shifted from the United Kingdom to U.S. shores, and the flow now includes Indian academics headed for employment in the United States. It is hardly a surprise that some key concepts of PSPC — migrancy, hybridity, liminality, and the like — have been developed by this stratum. They effectively convey its own conditions of existence.

## Conclusion

In the United States, as well as in India, the past two decades have been a time of a rightward political drift, based on a balance of political power that has tilted massively toward dominant classes. In both countries, anticapitalist movements have become weaker — just about nonexistent in the U.S. case — hence greatly diluting the social milieu that has historically served to both sustain Marxist intellectuals, as well as to ensure generational reproduction. This has left a double burden: on the last generation to have been radicalized en masse — the "68"ers — and on institutions of higher education, which have emerged to play a central role in the production of radical theory. Much of the decline of class analysis, and of the peculiar brands of radicalism that have risen in its wake, can be explained by this simple phenomenon.

In the United States, this process can be observed most clearly, since Marxist theorizing there has essentially been confined to the academic setting since the 1980s. Now, the increased importance of academia in the production of radical theory is true across much of the Atlantic world, and even beyond. The New Left took haven in college campuses across Europe after the defeats of the 1970s. But in this dynamic, the United States stands apart. Nowhere else was the defeat of working class anticapitalist groupings so complete, and organizations of the Left relegated to so marginal a status in the political culture; and nowhere else have academic institutions occupied so central a space for radical theorizing. This amounted to a fundamental shift in the locus of Marxist theorizing — away from a directly political milieu, which had been the hub for the Left historically, and into academia, where the left had hitherto been a marginal presence.

This shift played an important role for the fate of class analysis in South Asian studies, as it did for scholarship across the spectrum. As the central locus for Left scholarship, the university established two sets of constraints on intellectual production. One was the quite predictable limit to how long a distinctively Marxist current would survive, let along thrive, in any particular discipline. Over time, much of the New Left intelligentsia got absorbed into the professional life and norms of their disciplines. But this did not portend a return to the status quo ante — the academic culture of the 1950s — because of the second constraint now in operation. This was one that established a floor on how far the mainstream could regress to its previous incarnations. Because of the joint influence of social movements and the changing social ecology of campuses across the country, there was to be no going back on matters of social discrimination, and the scholarship relating to it. On this, the New Left converged with students flooding into the universities. Hence, while the *political* basis for *class* analysis was rapidly disappearing, the universities were gaining a *mass* base for a continuing focus on *nonclass* forms of radical theorizing.

Of course, the weight exercised by these constraints was felt unevenly across various fields, and this was very much the case in area studies. South Asia scholarship in the United States had been one of those least affected by the entry of Marxism. Consequently, the field has remained more powerfully influenced by traditional approaches than have cognate specializations like Latin American studies. In particular, the culturalism of traditional Indology was never seriously challenged, much less displaced, in much of the literature. But because of the transformation of academic practice — the second constraint alluded to in the preceding paragraph — this culturalism has been grafted onto a critique of colonialism and an appreciation of indigenous — i.e., South Asian — scholarship far more extensively than ever before.

The result has been an internal momentum toward a radicalism of sorts, but one that is strongly culturalist in approach — unlike in other area concentrations, where culturalism has also witnessed some revival, but has had to coexist with the pockets of class analysis and political economy that were established in the 1970s. In the particular context of South Asia scholarship, it has resulted first off in the emergence of various forms of post-Marxisms as the reigning form of anticolonial or anti-imperialist critique. An interesting offshoot of this development is that, because of its culturalism, this movement has not met with a great deal of resistance from the more traditional elements of the field. Indeed, the marriage between them has been quite happy, as scholars coming out of an Orientalist tradition have found a new vocabulary for their substantive arguments.

The penetration of these theoretical fashions into the Indian scene has been more limited, but real nonetheless. I have suggested that the proximate mechanism responsible for this is an institutional one: the increasing integration of intellectuals from elite universities into the U.S. orbit, and the waves of students that have followed in their wake. Interestingly, the growing influence of U.S. training fields like economics has now become a commonplace among analysts. It is widely recognized that the spread of neoliberal ideas into policy circles in the South has been aided by the growing importance of U.S. universities in the training of their economists.[35] It is surely plausible that the powerful presence of PSPC theory in U.S. humanities should also be transmitted to the South through similar channels.

There is no reason to expect any of this to change in the visible future. In the past, it has taken deep and enduring mass upheavals for a significant stratum of middle-class intellectuals to turn toward anticapitalist ideas and class theorizing. The way things stand now, the most realistic prognosis is that the visibility of class analysis will decline even further in the next decade or so, as the remnants of the New Left become less active or productive. Once the generational shift is complete to those academics who completed their training in the 1990s and later, the landscape will only get more barren and more hostile to all but the most token nods to class. On the brighter side, it is also likely that, at least in the United States, there will at least be a turn to a greater place for materialist analysis, since South Asian studies is finally recovering from its flight out of the social sciences. This does not, of course, betoken a return to class, but at least it will mean a relative diminution of culturalism as the reigning framework for scholarship.

❑

# 2. Was the Indian Labor Movement Ever Co-opted?

## Evaluating Standard Accounts

**Emmanuel Teitelbaum**

Indian labour studies have...been plagued by the scholars' sense of mission. There is a parrot-like deprecation of all that is considered evil in trade unions. The political affiliation of unions, multiple unionism, and outside leadership are bemoaned in every study. This preoccupation...has indeed made the scholars myopic to the realities of the situation. Humble down-to-earth empiricism is the need of the hour in Indian labour studies. Any empirical study cannot but explode the many myths surrounding organized labour. — E.A. Ramaswamy (1977), *The Worker and His Union*

THERE CAN BE LITTLE DOUBT ABOUT THE CENTRAL IMPORTANCE of the working class to political and economic development. Through its unique ability to challenge the structural power of capital, the working class can determine whether a country enjoys a robust social democracy or languishes under the oppressive rule of a fascist regime.[1] Working-class mobilization can also have profound implications for economic performance. An aggressive trade union movement may force consumption-investment tradeoffs,[2] disrupt flows of foreign direct investment,[3] or inhibit economic reform.[4] At the same time, unions can provide a constructive voice function,[5] helping to increase productivity and decrease turnover by institutionalizing industrial conflict;[6] and synergistic ties between political parties and unions can facilitate class compromise, bringing workers "on board" to support the enactment of key reforms[7] and to restrain militancy in an effort to attract new investment.[8]

Considering the importance of the working class in determining the prospects of democracy and development, it is surprising that social scientists place so little emphasis on the organizational capacity of the working class in their discussions of India's political and economic development. There are at least two explanations for why India's working class has been relegated to a position of low visibility and minimal causal weight in the development studies literature. First, the traditional working class is made up of wage laborers in industry, and as Agarwala (this volume) points out, the number of workers in the organized industrial sector is small relative to the total workforce, most of which toils in the unregulated informal sector. The small size of India's organized sector relative to the size of the informal sector has led some scholars to conclude that the mobilization of the traditional working class in India's formal sector is unimportant.

This view is easily dismissed on theoretical grounds. The political and economic importance of the working class lies in its ability to monopolize existing labor markets and thereby challenge the structural power of capital. In this equation, the mobilizational capacity of the working class vis-à-vis industrial capital is the crucial factor to consider, not the size of organized manufacturing relative to the informal sector.

Moreover, although organized manufacturing is small relative to the informal sector, it remains critical to the future of India's industrial development. Thus far, the Indian government has pursued two developmental strategies that attempt to skirt the issue of industrialization. The first has been to expand employment in the informal sector and to improve the productivity of informal sector workers, a strategy that appears to be related to a traditional Gandhian ideology that eschews large-scale urban-based industrial development.[9] The second strategy involves, as Francine Frankel writes, "leapfrogging the industrial revolution" by focusing on the development of the service sector and, in particular, the high-skill high-wage information technology (IT) sector.[10]

These strategies are bound to fail. Both the informal and IT sectors are unlikely to provide "good jobs" (those with high pay and benefits) to the masses of poor Indians. By its very nature, informal sector employment leaves workers highly vulnerable to exploitation. Indeed, the employment relationship in the informal sector can be best characterized as despotic and precapitalist.[11] The IT sector will benefit only the tiny percentage of Indians who are fortunate enough to graduate from one of India's elite universities. Comparing India's industrialization strategy with China's, Drèze and Sen argue that

> [e]ven if India were to take over the bulk of the world's computer software industry, this would still leave its poor, illiterate masses largely untouched. It may be much less glamorous to make simple pocket knives and reliable alarm clocks than to design state-of-the-art computer programmes, but the former gives the Chinese poor a source of income that the latter does not provide — at least not directly — to the Indian poor.[12]

Finally, it is important to note that India's ability to compete in the manufacturing sector is hampered by the inefficiencies associated with production in the informal sector. Put simply, backyard operations in Dharavi and small-scale units in Umbergaon cannot begin to compete with the economies of scale enjoyed by manufacturers in China, where entire cities (e.g., "Sock City," "Underwear City") devote their energies to manufacturing a single product. The development of medium- and large-scale manufacturing units in urban centers is therefore crucial to the growth of Indian industry. The importance of understanding the role of organized labor in this process cannot be overstated.

The second reason that the importance of India's working class to economic and political development gets minimized by social scientists relates to some faulty historical analysis that portrays organized labor as highly fragmented and, therefore, weak. Chronic failures of collective action, it is said, prevent workers in India's organized sector from successfully pursuing their collective interests in both the industrial relations and political arenas. Moreover, this weakness is thought to be progressive, meaning that the working class has become increasingly factionalized and ineffective over time.

The supposed source of this lack of organizational strength is the political incorporation of labor. It is argued that strong ties to political parties generate political infighting in what would be an otherwise united labor movement, and that the progressive fragmentation of the party system in turn results in greater fragmentation of the labor movement. Additionally, strong ties between parties and unions result in the political domination and exclusion of working-class interests. According to this view, the relationship between parties and unions is a zero-sum game in which *either* party interests *or* working-class interests get represented in the collective bargaining and political arenas. Since parties dominate unions, it is assumed that working-class interests get marginalized or, in other words, that political incorporation is tantamount to the political co-optation of labor.

Although consistent and logical, these arguments have not been tested with empirical evidence. The situation in Indian labor studies remains quite similar to that described by Ramaswamy in 1977.[13] Authors continue to parrot rather than substantiate claims about the fragmentation and co-optation of labor, claims that were initially propped up by a limited number of statements made by employers and party leaders in the 1960s. Moreover, many of these statements appear to be motivated by a bias, held by interview subjects and shared by scholars, toward portraying workers as lacking agency and any real grievances. Thus, Ramaswamy's plea that a "humble down-to-earth empiricism is the need of the hour in Indian labour studies" remains highly relevant today.[14]

As I demonstrate in this essay, a more critical evaluation of the arguments presented in standard accounts and an examination of a broader range of available evidence reveal a starkly different picture. Through an examination of original survey data, government statistics, and Indian industrial and labor law, I show that the Indian labor movement has been much more unified, much more contentious in the collective bargaining arena, and much more politically influential than previously assumed.

This essay proceeds as follows. In the next section, I discuss two of the most common arguments supporting the view that the political incorporation of labor led to its co-optation, namely, that the Indian labor movement is becoming increasingly fragmented over time and that political parties and the state undermine union bargaining power through interference in the industrial relations arena. In Section 2, I look at industrial protest statistics to test the theory that the political incorporation of labor following Independence led to labor quiescence in the industrial relations arena. I show that, in fact, unions engaged in increasingly higher levels of industrial protest following Independence until the 1980s. Further, the total volume of industrial protest in India continues to be high, even relative to European countries with famously contentious labor movements. In Section 3, I explore organized labor's influence in the legislative arena. India has some of the strongest legal protections for workers in the developing world and resistance to privatization has been quite effective. These legislative successes would not have been possible had working-class interests been marginalized in the political arena. Finally, in Section 4, I speculate on why social scientists have gotten the story so wrong. I argue that the main problem is that researchers have trusted too much in "key source" interviews with employers, trade union federation leaders and party leaders. All three groups have incentives to portray labor as disorganized and politically subordinated.

## 1. Did the Postindependence Incorporation of Labor Result in Its Permanent Co-optation?

There can be little doubt that shortly following Independence in 1947 unions were brought to heel by political parties and the state. Indeed, the labor quiescence witnessed in the years immediately following Independence resulted from the intentional and aggressive efforts of the Indian National Congress to subdue labor at the behest of conservative elements of the party.[15]

Congress employed two strategies in its effort to subdue labor. The first was to create its own party-affiliated union, the Indian National Trade Union Congress (INTUC) to compete with the communist-dominated All India Trade Union Congress (AITUC). The second was to set up an institutional framework designed to facilitate heavy state intervention in labor disputes. The most important piece of legislation with respect to this new institutional framework was the Industrial Disputes Act of 1947, which required unions to provide fourteen days notice before going on strike and provided "the appropriate Government" with the authority to refer disputes to courts, tribunals, or specially constituted boards for compulsory arbitration.[16]

In the years immediately following its enactment, the state leaned on this legislation quite heavily to intervene in industrial disputes and thereby prevented the resolution of disputes through bipartite collective bargaining. As Chibber notes, "[m]atters that were usually settled through collective bargaining were now dealt with through detailed regulations within labor law and the number of industrial disputes rapidly declined. Congress, had, at least momentarily, achieved labor peace."[17]

But was this peace a lasting peace? In this section, I will demonstrate that by the 1960s portrayals of labor as quiescent and dominated by political parties and the state no longer reflected reality. Yet impressions based on past patterns of state-labor relations have continued to dominate thinking on Indian labor relations. Generally speaking, social scientists assume that the political domination of unions and state interference in industrial relations that occurred immediately following Independence were perpetual and permanently damaging to organized labor. Specifically, it is possible to identify two myths perpetuated in social scientific pronouncements about Indian industrial relations over the past half-century: (1) that political domination fragmented the union movement, thereby generating a "multiplicity" of weak unions incapable of pursuing their collective interests; and (2) that political and state interference weakened organized labor in the collective bargaining arena. Below, I examine each of these myths in turn.

### The "Multiplicity" Myth

Perhaps the most common statement about Indian labor is that political divisions in the labor movement have led to a multiplicity of unions, thereby diminishing worker solidarity and the ability of workers to pursue their collective interests. This notion of union multiplicity is based on the rapid increase in the number of registered unions after Independence. Authors have repeatedly interpreted this increase to mean that the union movement was rapidly undergoing a process of fragmentation, with rival factions within unions breaking off to form their own organizations, both at the federation and local levels. Further, observers have commonly argued that these intractable rivalries were inspired by the interference of external union leaders with political aspirations.

In political economy, this perspective was standardized by Rudolph and Rudolph, who refer to the continual fragmentation of the union movement as "involution" and to the politics it generates as an "involuted pluralism." [18] According to Rudolph and Rudolph, this process of "involution," coupled with the state's domination of industrial relations, inhibits collective action. As a result, unions fail to effectively represent working-class interests in the political and industrial relations arenas. In recent years, this characterization of the union movement as disorganized, listless, and politically impotent has become pervasive in academic, journalistic, and official writings on Indian unions and industrial relations. Nearly every document pertaining to industrial relations in India mentions the continual division of the labor movement and accepts the weakness of the labor movement as established fact.

The pervasiveness of the characterization of Indian labor as continually fragmented is not the work of the Rudolph and Rudolph alone, however. The Rudolphs' conclusions rest, in part, on the work of the generation of scholars who preceded them. For example, Kennedy stated that by generating "extreme fragmentation," political rivalries generate unions that "are small and fatally weak in finances and claim as members only a minority of the work force they seek to represent."[19] Raman argued that political divisions in the union movement lead to a host of ills, including "the wasteful application of scarce leadership and material resources; lack of loyalty to their unions among members; worker indiscipline; complication of the issue of union recognition; and organizational weakness in the struggle for the workers' economic and social progress."[20] Further, scholarship since the publication of the Rudolphs' book in the late 1980s has done little to challenge perceptions of a fractious and weakened union movement. Ramaswamy's characterization is common:

> For all their apparent might, the fact is that our unions are in the midst of an unprecedented crisis. Their membership is shrinking. There is no end in sight to the rivalries which fragment them. With the leadership distanced from the ranks, there is growing revolt from within. Other mass movements distrust trade unions and their credibility in the wider society cannot get any worse.[21]

### *The Use of Government Data in Standard Depictions of a Fragmented Labor Movement*

While a chorus of voices has long been unanimous in singing the requiem of organized labor and class politics, no good evidence has been found to support the claim that the Indian movement is divided enough to hinder collective action. As I demonstrate later, the Indian working class was highly mobilized in collective bargaining long after Independence and continues to successfully negotiate bipartite agreements today. In politics, labor unions have successfully fought in favor of one of the most robust bodies of protective labor legislation in the world. Before turning to that discussion, however, I will scrutinize the conventional wisdom regarding the scale of divisions in the Indian labor movement.

The first major problem with standard depictions of the Indian labor movement is that they present government statistics on unions and union membership in a way that grossly overstates the problem of union "multiplicity." Table 1 presents the official figures from India's Ministry of Labour documenting the growth in the number and membership of unions in India between 1960 and 1995.

Most pronouncements about a hopelessly fragmented union movement in India focus on the statistic in the first column of Table 1 — the "number of registered unions" statistic. Indeed, the number of registered unions has increased more than fivefold over this period, from 11,312 in 1960 to 57,925 in 1995. The problem is that the number of registered unions in no way accurately reflects the number of *functioning* unions in India.

The Trade Unions Act of 1926, which governs the registration of unions in India, allows any seven individuals to register as a union but has no mechanism to verify the continued functioning or existence of unions that register. The Trade Unions Act requires unions to submit returns, but the penalty for not submitting a return is a mere five rupees per week up to a total of fifty rupees (section

Table 1: Unions and Union Membership in India, 1960–1995

| Year | Number of Registered Unions | Number of Unions Submitting Returns (Functioning Unions) | Membership of Functioning Unions | Members per Functioning Union |
|---|---|---|---|---|
| 1960 | 11,312 | 6,813 | 4,013,000 | 589 |
| 1965 | 13,248 | 6,932 | 3,787,000 | 546 |
| 1970 | 20,879 | 8,537 | 5,120,000 | 600 |
| 1975 | 29,438 | 10,324 | 6,550,000 | 634 |
| 1980 | 36,507 | 4,432 | 3,727,000 | 841 |
| 1985 | 45,067 | 7,815 | 6,433,000 | 823 |
| 1990 | 52,016 | 8,828 | 7,019,000 | 795 |
| 1995 | 57,925 | 8,162 | 6,538,000 | 801 |

Source: *Indian Labour Yearbook,* various years.

Banners showing rules on security and the prohibition of child labor on a construction site in Bangalore, India. (ILO/Crozet M., March 2002)

31) and it is not clear that fines are ever collected. State ministries of labor may eventually delete a union from the registry, but there is no set time frame in the law for doing so (section 10). Consequently, at any given time, thousands of unions are "registered" but either do not function or do not exist.

To the extent that we trust these government statistics (I point out problems with them below), a better indication of the trend in the number of functioning unions is the statistic in the second column of Table 1, the number of unions submitting returns. Aside from the period immediately following the Emergency, this number has stayed fairly constant at around seven or eight thousand unions. At the same time, the membership of unions submitting returns has increased, so that according to these data the average size of unions (or members per union) has increased by roughly 30 percent between 1960 and 1995.

Just as importantly, studies citing the total number of individually registered unions do not recognize the obvious fact that many registered unions are joined together in *federations*. The number of federations submitting returns to the Ministry of Labor is relatively small and has been declining in recent years. In 1987, seventy-one federations submitted returns. By 1992, the number of federations submitting returns had fallen to forty-nine and by 1997 to nineteen.[22]

***Evidence from Original Survey Data***

While they may be of limited use in analyzing *trends* in the number and average size of unions, there are substantial technical problems with the union statistics published by the Government of India. These technical difficulties present a host of problems when we try to draw conclusions about the *actual* organizational capacity of unions. First, union membership statistics are based on self-reported data, which poses problems of reliability since unions have obvious incentives to inflate their reported membership figures. Additionally, the

Billboard showing objectives regarding security measures in the Mahindra Jeep factory in Bombay, India. Research shows "that the Indian labor movement has been much more unified, much more contentious in the collective bargaining arena, and much more politically influential than previously assumed." (ILO/Crozet M., March 2002)

Indian government has no way to force or even encourage unions to submit their returns. Many (if not most) unions shirk their responsibility to submit a return and there is no way to know what percentage of the data is missing. Consequently, even though unions submitting returns may have an incentive to inflate their membership figures, overall union membership may be grossly *understated* due to non-reporting.

A third major problem with the reliability of the government's statistics is the variation in the capacity and willingness of state governments to report their statistics to the central government. From Independence until the early 1970s, trade union statistics based on annual returns were reliably reported by the state governments to the central government and were published annually by the Ministry of Labour in Chapter 4 (Industrial Relations) of the *Indian Labour Yearbook*. However, starting with the publication of statistics from the 1970 returns,[23] the central government began to "estimate" the figures for major states that had failed to report trade union statistics by simply repeating figures reported in the previous year. In 1970, three major states failed to complete returns.[24] By 1978, the number of major states for which trade union figures were "estimated" doubled to six.[25] After 1978, the Ministry of Labour stopped publishing state-wise trade union statistics, but noted in their reporting of national trade union statistics the states for which data were missing. By 1988, the number of states not reporting had grown to fifteen and included most major states in the Union.[26] In short, by the mid-1970s, officially published trade union statistics told us little about the actual organizational strength and by the mid-1980s they were utterly useless, even with respect to discerning trends in the organizational capacity of the union movement.

A final problem with using Government of India data to discern the organizational capacity of unions is that national-level statistics cannot measure fragmentation of the union movement that may be occurring in individual companies or production units. From the perspective of industrial relations, it is important to know the degree of enterprise-level fragmentation since most collective bargaining in India occurs between unions and managers at individual firms.

A better way to illuminate the organizational structure of the union movement is to gather firm-level data through surveys of randomly selected manufacturing companies. In this section, I present results from two original surveys conducted in three Indian states: Kerala, Maharashtra, and West Bengal. These three states were selected because historically they have witnessed high levels of labor activism. Generally speaking, the results of these two surveys suggest that the organization capacity of Indian unions is much greater than commonly believed. Fragmentation at the firm level is far less than we would expect based on the Rudolph's "involuted pluralism" characterization. Further, a large percentage of unions are affiliated to a small number of national federations, shedding substantial doubt on claims about the continual fragmentation of the union movement along political lines. Finally, the results of these surveys show that union density is much higher than commonly believed, indicating that government data underreport the number of unionized workers.

Table 2 presents data on the number of unions in individual production units from an in-person survey of directors and managers at eighty-seven manufacturing companies in Kerala, Maharashtra, and West Bengal.[27] Defying the common

Table 2: Union Structure in Four Regions of South Asia
(Percentage of unionized production units)

| | Kerala | Maharashtra | West Bengal |
|---|---|---|---|
| 1 Union | 46 | 48 | 28 |
| 2 Unions | 25 | 41 | 44 |
| 3 Unions | 18 | 7 | 19 |
| 4+ Unions | 11 | 4 | 9 |
| N | 28 | 27 | 32 |

*Source*: Survey of 87 randomly selected personnel directors and senior managers in four regions of South Asia (Kerala, Maharashtra, West Bengal and Sri Lanka). The survey was taken during interviews conducted between November 2002 and 2004. For details regarding the sample selection and response rates, consult the online data appendix: http://home.gwu.edu/~ejt.

Table 3. Regional Variations in the Structure of the Union Movement

| Type of Union | (Percentage of companies surveyed)* | | |
|---|---|---|---|
| | Maharashtra | Kerala | W. Bengal |
| Major Party Federation | 30 | 45 | 74 |
| CITU | 3 | 33 | 64 |
| AITUC | 1 | 8 | 7 |
| INTUC | 16 | 23 | 40 |
| INTTUC | NA** | NA** | 16 |
| BKS | 13 | 0 | 0 |
| BMS | 4 | 17 | 2 |
| Small Party Federation | 7 | 3 | 7 |
| Independent Federation | 16 | 1 | 3 |
| Enterprise Union | 31 | 1 | 5 |
| Any Union | 72 | 48 | 79 |

*Source:* Telephone survey of 294 randomly selected managers and directors. Surveys conducted between March 2003 and May 2004. For more details regarding the sample selection and response rates, consult the online data appendix: http://home.gwu.edu/~ejt.
*Notes:* * Figures do not add up to 100 as companies surveyed may have more than one union. **Union does not have a member presence in these states.

view that the Indian labor movement is hopelessly fragmented, the vast majority of companies surveyed have one or two unions operating in their factories. On average, companies in Maharashtra had the fewest number of unions operating in their factories, with 48 percent of companies reporting the presence of only one union, 41 percent reporting the presence of two unions, 7 percent reporting the presence of three unions, and just 4 percent reporting the presence of four or more unions. In West Bengal and Kerala, fewer than 30 percent of companies reported the presence of more than two unions in their factories. In Kerala, fewer than 11 percent of companies report four or more unions operating in their factories, and in West Bengal the figure is 9 percent. In short, these data suggest the inaccuracy of the "involuted pluralism" argument at the level of individual firms. Despite the supposed presence of almost sixty thousand officially registered unions, unionized companies are bargaining with one or two unions in their factories.

Table 3 presents data on union affiliation to major federations from a telephone survey of 294 managers and directors from private-sector manufacturing companies in three Indian states: Kerala, Maharashtra, and West Bengal. In this survey, I asked managers and directors which unions operated in their factories. I then categorized the unions as belonging to "major party federations," "small party federations," "independent federations," or "enterprise unions." "Major party federations" are union federations affiliated to major political parties. In the three regions where the survey was conducted there are six major party federations: (1) the Center for Indian Trade Unions (CITU), affiliated to the Communist Party of India (Marxist) (CPM); (2) the All Indian Trade Union Congress (AITUC), affiliated to the Communist Party of India (CPI); (3) the Indian National Trade Union Congress (INTUC), affiliated to the Congress Party; (4) the Indian National Trinamool Trade Union Congress (INTTUC), affiliated to the Trinamool Congress; (5) the Bharatiya Kamgar Sena (BKS), affiliated to the Shiv Sena; and (6) the Bharatiya Mazdoor Sangh (BMS), affiliated to the Bharatiya Janata Party (BJP). "Small party federations" are union federations affiliated to small political parties. "Independent federations" are union federations that hold no affiliation to a political party. "Enterprise unions," also known in South Asia as "in-house unions," are company-specific unions that are typically governed by the workers of a given enterprise and hold no affiliation to an external union organization or leadership.

If we were to rely simply on government data as presented in previous studies of the structure of the union movement in India, we would expect the average size of a union to be around eight hundred members. This would mean that each union would organize one or a handful of companies, in which case most companies would report the presence of either a company-specific union or a federation affiliated to a small political party.

Defying this expectation, a rather large percentage of companies report the presence of unions affiliated to relatively encompassing major party federations and very few report the presence of a company-specific union, i.e., a union with "internal leadership only." The CITU and INTUC dominate the union movements in Kerala and West Bengal. In Kerala, 33 percent of companies surveyed report the presence of a CITU union and 23 percent report the presence of an INTUC union. Overall, 45 percent of companies in Kerala report the presence of a union connected to a major party federation. In West Bengal, 64 percent report the presence of CITU and 40 percent report the presence of INTUC. Overall, 74 percent of companies in West Bengal report the presence of a union connected to a major party federation. By contrast, a relatively small percentage of companies (less than 1 percent in Kerala and 5 percent in West Bengal) report the presence of company-specific unions in these two states. Maharashtra is the region with the highest percentage of companies (31 percent) reporting the presence of company-specific unions. Yet an almost equal number of companies (30 percent) in Maharashtra report the presence of unions affiliated to major party federations.

Finally, if the organizational capacity of unions were truly on the wane, we would expect to observe low union density. Based purely on data from voluntary returns, the ILO estimates union density in India to be around 25 percent.[28] Yet the data from this survey suggest that unionization rates among manufacturing companies are quite a bit higher. In Kerala, 48 percent of companies reported the presence of at least one union. In Maharashtra, the figure was 72 percent and in West Bengal a whopping 79 percent of surveyed companies were unionized. Admittedly, the high levels of unionization original survey data show are due in part to the fact that the sample is taken from directories of manufacturers, which are primarily comprised of large- and medium-scale enterprises. Nonetheless, the large differences between these figures and the official statistics clearly throw statements about union membership in India being low and falling into question.

#### *Moderate Fragmentation Probably Generates Healthy Competition, Not Quiescence*

In addition to lacking empirical support, the argument about a multiplicity of unions weakening organized labor suffers from serious analytical flaws. Quite simply, there is no clear argument as to why we might expect union fragmentation to prevent collective action. In fact, a degree of competition in the union movement *benefits* workers by producing exit options that force union and political leaders to pay greater attention to worker demands.[29] By allowing workers to "vote with their feet," union competition may prevent state and political domination of unions.

In his study of textile workers in Coimbatore, Ramaswamy notes that union rivalry has prevented union leaders from "reprimanding an errant rank and file."[30] In their discussion of the effects of the alleged fragmentation of the Indian labor movement, Rudolph and Rudolph inadvertently suggest the veracity of this claim:

> The cutting edge of fragmentation and involution is found in the private industrial sector, where a work force whose numbers have stagnated intersects with the phenomenal growth of registered unions. Fragmentation generates conflict. Private-sector industrial disputes are about ten times as frequent as those in the public sector.[31]

In making this statement, Rudolph and Rudolph contradict their central argument about the relationship between fragmentation and the strength of organized labor. If union fragmentation leads to union weakness and state domination of unions, we should see greater union quiescence in the private sector relative to the public sector, not higher levels of conflict.

Like so many authors who have addressed the subject of the structure of the Indian labor movement, the Rudolphs misjudge both the scale of union fragmentation and the effects of union competition on the representation of working-class interests. The level of competition has remained more or less constant over the past five decades and, as I demonstrate in sections two and three, this competition has been healthy for the representation of worker interests both in the industrial relations and political arenas.

### *The "Political Interference" Myth*

The second standard myth about unions in India is that they have become ineffective or quiescent in collective bargaining because they are dominated by outside political interests.[32] This domination is argued to occur in two forms. The first is interference by political parties in the collective bargaining process. For example, Raman argues that external political leadership infuses "extraneous political issues" in labor-management negotiations that distort negotiations and make employers reluctant to enter into collective bargaining agreements.[33]

Table 4: Labor Institutions and Collective Bargaining

| | | |
|---|---|---|
| POLITICAL INTERFERENCE | | |
| | Percentage of companies reporting a political strike since 1991 | 62 |
| | Percentage of companies reporting political intervention in an industrial dispute since 1991 | 17 |
| COLLECTIVE BARGAINING | | |
| | Percentage of companies currently bound by a collective bargaining agreement | 64 |
| STATE INTERFERENCE | | |
| | Percentage of companies reporting at least one dispute referred for compulsory adjudication in the last year | 15 |
| | Percentage of companies reporting at least one collective dispute referred to an industrial tribunal for compulsory adjudication since 1991 | 16 |
| | Percentage of companies reporting at least one dispute referred for voluntary arbitration proceedings since 1991 | 8 |
| | Percentage of companies having at least one dispute called before the Ministry of Labour for conciliation proceedings since 1991 | 31 |
| | Percentage of disputes successfully resolved in conciliation once referred to the Ministry of Labour | 38 |

*Source*: Survey of 110 randomly selected personnel directors and senior managers in three Indian states (Kerala, Maharashtra, and West Bengal). The survey was taken during interviews conducted between November 2002 and 2004. For details regarding the sample selection and response rates, consult the online data appendix: http://home.gwu.edu/~ejt.

A related concern is that "politically engineered" strikes such as ***hartals***, ***bandhs***, and token strikes have diverted limited union resources to activities that do not directly benefit unions. Behind these arguments lies the assumption that workers are easily taken advantage of because they lack education and agency. Crouch, for instance, claims that it "is relatively easy for trade union leaders to 'exploit' the workers in that the workers tend to be loyal to leaders rather than to principles."[34]

The second form of political domination is thought to occur as a result of antiunion industrial relations policies and institutions. A number of scholars have argued that the state has interfered in Indian industrial relations to the detriment of the bipartite resolution of disputes in the collective bargaining arena. For example, writing in 1958, Myers stated that "[c]ompulsory adjudication remains the cornerstone of labour dispute settlement in India, and is likely to continue for the near future, at least."[35] Similarly, Ramaswamy argues that state intervention in industrial relations is a sign of the failure of collective bargaining:

> While the state has emerged as a regulator of labour-management relations everywhere, there are vital differences between industrial relations systems in which the state enters the relationship on the breakdown of bipartite bargaining, and those where the state assumes the role of arbiter in lieu of a bargained relationship. It is clearly the latter position which obtains in India.[36]

Raman concludes that "political involvement of trade unionism in India has meant the initiation, control, and exploitation of the labor movements by political parties."[37] Rudolph and Rudolph claim that

> because the state, INTUC, and most national federations have a vested interest in the system of corporatist dependency, they pay only lip service to the widely accepted goal of open-ended collective bargaining agent and the right to strike.... The pervasiveness of compulsory adjudication and arbitration and the increasingly limited circumstances under which strikes are legal perpetuates government's tutelary relationship to unions.[38]

"The common assumption behind these statements is that the Industrial Disputes Act of 1947 pushed conflict out of the collective bargaining arena and into the state's industrial relations "machinery."[39] This shift from collective bargaining to state-mediated conflict resolution is thought to disadvantage unions for three reasons. First, standard accounts generally assume that the institutions set up by the Industrial Disputes Act is biased toward employers, although no evidence has ever been presented to support this assumption.[40] Second, cases referred for adjudication typically can drag on for many years due to court clog, benefiting employers who prefer the status quo. Third, it is argued that the rise of tripartite (state-sponsored) negotiation has resulted in an increased dependence on educated external leaders who can interpret and negotiate this complex set of institutions.[41]

Considering the motivations of the Congress Party in the 1950s, these arguments bear an initial plausibility. In creating its own politically loyal union federation and in enacting the Industrial Disputes Act, Congress hoped to shunt disputes away from the uncertain and conflict-ridden realm of bipartite negotiations and into the sure-footed, paternalistic care of the state. But did this strategy work?

***Interference by Political Parties in Industrial Relations***

We first turn to the issue of whether interference by political parties has resulted in the disempowerment of unions in industrial relations. Table 4 presents data from an original survey of randomly selected personnel directors and senior managers from 110 manufacturing companies. These companies were randomly selected for in-depth interviews from a pool of 294 managers who participated in the previously described telephone survey.

In the survey, I asked two questions to measure the level of political interference in a given company: whether the company had been affected by a "political strike" since India embarked on its program of economic reform in 1991, such as a *bandh*, *hartal*, general strike, or token strike; and whether the company had experienced direct intervention by a politician to negotiate a resolution to an industrial dispute since 1991.

Sixty-two percent of companies reported experiencing a political strike. While this is a substantial percentage, it is important to note that a company can be affected by a political strike regardless of whether its union is affiliated to the party calling the strike. Since bandhs and general strikes shut down cities, a large number of companies are affected by political strikes because it is impossible for workers to travel and not because that company's union is directly involved in supporting the strike. Thus, a political strike represents an *indirect* form of political interference rather than an instance in which a political party consciously attempts to influence enterprise-level industrial relations.

The second question more precisely addresses the level of direct political interference in the collective bargaining arena. Notably, only 19 percent of companies reported experiencing some form of direct political intervention in an industrial dispute since 1991. It is also important to note that the statistic does not indicate anything about the *terms* of these political interventions. When I asked about the nature of these interventions, I was commonly told that they were made at the request of and in support of unions. In sum, a connection between political parties and unions does not appear to translate into overt interference by politicians in the collective bargaining arena to the detriment of workers.

### *State Intervention in Industrial Relations*

In the same survey, I also asked a series of questions designed to measure the extent to which state intervention in industrial relations reduced the propensity to resolve disputes through collective bargaining. The Industrial Disputes Act of 1947 provides the state with a broad range of powers to settle industrial disputes. These include (a) voluntary mechanisms, such as voluntary nonbinding conciliation proceedings or voluntary binding arbitration proceedings and (b) compulsory arbitration and adjudication.

Voluntary conciliation proceedings are typically presided over by a labor commissioner, but are sometimes conducted by a specially appointed board. Labor courts and industrial tribunals conduct arbitration and adjudication proceedings. While they have overlapping jurisdiction on some issues, labor courts are primarily responsible for adjudicating disputes pertaining to individual workers whereas industrial tribunals adjudicate collective disputes between the management and a union.[42]

I asked managers whether they were covered by a collective agreement and whether they had any disputes referred for compulsory adjudication (collective or individual) in the last year. Sixty-four percent of companies reported that they were currently bound by a collective bargaining agreement but only 15 percent reported having a dispute referred for compulsory adjudication (or arbitration) in the previous year. Are disputes referred for adjudication primarily disputes with individual workers or collective disputes? I also asked managers whether they had any collective disputes referred to an industrial tribunal (which have jurisdiction over collective disputes) for compulsory adjudication since 1991. Only 16 percent reported that one or more collective disputes had been referred to an industrial tribunal for compulsory adjudication since 1991, suggesting that the bulk of disputes being referred for compulsory adjudication in the previous year were disputes between companies and individual workers and not collective disputes.

In addition to questions about compulsory adjudication and arbitration, I asked managers questions about how frequently they rely on voluntary state-sponsored mechanisms to resolve industrial disputes. Only 8 percent of companies reported a dispute that had been referred for voluntary arbitration pro-

Table 5. Employer Perceptions of Obstacles to Growth

| POTENTIAL OBSTACLE | Percent responding "moderate obstacle" or "major obstacle" |
|---|---|
| 1. Infrastructure | 63 |
| 2. Corruption | 61 |
| 3. Labor regulation | 61 |
| 4. Policy instability/uncertainty | 51 |
| 5. Other taxes | 47 |
| 6. Labor protest/strikes | 44 |
| 7. Worker absenteeism | 42 |
| 8. Functioning of judiciary | 38 |
| 9. Environmental regulations | 33 |
| 10. Financing | 32 |
| 11. Customs duties | 28 |
| 11. Riots/political instability | 28 |
| 13. Inflation | 26 |
| 13. Customs administration | 26 |
| 15. Income tax Administration | 23 |
| 16. Import restrictions | 20 |
| 16. Income taxes | 20 |
| 18. Worker violence | 19 |
| 19. Foreign currency/exchange regulations | 15 |
| 20. Street crime/theft | 13 |
| 20. Organized crime | 13 |

Source: Survey of 88 randomly selected directors and senior managers in four regions of South Asia (Kerala, Maharashtra, West Bengal and Sri Lanka). Directors and managers were asked to identify each item as "no obstacle," a "minor obstacle," a "moderate obstacle," or a "major obstacle" to business and economic growth. The survey was taken during interviews conducted between November 2002 and May 2004. For more details regarding the sample selection and response rates, consult the online data appendix at http://home.gwu.edu/~ejt.

Table 5: Employer Perceptions of Obstacles to Growth

*Source:* Telephone survey of 294 randomly selected managers and directors. Surveys conducted between March 2003 and May 2004. For more details regarding the sample selection and response rates, consult the online data appendix: http://home.gwu.edu/~ejt. *Notes:* * Figures do not add up to 100 as companies surveyed may have more than one union. **Union does not have a member presence in these states.

ceedings since 1991. And while 31 percent of companies reported bringing one or more industrial disputes before the commissioner of labor for conciliation proceedings since 1991, only 38 percent of these disputes had been successfully resolved in conciliation. The remainder were shunted back into the collective bargaining arena for bipartite negotiation. These results suggest that like compulsory adjudication and arbitration, voluntary state-sponsored tripartite mechanisms of dispute resolution pose no threat to collective bargaining.

## 2. Trends in Industrial Conflict

Post-Independence trends in industrial disputes provide another reason to doubt the typical portrayal of unions in India as increasingly divided and weak. If, as conventional wisdom states, unions were undergoing a process of contin-

Figure 1: Industrial Dispute Volume in India 1966-1995

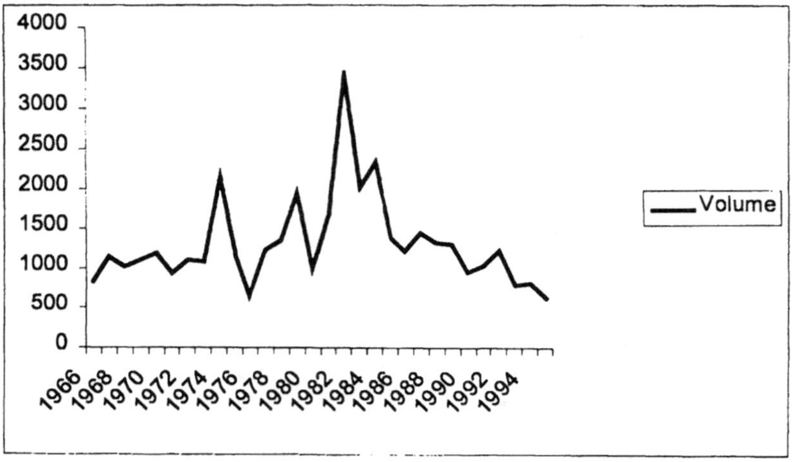


*Notes*: Dispute volume is calculated as the number of worker-days lost per 1000 organized sector workers. This figure represents the aggregate dispute volume for 15 major Indian states (see text for details). Industrial disputes data are from various issues of the *Indian Labor Yearbook*. The number of organized sector workers comes from various issues of the *Annual Employment Review*.

ual division and suffering from political domination in the industrial relations arena, we would expect collective action to become increasingly difficult and union assertiveness to decline.

In fact, the available evidence suggests the opposite is true. In the post-independence period, Indian unions have been anything but quiescent. As evidenced by India's high volume of industrial disputes, Indian labor unions have been quite aggressive in pursuing working-class interests in the industrial relations arena.

Figure 1 displays the aggregate volume of industrial disputes in India's fifteen most populous states.[43] Dispute volume is measured as the number of worker-days lost to industrial disputes per one thousand organized sector workers.[44] As Figure 1 shows, the general trend in dispute volume is upward until the mid-1980s and in general decline thereafter. Further, the trend is almost universal across Indian states. Only Kerala displays a consistently downward trend in dispute volume, but it starts with unusually high levels of industrial conflict — between three thousand and five thousand worker-days lost per one thousand organized sector workers (or between three and five worker-days lost per worker).[45]

Further, regardless of the states or periods chosen, the strike volume witnessed in India is high by international standards. Ranging from about five hundred to thirty-five hundred worker-days lost per one thousand organized sector workers, the volume of industrial disputes in India is comparable to that of European countries with routinely contentious industrial relations such as France or Italy.[46] Levels of strike volume in West Bengal during the 1980s (between six and twelve days lost *per worker*) compare with the unsurpassed strike activity in pre-war Nordic countries before labor was incorporated by the state. Even relatively peaceful states like Gujarat, Orissa, and the Punjab experience dispute volume levels of between five hundred and one thousand worker-days lost per one thousand organized sector workers.[47]

## 3. The Influence of Organized Labor in the Political Arena

Another major reason to doubt the consensus view of Indian labor as divided and politically ineffective is that India is generally recognized as having some of the strictest legal protections for organized sector workers anywhere in the world.[48] A complex web of regulations govern Indian industrial relations, with forty-nine central government acts alone governing various aspects the employment relationship.[49] Thirty-three of these acts govern the organized industrial sector. Twenty-one of them apply to the industrial sector as a whole,[50] while twelve provide sector-specific worker protections.[51]

Further, state legislatures (Vidhan Sabhas) have enacted many pro-worker amendments to these central acts. Some of these state-level amendments place stringent restrictions on the employment relationship. Ironically, one of the most pro-labor bodies of legislation is comprised of state-level amendments to the Industrial Disputes Act of 1947. In particular, by amending the Industrial Disputes Act, many states have placed fairly onerous restrictions on the ability of employers to shed labor. For example, in 1980 Maharashtra passed an amendment to section 25C that requires employers to pay workers 100 percent of their wages for a period of forty-five days if they are laid off for any reason aside from a failure in the supply of electricity. In 1984, Rajasthan passed an amendment to section 25Q stipulating that employers who lay off workers or reduce the size of their workforce without the permission of the government are subject to a penalty of up to three months imprisonment and/or a fine of up to two thousand rupees. In 1980, West Bengal passed an amendment to section 25C stipulating that laid-off workers are entitled to receive 50 percent of their salary indefinitely.[52]

As stated earlier, most scholars have viewed this large body of labor legislation as an attempt by meddling political parties to shift disputes from the collective bargaining arena to a state-controlled, employer-friendly process of arbitration, i.e., as a mechanism for co-opting organized labor. If this were in fact the case, we would expect employers to have a favorable or at least neutral impression of Indian labor legislation. Yet survey evidence suggests that employers are highly pessimistic about the implications of India's labor laws for economic expansion.[53] A World Bank survey of 263 private sector firms conducted in the late 1990s asked employers to rate eighteen potential obstacles to the smooth functioning and growth of business on a four-point ordinal scale ("major obstacle," "moderate obstacle," "minor obstacle," and "no obstacle"). Sixty-four percent of employers felt that labor regulation represented a 'moderate' or 'major' impediment to the operation and growth of business.[54] By this calculation, labor regulation ranked second (behind inflation) as a perceived obstacle to growth.

I repeated this survey with a similar list of items to confirm the negative sentiment regarding labor regulation among employers in the manufacturing sector. Table 5 reports the results of a survey of eighty-eight randomly selected directors and senior managers in Kerala, Maharashtra, and West Bengal. In this survey, employers were asked to identify twenty-one potential items as a "major obstacle," "moderate obstacle," "minor obstacle," or "no obstacle" to the functioning and growth of business. Sixty-one percent of employers deemed labor regulation to be a "moderate" or "major" impediment to the operation and growth of business, again placing labor regulation second in importance on the list of twenty obstacles. Labor regulation was deemed to be only slightly less important than infrastructure, which 63 percent of employers rated as a moderate to major obstacle, and was tied with corruption as a perceived obstacle to economic growth.

Labor's political strength is further evidenced by the absence of any substantial "reform" of its labor law, despite consistent calls for reform by employers and the World Bank.[55] Additionally, as Candland argues, union resistance has substantially inhibited the pace of broader economic reforms.[56] Most notably, the privatization of central government enterprises has been very slow. Within the first nine years of the privatization process, Candland notes, India had "not completed the privatization of any of its 248 enterprises," whereas in Pakistan, where unions have less political influence, privatization "has been anything but cautious."[57]

It is hard to imagine that such a large body of pro-worker labor legislation would have been passed through national and state legislatures, or have been consistently enforced, if labor were fragmented and politically weak. It is unlikely that employers would have a negative opinion of this legislation if it were effectively serving to co-opt the interests of organized labor and quelling industrial unrest. It is also unlikely that labor would so substantially inhibit the enactment of economic reforms if it were not politically influential.

## 4. Why Do Social Scientists Get It Wrong? Class Bias in Interview Data

With so much evidence pointing to the continuing vibrancy of the Indian labor movement, it is surprising that observers have consistently characterized Indian labor as fragmented and weak. What explains this misreading of the situation? Why have scholars looked past or even misread trade union and industrial relations statistics suggesting a highly unified and militant labor movement? Noting the large body of pro-labor legislation on the books and the overwhelmingly negative reaction of employers to this legislation, why have social scientists failed to conclude that labor is politically influential? Why, despite organized labor's ability to unilaterally slow the process of privatization, have observers maintained the view that fatal divisions and political co-optation prevent Indian workers from defending their collective interests?

To answer this question, it is helpful to return to Ramaswamy's assessment of Indian labor studies, made nearly three decades ago.[58] Ramaswamy argued that Indian labor studies suffered from two flaws. The first was an excessive concern with the activities of union leaders, particularly at the federation level, that blinded scholars to the everyday activities of unions at the grassroots level. Unfortunately for Indian labor studies, grassroots activities encompass the most important functions of the union. As Ramaswamy puts it, "national federations do not enroll members, negotiate with employers, or [engage in] conflict with rival unions."[59] Consequently, a narrow focus on interviewing trade union leaders resulted in a severe paucity of "behavioural and attitudinal data pertaining to the ordinary member."[60]

Students of Indian industrial relations have generally ignored the example Ramaswamy set in his careful study of textile unions in Tamil Nadu. Rather than a careful investigation of union activities, the studies cited in this article rely heavily on key source interviews with trade union, political, and business elites.[61] In later work, Ramaswamy himself turns away from the careful empiricism of his earlier work and begins to parrot many of the conventional views regarding union multiplicity and the political domination of unions that he once described as suspect.[62]

In his original assessment of the Indian labor studies literature, Ramaswamy also suggested that data and objectivity were supplanted with the "scholars' sense of mission,"[63] the "mission" presumably being the advocacy of a business-friendly industrial relations climate and the related need to portray unions as fragmented and aimless yet potentially dangerous. While Ramaswamy was correct in pointing to an antiunion bias in Indian labor studies, it is likely that this bias stems as much from the biased information provided by key source informants as with the intentions of the scholars themselves. Interviews with federation leaders, employers, and party leaders, upon which the studies cited in this article typically rely, are generally poor sources for information regarding the strength of organized labor. All three groups (federation leaders, employers, and political leaders) have incentives to portray unions as subordinate and, therefore, to portray them as less cohesive and organized than they actually are.

Employers have the most obvious reason to portray unions in a negative light. First, employers want to give the impression that they are in control of the industrial relations situation in their company; thus they portray the union(s) in their production units as quiescent. Second, employers want to demonstrate that they treat their workers well and to minimize any claims to the contrary. Stressing outside interference and union infighting is a strategy used to delegitimate worker grievances. When employers cite union division and rivalry as the source of an industrial dispute, they distract from the fact that workers are united in their basic desire for improvement in their material condition. By linking wage demands to the interests of outside union leaders in defeating their rivals, employers can obscure the fact that workers have a legitimate, collective interest in improving their wages. Such depictions attempt to deny the salience of class conflict and to undermine the legitimacy of class-based mobilization.

Political parties and union federations also have incentives to portray local unions as subordinate. However, the extent to which parties and federations do so is contingent on the ideology of the party and the federation. Writing in 1966, Crouch described the cross-federation variation in the degree of emphasis placed on "responsible unionism" this way:

> The Indian trade union federations, whatever their ideology, have at least in their official pronouncements tended to place greater emphasis on the long-run national interest than on the short-run wage demands of the workers....The Gandhians of INTUC, of course, have no difficulty in justifying the placing of national interest above working class interest. From the ideological point of view, the Marxists in AITUC, are equally able to argue that economic development which results in greater independence from capitalist countries is necessary even if the immediate interests of the working class suffer....It is the in the HMS and HMP where in theory there is more reservation about placing the workers' immediate interests in second position...because the HMS has tended to think of itself as being similar to the democratic socialist unions of the West....Nevertheless, HMS continues to generally support the government's policies of economic development.[64]

In my own interviews, conducted during the 2002–2003 and 2003–2004 academic years, I also found that leaders of INTUC (Congress-affiliated) unions demonstrated a high propensity to advocate a philosophy of "'responsible' unionism" and to portray affiliated unions as quiescent. This tendency is rooted in the party's heavy emphasis on a Gandhian ideology that eschews industrial conflict and emphasizes class compromise. For example, one INTUC union leader said that the purpose of trade unionism is just as much to get the worker to "understand his responsibilities" and the financial position of the company as it is to get the management to agree to higher wages and benefits.[65] Another INTUC leader stressed that rather than threatening to withhold labor, INTUC's basic strategy is to achieve wage gains by using productivity as a bargaining chip:

> We control the productivity. Our basic approach is this. First, the company should survive. If the company survives, then there is continued employment. The government lays down laws regarding the minimum wage. If you want more than the minimum wage, then you have to support the company. You have to allow the company to rationalize the deployment of persons, to modernize technology, and to increase productivity.[66]

In this leader's view, the union plays a crucial role in convincing workers of the need for mutually beneficial productivity increases. The management is unable to convince workers themselves, because a large percentage of workers are illiterate: "To convince the worker, they require a really strong person who can deliver the goods....They cannot negotiate with every person because our people are not that much educated."[67]

However, it is far from clear that workers always buy into this ideology of responsible unionism. As Crouch noted, "[a]t the national level, the trade unions are very 'responsible,' placing the national interest first. At the local level in a competitive situation, it is not always possible for leaders, who want to remain leaders to do this."[68] In other words, as I argued in section three, union competition generates pressure for union leaders to put worker interests first. The degree to which parties and national federations can impose an ideology of "responsible" unionism depends on the degree of competition faced by local union leaders.

To sum up, employers, federation leaders and party leaders have clear incentives to portray unions as subordinate and dominated by outside interests, to minimize common grievances, and to deny the existence of a unified and highly mobilized working class. When scholars rely too heavily on information gathered from interviews with political, business, and trade union elites (particularly INTUC leaders), they reify the class bias inherent in the statements of these dominant groups. While the statements of elites may seem to provide support for standard theories of politics or industrial relations, they often have no basis in reality and thus provide a poor test of such theories.

## Conclusion

In this essay, I have challenged prominent misconceptions about the organizational capacity of unions in India. Specifically, I have demonstrated that the standard view of Indian labor as fragmented, weak, and dominated by political parties and the state does not stand up to scrutiny. The common argument that the Indian labor movement is constantly undergoing a process of fragmentation and that a proliferation of unions inhibits collective action among workers is based on a flawed understanding of government statistics. More reliable original survey data suggest that the Indian labor movement is competitive but stable, with a fairly limited number of union centers competing for membership at the enterprise level. On average, companies tend to negotiate with one or two unions. Only a very small percentage of companies bargain with more than three unions.

Original survey data also suggests the fallacy of statements regarding the domination of the union movement by political parties and the state. Most companies (64 percent) are bound by collective bargaining agreements. Only a small percentage of companies report direct interference by a political party in industrial relations (17 percent) and an even smaller percentage report having collective disputes referred by the state for compulsory adjudication (15 percent).

Industrial disputes data and an examination of Indian labor legislation show that unions have aggressively pursued working-class interests in both the industrial relations and political arenas. Industrial disputes data suggest that the view of Indian labor unions as quiescent was outdated by the 1960s, when the level of protest surpassed that of many countries in Europe. Protest in Indian states subsequently climbed to reach average levels exceeding three-and-a-half worker--days lost per organized sector worker in the mid-1980s. Unions were also highly effective in pursuing protections in the political arena. Labor activism has resulted in a thick web of pro-worker labor legislation that has withstood the pressures of economic liberalization and increased exposure to trade.

Finally, this essay has speculated as to why so many social scientists have gotten it wrong. I argued that the tendency to overlook the mountain of evidence suggesting the continued prevalence of class conflict and the aggressive representation of working-class interests in India has been due to an over-reliance on interviews with business, political, and trade union elites. All of these groups have incentives to portray labor as divided and/or subordinate. It is important to interrogate and not simply parrot the class bias inherent in statements made by these elites. In short, Indian labor studies should return to the careful empiricism of Ramaswamy's earlier work when exploring hypotheses regarding the organizational structure of India's trade union movement.

ACKNOWLEDGMENTS: Research for this article was aided by a Social Science Research Council International Dissertation Research Fellowship, a Fulbright-Hays Doctoral Dissertation Research Abroad Fellowship, and a National Science Foundation Dissertation Improvement Grant. The author would like to thank Ronald Herring, Rina Agarwala, and Tom Fenton for helpful comments on earlier drafts. He would also like to thank the staff at Indiastat.com for their help in compiling data on the number of workers in India's organized sector.

❑

# 3. Workers' Organizations in Pakistan

## Why No Role in Formal Politics?

**Christopher Candland**

WHY HAVE PAKISTAN'S WORKERS EXHIBITED CONSIDERABLE INFLUENCE through street and factory protest but almost none in formal politics? Workers' organizations have obtained (or had once obtained) a significant measure of political power in India, Bangladesh, Sri Lanka, Afghanistan, and Nepal, but not in Pakistan. Organized workers in Pakistan have had little or no influence on political parties or the state.[1] Pakistan's contrasting experience allows us to see how specific political practices shape workers' organization and thus help us to understand better workers' organization elsewhere, especially where economic conditions are similar but political practices are different.

This essay begins by considering why Pakistani workers generally fail to mobilize on class lines but tend to mobilize on the basis of ethnicity, language, and religion. The first part of this essay considers the political forces that undermined workers' organizations in Pakistan and the common origins of these forces. These germinated and took root before Pakistan's creation and were fully mature in the 1950s when Pakistan joined the U.S. anticommunist Southeast Asian Treaty Organization (Seato) in 1954 and Pakistan's military first took formal control over the state in 1958. The second part of this essay addresses two questions: Why was labor repressed under Zulfikar Ali Bhutto's professedly pro-worker government (1972–1977)? Why are military governments seemingly hostile to workers' organizations?

### Workers and Workers' Organizations

The subject of this essay — workers' organizations — refers to the organizations of the nonagricultural labor force and, overwhelmingly, to male workers. This focus is a result of definitions for counting and legally recognizing workers and their organizations. Pakistani unions — the only organizations permitted under law to represent workers before employers and government — are the domain of workers from larger manufacturing sectors in nonfarm activities. These are predominantly male, salaried, government-recognized workers. There are other kinds of workers. Women, of course, staff a vast world of work, including paid and unpaid home-based work. But, of the officially recognized Pakistani labor force — regular (i.e., legally recognized) paid employees — fewer than 15 percent are female.[2] In comparison, 29 percent of the officially recognized Indian labor force are female.[3] Whether women are employed in this recognized labor force or elsewhere, they also work for their families. Family demands and social sanctions often make it near impossible for women to organize unions.[4] Pakistan's female workers are not well represented in Pakistani unions.[5] Agricultural workers, for their part, are prohibited from forming unions in Pakistan. This is not to say that these workers' organizations in Pakistan entirely exclude agricultural or "informal" sector workers. Some of Pakistan's labor leaders began by organizing *bidi* (hand-rolled cigarettes) and power-operated weaving loom workers. But the focus of this essay is workers in the "organized sector" (a Pakistani and Indian term for registered factories with relatively large numbers of employees).

## Class and Other Worker Identities

In most of South Asia, workers tend to organize on the basis of a shared political ideology. In Pakistan, major trade union federations are identified with specific ethnic or linguistic communities. It might appear, then, that the ethnic, linguistic, or religious bases of social power in Pakistan have limited the ability of working class movements to develop into a broader, national working class consciousness. Students of working class solidarity in Pakistan have lamented the manner in which workers organize along ethnically and linguistically exclusive lines. But, under some conditions, appeals to a common ethnicity, language, or religion might be the most effective (or only) avenue for working class assertion. The movement for Pakistan itself — a country for South Asian Muslims — reflects the way in which working class demands can be expressed through nonclass identities. Muslim landless agricultural workers, especially throughout Eastern India, embraced the movement for Pakistan as a struggle against economic servitude and exploitation. To the Muslims of India who supported Pakistan in the early 1940s Pakistan was appealing as a peasant and industrial working class utopia.[6]

Class solidarity everywhere — including working class solidarity — overlaps with solidarities based on ethnicity, language, nationality, and other non–class-based identities. Recovering the concept of class for political economy analysis requires attention to the conditions under which these nonclass identities strengthen or undermine class identity and one another. It is not sufficient to consider only how nonclass identities undermine class consciousness. Pakistani workers, sometimes with great effectiveness, organize on the basis of ethnicity, gender, language, and religion. These nonclass social bases for workers' organization have facilitated workers' collective action. Social solidarity on the basis of ethnicity, gender, language, or religion can be fierce. At the same time, nonclass social bases for workers' organization can prevent a broader foundation for wider working class solidarity and greater political influence.

Why have ethnicity, language, and religion taken on such importance in Pakistani workers' organizations? In workers' neighborhoods in Pakistan, as elsewhere in South Asia, residents need intermediaries to ensure the provision of basic services, for healthy relations with the police, and for the supply of jobs. In these neighborhoods, these intermediaries are representatives of distinct ethnic, language, and religious groups. Employment has long been made available through jobbers, contractors, and other informal middlemen, working through channels within distinct ethnic groups. Negotiation and bargaining occurs mostly within informal structures defined by ethnicity and language. In this way, workers of the same ethnicity, gender, language, and religion form working class organizations. These community identities then become reinforced and transposed to the political level, where political elites are well trained in manipulating ethnic rivalries. Thus, working class identities are diverted at the local level and transposed into ethnic rivalries at the level of formal politics. Whether through Basic Democrats, as under Field Martial Ayub Khan in the 1960s, through Zakat Committees, as under General Zia ul Haq in the 1980s, or through Union Councilors, as under General Pervez Musharraf today, the central government establishes the local level political structures. Labor brokers too are instruments of state power. Thus, even the articulation of working class interests (e.g., for employment and timely payment of wages) helps to solidify the informal power structures that maintain Pakistan's largely feudal system.[7] As labor activism emerges in distinct ethnic neighborhoods, patron-client relations determine the leadership structure. Leaders typically treat workers as clients, not as political allies. Unions are typically the creation of leaders who have loyal followings only among their ethnic group. Workers do not expect a democratic labor movement, but a leader who can produce jobs and deliver on workers' demands.[8]

The speed with which Pakistan was created and the ideological justification underpinning its establishment produced major obstacles to working class organization, specifically the displacement of more than 12 million people and promotion of a state-sanctioned religious ideology. The persistence of feudal relations and the government's legal controls undermined trade unionism. The Left was criminalized and internally divided.

The weakness of workers' organizations in Pakistan may appear to be overdetermined in the sense that more explanations are advanced than needed. But the determining forces all have a common origin: the centralizing and repressive practices of the ruling classes that controlled the state. The major obstacle to workers' representation in formal politics in Pakistan is a ruling class obsessed with its own security. This obsession led to the preservation of colonial instruments of control, anticommunist international alliances, and neo-classical economic ideologies. The opposition of the ruling classes — the bureaucratic and military elite — to workers' organizations is central to understanding why class identities, despite their importance to everyday social relations, fail to be replicated in formal politics.

Pakistani labor leaders and labor scholars share this perspective,[9] as I learned from more than a decade of close research on and participation with hundreds of workers and labor organizers in Pakistan.[10] Since 1991 I have conducted extensive interviews with dozens of labor organizers. I also tap a collection of interview transcripts conducted with senior trade union leaders in 1973 and thousands of Pakistan newspaper clippings related to labor published since 1947.[11]

## Union Strength in Comparative Perspective

What can a comparison of trade union and union membership growth in India and Pakistan tell us about working class solidarity in Pakistan? India is a good comparative case for Pakistan because, while economic conditions are similar, state ideologies and political practices differ sharply.

The size of the Pakistani labor force is roughly one-eighth of India's, but as a percentage of the number of nonagricultural workers, the numbers of union members are roughly equivalent in both countries. In the early 1990s, 5.4 percent of India's nonagricultural labor force was unionized,[12] while 5.5 percent of Pakistan's nonagricultural labor force was unionized. Given the general encouragement of unions in India and the general discouragement (and occasional outright repression) of unions in Pakistan during each country's formative decades, this should be surprising. But we need to consider how reported statistics are derived as well as what these statistics mean. Indian trade unions provide their own figures. The Government of India reports these figures as received, usually without verification. A comparison of figures, verified by periodic Indian government tallies of union figures, reveals that Indian unions exaggerate their membership by approximately 90 percent.[13] Indian unions turn in more realistic figures following regular government verifications of their trade union center figures. At the same time, many unions submit no returns at all, resulting in the absence of these unions and their members from official figures. These two features of labor data collection in India — voluntary reporting and self-reporting — account for the relatively low numbers of unions and members and for the dramatic fluctuation in reported union membership in India. In Pakistan, in contrast, the Ministry of Labour, Manpower and Overseas Pakistanis collects and reports figures that it has verified through its mechanisms for recognizing unions and through its examination of named employees on union rolls.

Even perfectly reliable and comparable numbers of unions, union members, or industrial disputes, on their own, say little about workers' organizations. Statistics can disguise more than inform. The statistics in figure 1, for example, do not reveal that most Pakistani unions are unions in name but not in practice, as unions do not have the right to bargain collectively. Throughout Pakistan, fewer than two thousand unions have collective bargaining rights. Each of these unions is restricted to a single workplace. In India, in contrast, there is no mechanism for recognizing unions as the collective bargaining agent for workers, except in three states, Karnataka, Orissa, and West Bengal. (Workers in these states hold secret ballot elections.) In most of India, employers are inclined to negotiate with any union (of seven or more workers) that poses a credible threat to production.[14] These fuzzy rules in Indian industrial relations have led workers to protest political party-based unionism. The upshot of these considerations is that the numbers — in figures 1, 2, and 3 —

Figure 1: Pakistani and Indian Union Growth (in thousands) 1952–1997

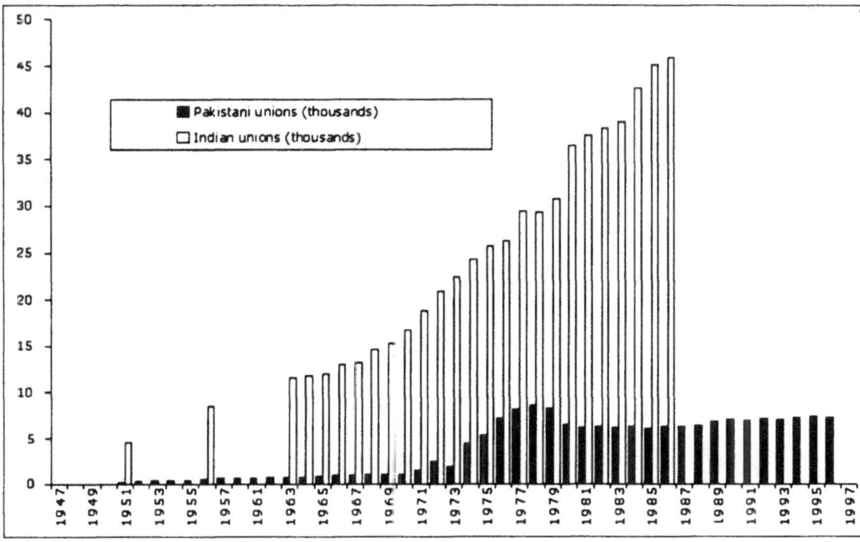


Sources: Government of Pakistan, Ministry of Labour, Manpower and Overseas Pakistanis, *Pakistan Labour Gazette*, various issues and Government of India, Ministry of Labour, *The Indian Labour Yearbook*, various issues. Note: Data in pre-partition Pakistan are for West Pakistan only. Periodic changes to the definition of employment make it fruitless to trace over time union membership as a percentage of employment (union membership density). While data are available for later years these are derived in different ways than those for earlier years.

ecome meaningful only when interpreted in the context of the reported experiences of labor leaders and workers.

A sketch of political and economic developments in Pakistan from the perspective of labor leaders will be useful here. Pakistan inherited very little industry at Partition. The industrial labor force, accordingly, was very small. But it grew rapidly, as did unions and union membership. Between 1948 and 1955, unions and union members grew at a rate of 10 percent per year. At the same time, the ruling classes suppressed workers' organizations and denied workers' basic rights. Indeed, unions were not recognized as legal entities until 1959. The government often denied citizens the right to assemble. In 1958, President Iskander Mirza, rather than face the prospect of defeat in the general elections scheduled for 1959, asked the commander in chief of the armed services, Mohammad Ayub Khan, to assume power. The military obliged. The bureaucracy thereby maintained its influence in government by trading civilian government for military government.

While the martial law government initially succeeded in controlling workers and workers' organizations, workers grew militant. Pakistan's war against India in 1965 dampened workers' unrest, but only temporarily. In 1968, outraged over Field Marshal Ayub Khan's national celebration of his "first decade of development," factory workers gave teeth to a movement that forced the military to promise to hold what would be Pakistan's first general election. The elections

Figure 2: Pakistani and Indian Union Members Growth (in millions), 1947–1996

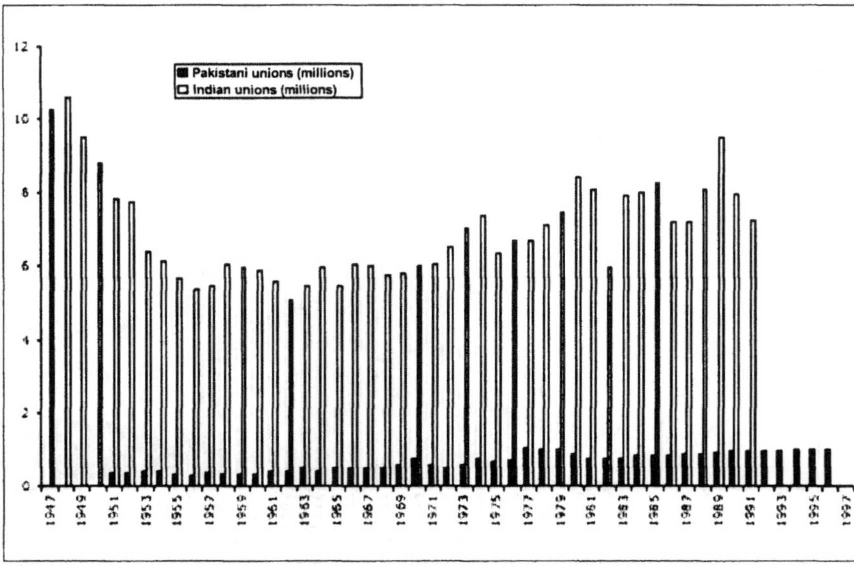


Sources: Government of Pakistan, Ministry of Labour, Manpower and Overseas Pakistanis, *Pakistan Labour Gazette*, various issues and Government of India, Ministry of Labour, *The Indian Labour Yearbook*, various issues. Note: Data in pre-partition Pakistan are for West Pakistan only. Periodic changes to the definition of employment make it fruitless to trace over time union membership as a percentage of employment (union membership density). While data are available for later years these are derived in different ways than those for earlier years.

led to the creation of Bangladesh out of East Pakistan and a short period of civilian government in West Pakistan. Before the military government arranged promised elections, it amended laws significantly, especially for workers and students. Workers and students were the base of the movement against military government during the 1968–69 popular movement. The military government promulgated the Industrial Relations Ordinance (IRO), which recognized — in principle — workers' rights to form unions and to bargain collectively. Under the IRO (discussed in detail below), unions and union membership grew in the initial years of the pro-worker government of Zulfikar Ali Bhutto. In 1975, Bhutto amended the IRO to stem the proliferation of unions. The amendment did reduce union numbers but did not affect membership growth. By 1975, the bureaucracy and the military recovered from their national disgrace in the debacle in East Pakistan and began again to assert themselves against workers' organizations. In 1977, Bhutto was replaced in a military coup d'etat by General Zia ul Haq, who imprisoned union leaders and suppressed unions and union members during the eleven years he ruled. (He died in 1988.) The impact of these political and economic developments on unions, union membership, and industrial dispute trends can be seen in figures 1, 2, and 3.

The origins of Pakistan's anti–working class environment can be traced to social forces that emerged during the movement for Pakistan, which Yunas Samad insightfully refers to as "a brief moment of political unity," and to the first decade of the new state.[15] The peculiarities of Pakistan's precipitous creation produced powerful obstacles to trade unionism. The majority of industrial workers at the time of Partition were refugees and thus the basis of workers' mobilization was predominantly cultural and not political or economic.

In India, unlike Pakistan, ethnic mobilization and working class organization are not generally in conflict because Indian governments and political parties have not been hostile (at least not consistently) to workers' movements and organizations. The greatest obstacle to workers' organization in Pakistan is government opposition to workers' movements and organizations. Lacking institutions other than those of the colonial era, which was designed to control and extract resources from a subject population, the classes in control of the state — the bureaucracy, the military, and, until 1958, the Muslim League leadership — opted for a centralized approach to governance. The economic development strategies adopted by the ruling classes treated workers not as human beings but as factors of production. In contrast, Indian economic development strategies recognized the importance of workers and workers' organizations. Indeed, the Constitution of India itself confirms the importance of workers and workers' organizations to Indian democracy and development. Additionally, the government of Pakistan joined SEATO, the U.S.-backed military alliance that regarded worker activists and workers' organizations as potentially subversive. The involvement of the U.S. Federation of Labor-Confederation of Industrial Organizations (AFL-CIO) and of the pro–United States International Confederation of Free Trade Unions (ICFTU) strengthened the state's effort to depoliticize the Pakistani labor movement. Let us examine these four obstacles to workers' solidarity — partition and migration, colonial institutions, anticommunist international alliances, and neo-classical development strategies — in greater detail.

### *Partition and Migration*

The precipitous partition of British India in August 1947 resulted in large-scale communal riots, the displacement of more than 12 million people, the severing of a once unified trade union movement, and the creation of two new mutually hostile states. Partition caused the loss of many leaders and rank-and-file activists in areas that were to become Pakistan. Urban workers came almost exclusively from eastern Punjab, the United Province, and other Muslim minority areas that would become part of independent India. As people who had lost their homes and livelihoods, the refugee working classes were susceptible to communal sentiments. In addition to being imbued with a communal consciousness, these groups were largely dependent on the state for their rehabilitation. Having sacrificed greatly to join Pakistan, they readily projected themselves as more authentic Pakistanis. The Urdu-speaking community, for example, referred to themselves as *muhajir*, a reference to the flight of some of the earliest Muslims from Mecca to Medina.

After the Partition of the subcontinent, 20 percent of the population of West Pakistan consisted of refugees from the territory that made up independent India. India's population after Partition, in contrast, was about 1 percent refugees from the new country of Pakistan. More than 7 million Muslim migrants left territories that, by 15 August 1947, had already become independent India.[16] The impact of the immigration on Pakistan was overwhelming in urban areas. Many of Pakistan's major cities — Faislabad, Gujranwala, Karachi, Lahore, Llyalpur, and Hyderabad — became immigrant majority cities by 1951.[17] Most industrial workers in these cities were refugee immigrants from India or immigrants from other areas of Pakistan. In Karachi, Pakistan's major industrial city, more than 57 percent of the labor force in 1959 were immigrants; more than 24 percent were migrants from other areas of Pakistan.[18] The migrant population continued to grow.

Further, the migrant labor force remains largely male and, consequently, the articulation of its demands is almost exclusively masculine. Union demands include jobs for sons, in the case of the accidental death or dismemberment of workers, and dowry funds for daughters.

The displacement of people at the time of Partition allowed religious and ethnic identity to undermine working class identity. The social stratification of workers is reflected in residential patterns in Karachi, Lahore, Hyderabad, and other centers of immigration, where there are Baloch, Pathan, and other ethnically defined residential colonies. Politicians and employers are skillful at exploiting and encouraging ethnic identities at the local level. To ensure that workers have minimal opportunity for collective action, employers hire workers who do not speak local languages or have access to local social networks. Coal miners in rural Sindh, for example, are Pathan migrants from the Northwest Frontier Province, who speak neither Urdu nor Sindhi, the languages of the region where they work. Therefore, none have access to local social networks. The workers live in barracks near the pits, far away from the nearest human settlements.

At the same time, labor protests have typically been organized and articulated along ethnic lines. In Karachi, for example, Pathan workers led many of the workers' movements. The basis of their mobilization, as we have noted, was predominantly cultural not political. Notions of community honor, rather than demands for political equality, predominated. The high level of mobilization over such culturally articulated demands was easily dissipated. Occasionally, working people have been able to overcome divisive ethnic identities and mobilize on the basis of class identity. Workers have demonstrated an ability to participate in collective action. The labor movement has evidenced a high degree of militancy and street power. But workers have not been able to sustain a high level of mobilization or convert that into representation in formal politics. Given the tight circumscription of labor by law, workers have typically expected little from trade union action. At the same time, the predominance of immigrants and migrants in the Pakistani economy can weaken workers' solidarity. As Karamat Ali has written

> the migrant worker, once he decides to migrate, has already preferred to opt for an individual solution to improve his living conditions and

Labor-management administrator meeting with dockworkers in Karachi harbor. "Union demands include jobs for sons, in the case of the accidental death or dismemberment of workers, and dowry funds for daughters." (ILO/Jacques Maillard, 1985)

therefore it would be a long time before he could realize the importance of collective action.[19]

The mass migration caused by Partition far more powerfully undermined workers' solidarity in Pakistan than in India.

### *Colonial Institutions of Government*

The government of Pakistan — the manager of the new state — was poised to create a centralized structure and a repressive approach to governance even before Pakistan was created. Mohammad Ali Jinnah, the All India Muslim League leader, chose to assume the office of governor general, a colonial-era institution, rather than to head the elected government.[20] For nearly a decade after independence, the government operated under the colonial Government of India Act of 1935. Government instruments of control — such as article 144 of the Code of Criminal Procedure (CCP) banning public assembly — were used with great frequency from Pakistan's earliest existence. The Pakistan Army's annexation of the state of Khalat, now a part of Balochistan, was the act of a colonial power. Until 1951, the commander in chief of the armed forces was a British officer, and a British military officer served as the chief of the Pakistan Air Force until 1956. Colonial institutions were designed to extract local resources for the personal gain of public officials and to subject the population to military, police, and bureaucratic control, not to promote social welfare and economic development. These institutions remain strong in "postcolonial" Pakistan. The readiness of the government to abandon domestic interests to serve first the U.K. and then the U.S. government helped nondemocratic colonial institutions to become embedded in the Pakistani political economy.

In Pakistan's early years, the government made no effort to formalize industrial relations. The early 1950s, however, witnessed many strikes. Concerned about rising industrial unrest, especially in East Pakistan, the government adopted a two-pronged strategy. It announced its intention to meet workers' demands for better rights to organize while enacting legislation to control workers and to make unionization impossible. In February and May 1952, the government ratified two of the most important International Labour Organization conventions, the Freedom of Association and Protection of the Right to Organize Convention, 1948 (number 87) and the Right to Organize and Collective Bargaining Convention, 1949 (number 98). But with the introduction of the Essential Services Maintenance Act (ESMA) that same year, the only significant labor law in the pre–martial law period, large categories of workers were denied the right to collective representation in unions. The ESMA gives the government complete discretion to restrict or ban trade unions and collective bargaining in any industry deemed by the government to be essential to the welfare of "the nation," and it makes absence from or stoppage of paid or unpaid work in designated essential industries a penal offense. Work actions in almost all industries are proscribed.[21] No court has jurisdiction to entertain complaints of workers affected by the application of the ESMA.

Under the ESMA, which is still in effect today, agricultural workers are also prohibited from unionizing, as are workers in other "essential" service sectors, such as education. Given these legal prohibitions against union organizing, it is not surprising that Pakistan's union membership, as a percentage of the economically active population, was only 0.7 percent in 2000. In comparison, India's union membership, as a percentage of the entire economically active population, was 1.7 percent in the same year.[22]

After Ayub Khan's declaration of martial law in 1958, labor laws were promulgated to formalize industrial relations and to control the labor movement through government regulation. For example, the 1959 Industrial Disputes Act, which superseded the colonial-era Trades Union Act of 1926 and the Industrial Disputes Act of 1929, made conciliation, arbitration, and adjudication compulsory, limited nonworkers (so-called outsiders) to no more than 25 percent of trade union offices, and banned unions from collecting funds for political activities. The laws for the regulation of industrial labor in Pakistan by 1959 can already be characterized as restrictive and repressive. Of course, Indian governments have also unleashed considerable oppressive power against Indian workers, but anti-worker violence has been much more the norm in Pakistan.

### *Anticommunist Alliances*

Pakistan's creation coincided with the onset of the cold war. The government of Pakistan opted to join the United States in an anticommunist alliance that promoted the repression of worker activists and organizers. Although the Communist Party of India supported the creation of Pakistan, communists in Pakistan were hounded. Mohammad Ali Jinnah himself blamed communists for the language riots in East Bengal in March 1948. The government banned the Communist Party of Pakistan in 1954. By 1958, the possession of communist literature was a punishable offense, and university libraries were purged of communist literature. At the same time, U.S. governmental and quasi-governmental organizations provided plentiful anticommunist labor education and training materials.[23] As Karamat Ali has argued, the government controlled workers not only in factories (by allowing owners of industry to deny workers the right to bargain collectively), but outside factories as well through its anticommunist ideology.[24]

With the strategic relationship between Pakistan and the U.S. governments and militaries in place, U.S. influence over Pakistan's trade union movement increased considerably. Pakistan's incorporation into first bilateral and later multilateral military and economic alliances with the United States led to the suppression of left-oriented trade unions associated with the Pakistan Trade Union Federation and forced the creation of a depoliticized, anticommunist federation, eventually named the All Pakistan Confederation of Labor (APCOL). The Brussels-based International Confederation for Free Trade Unions (ICFTU) established offices in Karachi and Lahore, extended financial and other assistance to APCOL, and sent Pakistan trade unionists on tours to the United States to encourage them to emulate U.S.-styled "independent" (i.e., apolitical) trade unionism. Minister of Labour Abdul Malik ran APCOL, the country's largest federation, during the height of industrial and union growth in the country.[25] At first, the government enforced trade union unity through APCOL, but with the advent of the cold war international trade union movements began to divide along ideological lines. In the 1960s, the APCOL fractured, resulting in a half dozen federations. The ICFTU, like the World Federation of Trade Unions (WFTU), accepted the affiliation of rival federations in Pakistan.

Major ideological differences in Pakistan's labor movement can be traced to pre-independence disagreements of the kind that split the Indian Federation of Labour, under the leadership of the socialist M. N. Roy, from the more radical All India Trade Union Congress. But the affiliation of Pakistani federations with the ICFTU and the WFTU quickened and solidified political rivalries within the labor movement.

### *Neoclassical Development Strategies*

The fourth major obstacle to workers' solidarity in Pakistan is an economic counterpart to the U.S. anticommunist military alliance. Under Field Marshal Ayub Khan, economic advisors from the United States were invited to assist Pakistan in engineering rapid industrial growth. (One Planning Commission advisor complained that economic planning in Pakistan had been "insidiously taken over" by these American advisors.)[26] The Pakistani government's program of rapid industrialization was based on W. Arthur Lewis's strategy of squeezing maximum profits by paying nonagricultural workers "a subsistence wage plus a margin."[27] Poor migrants from rural areas were essential to this neo-classical model of (industrial) growth. The key to rapid growth, Pakistani planners and their U.S. advisors argued, was keeping the rural population at subsistence levels while paying workers a near-subsistence wage. The closer the wages could be held to subsistence levels, the faster profits would accumulate and, by assumption, be reinvested in what Lewis referred to as "the capitalist sector."[28]

In Lewis's neoclassical model, the state's duty was to intervene only to maintain this unlimited supply of subsistence waged labor. Land reforms, thus, served no purpose in Lewis's model of economic growth. As the then chairperson of the Planning Commission, Mahbub ul Haq, declared, "it would be tragic if policies appropriate to a Keynesian era were to be tried in countries still living in a Smithian or Ricardian world."[29] The state was to assume a pivotal role in repressing workers and their organizations. The ideological, political, and economic interests of the classes that controlled the state prevented workers from exercising their rights. To serve rapid industrial growth, Field Marshal Ayub Khan's government denied workers such fundamental rights as the freedom of association and of representation. The denial of these rights together with rapid loss of purchasing power, affecting waged labor most, helped to promote the major industrial unrest of the mid 1950s. While India was also the recipient of antilabor, neoclassical U.S. economic ideology, Nehruvian Socialism countered this advice.[30]

### *The Military and Its Elections*

In the early 1960s, Communist and Left activists began mobilizing in communities where workers were becoming militant.[31] By 1967, militant activists were strong in workers' communities and in factories, and, in 1968, industrial workers took to the street to oppose the government of Field Marshal Ayub Khan and to demand the restoration of democracy. For six months, the military government attempted to suppress the protests, employing the same techniques that colonial rulers had. The government prohibited demonstrations under the colonial-era Defence of Pakistan Rules, arrested the protest leaders, and shot and killed hundreds of protesters. In March 1969, Ayub Khan conceded by promising elections and handing power to his army chief of staff, General Yahya Khan.

The single most important labor law in Pakistan came into effect after Ayub Khan was forced from the presidency. In an attempt to both mollify and depoliticize industrial workers in preparation for a return to civilian government, Ayub Khan's martial law government consulted with labor leaders and promulgated a new labor law, the above-mentioned Industrial Relations Ordinance. The IRO enabled the Yahya Khan government to depoliticize the labor movement through seemingly democratic means. Deputy Martial Law Administrator Noor Khan, who had earlier organized a tripartite conference to prepare for promulgation of the IRO, borrowed the model that had worked well for him when he managed Pakistan International Airlines, then a military enterprise.[32] The IRO required that trade union leaders be workers, currently employed, and elected by fellow workers. This stipulation ensured that Pakistan's trade union representatives would be ill equipped to negotiate labor law and labor courts (where English is still used). The IRO also instituted enterprise unionism in Pakistan, permitting trade unionism only at the factory level.

Ayub Khan's IRO forced radical and reformist labor leaders together as caretakers of a legal framework for the protection of the rights of workers in the formal economy. The IRO required unions to devote their energies to complicated legal requirements for a fraction of the labor force. The labor leaders celebrated the adoption of law that would grant industrial workers their rights to organize, bargain collectively, and strike. The disorganized militant movements of the 1960s could not be sustained under a state-dominated form of trade unionism. The IRO provided rich windfalls for the very labor leadership that had sidelined itself in the 1960s. Unionists who were better equipped to deal with the legal framework gained control over significant categories of workers in the organized industrial sector. But those workers who led the movement lost their command of the labor movement.[33]

In the section that follows, we consider why the pro-worker government of Zulfikar Ali Bhutto unleashed violence against workers. We also consider whether military governments are necessarily opposed to workers' organizations.

## Labor Repression and Bhutto's Pro-Worker Government

In his first address to the nation as president of Pakistan, Zulfikar Ali Bhutto promised to usher in a period of social and economic justice. He enjoined industrialists not to dismiss workers and, in words echoing his "Election Manifesto," referred to workers as "our masters" and the "producers of wealth."[34] Within two weeks of assuming office, Bhutto made good on his election pledge to nationalize most basic industries, assuming the management of thirty-three private businesses through the proclamation of the Economic Reform Ordinance of 1972. In his remarks to a tripartite labor conference in Rawalpindi in November 1973, Bhutto claimed that his "electoral success was made possible because [of] the toiling masses, particularly peasants and labourers [who] co-operated with the Pakistan People's Party. We cannot forget their kindness."[35] At the start, Bhutto did deliver a great deal to regularly employed workers: He promulgated the country's first pension benefit program as well as programs for workplace injury compensation, workers' profit sharing, and workers' participation on management boards. But in 1974, Bhutto vowed that if workers did not end their protests, then "the strength of the street will be met by the strength of the state."[36] Indeed, many of the workers who led the movement of 1968–69 were arrested and shot under Bhutto's government. In June 1972, for example, police shot to death workers at a protest at the Sindh Industrial and Trading Estates.[37] How are we to explain the simultaneous embrace of workers' right to political power and new heights of state violence, as alleged by workers and labor leaders of the day?

The leadership of the Pakistan Peoples' Party, including Bhutto himself, claimed that severe action against industrial workers was required because agents of unnamed foreign governments had allies in the trade union movement who were using industrial unrest to destabilize the country.[38] For their part, trade union leaders claim that Bhutto was never serious about undertaking pro-worker reforms and that he betrayed his feudal origins soon after taking power.[39] An explanation that accommodates both these perspectives returns our attention to the military and the bureaucracy. While Bhutto initially encouraged the growth of organized labor, as figures 1 through 3 suggest, the bureaucracy and police violently repressed it. A story related to me by Gul Rahman, president of the Pakistan Workers' Confederation, support this "treason of the bureaucrats" explanation. In 1973, Rahman met Bhutto, who promised then that he would ensure that workers at the Swat Textile Mill, who were not being paid, would get their back wages within one week. Bhutto conveyed the directive to the NWFP chief minister and to the minister of the interior, who claimed that they were unable to get the owners to pay the workers. "How long is a week!" Bhutto is said to have pleaded. Workers were only paid months later when the Azad Mazdoor Federation, the predecessor to the Muttahida Labour Federation, surrounded the management and refused to release them (*gherao*) until they arranged for workers to be paid.[40] The incident suggests that it was not so much Bhutto who turned against Pakistan's workers, but the bureaucracy and the owners of industry who turned against Bhutto.

## The Military and Workers' Organizations

Are military governments necessarily opposed to workers' organizations? After all, military personnel are often recruited from the working classes. And bounded solidarity — the kind of solidarity that keeps many unions together — is high among comrades in arms. But militaries in highly unequal societies will regard strong workers' solidarity as threatening to command loyalty and organizational integrity. Unless specifically tasked to create a new order from existing inequalities, militaries typically prefer the existing state of affairs, including a highly unequal economy and the exclusion of civilians from decision-making. Militaries recognize, as Nicolo Machiavelli put it, that

> there is nothing more difficult to carry out, nor more doubtful of success, nor more dangerous to handle, than to initiate a new order of things. For the reformer has enemies in all those who profit by the old order, and only lukewarm defenders in all those who would profit by the new order.[41]

Workers in Pakistan have been steadfast proponents of a "new order of things" — an order that would include an elected government and policies designed for greater economic justice. But Pakistani workers have been fervent in support of their rights: workers' demonstrations and sacrifices in 1968–69, for instance, secured from the military government a promise to restore civil and electoral rights. Workers then helped to elect a president who vowed to attack economic injustice and inequality.

Militaries and military governments are not necessarily opposed to working class organizations. But militaries and military governments that are allied with the United States have been uniformly hostile to workers' movements and organizations. Pakistan's military governments have differed, although they all share a hostility toward workers organizations: Field Marshal Ayub Khan was a secular modernizer who controlled electoral politics, but he permitted a strong civil society; Zia ul Haq was a radical Islamist who poisoned the environment for civil society associations. What these military governments had in common was their

Pakistani dockworkers unloading metal waste from a freighter. "A government that is openly hostile to workers' rights is hostile to workers' organizations, and this can only undermine the foundations for working class consciousness." (ILO/Jacques Maillard, 1985)

alliance with the United States and the suppression of working class organizations. A thorough engagement of the question of why militaries tend to be anti–working class would have to consider more than one country or region. There is not opportunity here to consider even the essential scholarship on military governments. But Ellen Kay Trimberger gives us some immediate assistance. In the four cases of "revolutions from above" (defined as military-bureaucratic pro-working class coups d'etat) that she discusses — Meiji's in Japan in 1868, Ataturk's in Turkey in 1919, Nasser's in Egypt in 1952, and Velasco's in Peru in 1968 — the military took control in reaction to European or U.S. military intervention.[42] Scholarship on the military in Pakistan provides additional insights, including new perspectives on U.S. military training and the diffusion of military-technocratic roles.[43] This scholarship brings our attention back to the conflict between command loyalty and solidarity. Workers' solidarity might permit dissent; command loyalty does not.

Periods of civilian rule in Pakistan are not necessarily less violent toward workers than periods of military rule because the institutions of government do not rematerialize with a change of regimes (i.e., systems for selecting the senior managers of the state). That Bhutto rose to power through an electoral contest rather than military seniority did not automatically transform the institutions (i.e., the patterns of thought and behavior) of the state. As gauged by industrial disputes, one finds no discernable difference in labor militancy across regime type in Pakistan. (See figure 3.) High levels of industrial unrest stretched across two military governments — of very different stripes — and one civilian government. The industrial unrest in the wake of the December 1998 IMF-sponsored structural adjustment program also spread across military "caretaker" governments and elected civilian governments. If there is a correlation between regime type and industrial labor militancy, it is seen in Zia ul Haq's and Zulfikar Ali

Figure 3: Pakistan Industrial Disputes, Workers Involved, and Workdays Lost, 1947–2003

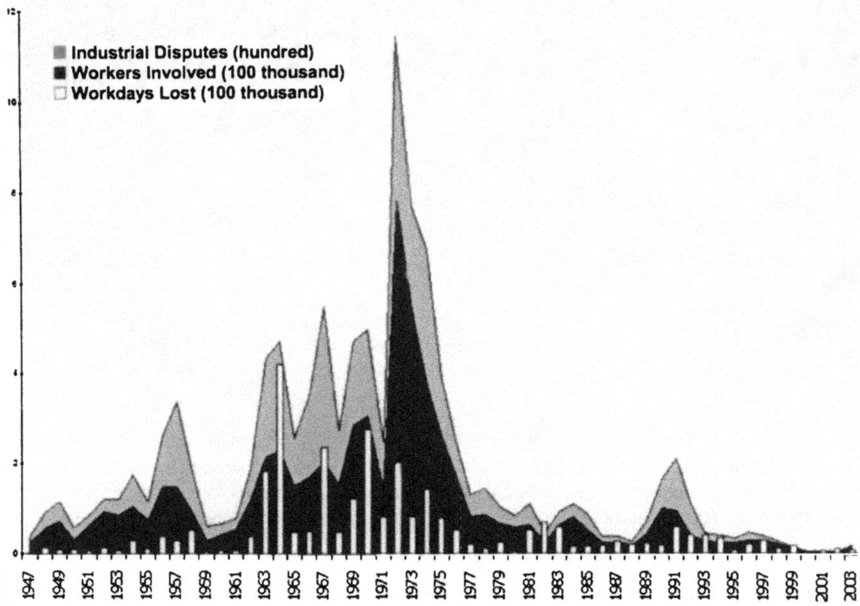


Source: Government of Pakistan, Ministry of Labour, Manpower and Overseas Pakistanis, *Pakistan Labour Gazette*, various issues. Note: Data in pre-partition Pakistan are for West Pakistan only. The Government of India differentiates between industrial disputes caused by strikes and those caused by lockouts; Pakistan does not.

Bhutto's' regimes. Each managed to reduce union membership and prohibit industrial disputes. The period of "industrial quiescence" that followed the adoption of the IMF program at the end of 1998 suggests that state institutions are now capable of keeping labor a "passive pedestal" for the ruling classes.[44] To be clear, it is not that the Pakistani ruling classes are more anti-worker or more avaricious than, say, Indian or Bangladeshi ruling classes. It is rather that the Pakistani state prefers that workers be politically disempowered.

The creation of Pakistan was not itself an obstacle to working class identity or to working class organization. Pakistan's ruling classes — the elite of the bureaucracy and the military — have erected most of the major obstacles to workers' organization. The military has thwarted the articulation of workers' interest at local levels in ways that might allow some transference to a national level (i.e., from the workplace to the national assembly); written and promulgated the major repressive labor laws in Pakistan; undermined democratic social institutions and interfered with political parties; banned parties and specific candidates, killed others, and rigged votes; set upon farmers' groups, who, by law, are prohibited from organizing; and murdered human and women's rights activists. The severity of the obstacles, in comparison to India, is clear. While the Indian military has never played a leading role in political decision-making, the military in Pakistan has often organized political actions and has played a decisive role in most political decisions, even during those few periods when elected, civilian governments were in the legislature.

## Conclusion

A complete exploration of the inability of working class solidarity to achieve political influence in Pakistan would require consideration of the history of left political parties in Pakistan and their fatal encounters with military governments. The exploration would have to consider how colonial-styled government education policy led to the suffocation of critical social sciences;[45] and it would have to examine as well the agenda of "elite classes" in Pakistan, including the upper echelons of the military, the bureaucracy, and industry, as well as the construction and penetration into Pakistani society of the "ideology of Pakistan" — the conviction that Muslims living in Muslim-majority areas of British India constitute "a nation" to be represented by an "Islamic state." The various forces undermining opportunities for workers' solidarity in Pakistan — the displacements due to Partition, colonial institutions of government, new anticommunist alliances, and neoclassical economic ideologies — might appear to be an assortment of independent variables. But, as I have argued, they all proceed from a single source: a centralizing and repressive ruling class preoccupied with "national security" — in practice, its own preservation.

Explaining why something did *not* happen — why workers have failed to achieve the kind of political influence that they have been able to achieve in other South Asian countries — is likely to be less convincing than explaining why something *did* happen. Fortunately for our analysis we have an episode — from 1972 until 1974 — when the unusual happened. A proponent of the rights of the working classes became prime minister. In 1971, when the morale of the Pakistani military was so low (as a result of its failure to keep Pakistan united), it withdrew in disgrace from politics. Bhutto was then made the chief martial law administrator. This was the only time in all Pakistan's history that the military was not in official or de facto control of the state.[46] This was also the one time when workers' organizations grew in numbers and in confidence, and won significant government concessions, including more secure employment, better wages, sharing of profits, pensions, injury and death compensation, and participation in management decisions.

Economic development strategies, state ideologies, and ruling classes in Pakistan have been openly hostile to workers and their rights. A government that is openly hostile to workers' rights is hostile to workers' organizations, and this can only undermine the foundations for working class consciousness. These observations may seem simplistic, but they direct our analysis to the core obstacle to working class organizations: government. Pakistani governments, as we have shown, have undermined working class organizations.

Another lesson proceeds directly from the first. Class analysis requires a global perspective. Workers' organizations in Pakistan cannot be analyzed as if they operate within a single economy or polity. Workers' organizations would be stronger if Pakistan were not a front-line state in Washington's battle against its "enemies" in the region. The ruling classes could have tolerated a more social welfare-oriented policy, had U.S. foreign policy not been deeply suspicious of left labor organizers and strengthened undemocratic forces to undermine workers' solidarity.

The accomplishments of Pakistan's Movement for the Restoration of Democracy (1980–1988) and the Alliance for the Restoration of Democracy (1999–present) were largely due to working class backing. Despite repression, unions have been, since the founding of Pakistan, the major social force for democracy and for civilian rule. There is no reason to think that industrial workers and their unions will not continue to be the leading force for the restoration of democracy and civilian rule. Regrettably we also have no cause to think that the military will not continue to regard workers' movements and workers' organizations as threatening to "national security" (i.e., the military's security) and to restrict and repress workers' organizations.

ACKNOWLEDGMENTS: This essay began as comments for the Pakistan Labour History Conference, 26–28 December 1999, held in Karachi. The essay owes a great deal to Karamat Ali, director of the Pakistan Institute of Labour Education and Research (Karachi), for many conversations over several years. I thank Ron Herring for detailed comments on earlier drafts. I would like to dedicate this essay to Omar Asghar Khan (1953–2002) and S.P. Lodhi (1925–2006).

❑

# 4. From Work to Welfare

## A New Class Movement in India

**Rina Agarwala**

TWO GLOBAL TRENDS HAVE SHAPED THE FATE OF THE WORLD'S WORKERS since the late-1980s. One is an unpredicted decline in formally employed labor and subsequent growth in informal labor; the other is an unprecedented decline in state welfare rhetoric and policy. These simultaneous trends have resulted in an increase in the proportion of workers who do not receive secure wages or social benefits either from employers or from the state. Such informally employed workers represent one of the poorest and most marginalized populations of the liberalization era. Yet little is known about these workers' lives.

In this article I argue that the rigidity of early class analysis and the recent demise of any type of class analytics have turned attention away from examining the growing population of informally employed workers as a class. As a consequence, the recent literature on globalization and liberalization is increasingly concluding that the decreasing proportion of formally employed workers (and the subsequent rise in informal employment) the world over signifies a decline in all class-based organization. Such arguments have obscured our understanding of the current social dynamics of exploitation and resistance. It particular, they overlook (1) the changing composition of the class structure in countries that are implementing economic reforms, and (2) the class-based political strategies that informal workers are using to improve their current situation. In other words, by not examining informal workers as a class "in themselves," we are losing insights into how they are translating their positions into a class "for themselves." In an attempt to begin filling this gap, this article recovers class as an important analytical tool with which to examine (1) the current relations of power between the state, employers, and the majority of India's workers, and (2) how the structures of production within which informal workers operate affect their collective action strategies. Insights into how informal workers organize can have profound implications on our understanding of changing state-labor relations as national governments. attempt to liberalize their economies and simultaneously reign in their welfare functions.

## 1. Defining Informal Workers

Perhaps the largest impediment to work on the informal sector to date has been the lack of consensus on how to define and count informal workers. Since 1973 when Keith Hart first coined the term "informal sector workers" based on his research in Kenya,[1] scholars have used various approaches to understanding the population of poor, marginal workers that Hart sought to highlight.[2] As a result of the lack of agreement about the informal sector concept, few national-level data sets have attempted to collect information on the informal workforce.

Recent studies, however, have begun to reverse this trend by establishing definitions that are consistent at both the theoretical and operational levels. Much of the best theoretical work on the informal sector has come from scholars of Latin America. In 1989, Alejandro Portes, Manuel Castells, and Lauren Benton provided the following definition:

> The informal sector consists of economic units that produce goods and services legally, but engage in operations that are not registered or regulated by fiscal, labor, health, and tax laws. Informal workers include the self-employed, who own and run a business in the informal sector with few or no employees, as well as casual labor, who work through subcontractors either for an informal or a formal sector enterprise. The primary difference between informal and formal workers is that the latter are protected and regulated under state law while the former are not.[3]

The key advantage of this definition is that by focusing on the level of state regulation, rather than the type of enterprise, it ensures the inclusion of informal workers in both informal and formal sector enterprises, as well as regular workers in informal enterprises. In addition, it includes the vast numbers of (often women) workers who work alone either at home or in multiple locations (such as street vendors). This definition has been largely accepted in much of the recent literature on informal workers in developing countries. In 1999, the National Sample Survey Organisation of India operationalized this definition in its National Sample Survey (NSS) on Employment and Unemployment by including, for the first time, detailed questions on employment status, location of work, and enterprise characteristics.[4]

Since India launched its economic reforms in 1991, informal workers have replaced traditional factory workers as the government's *ideal* worker. Similar trends can be found across nations attempting to compete in the global market with cheap, flexible labor. Although informal workers operate outside the state's jurisdiction, the Indian government is supporting firms in hiring fewer formal workers and more informal workers by urging early retirement options for formally employed workers and failing to enforce laws that protect job security. Recent government reports in India stress "the important role informal labor plays in ensuring the success of India's reforms."[5] By the end of the 1990s, India's informal sector was estimated to account for over 60 percent of gross domestic product.[6] In 2002, the Indian government recognized the informal sector as the primary source of future employment for all Indians, and in 2004, the

Central Government appointed a high-profile committee to examine ways to further increase productivity in the informal sector.[7]

As a result of these trends, the proportion of informal workers in the labor force is growing.[8] The significance of the growth lies not only in its absolute amount, but also in its stinging contradiction to early development theories predicting the demise of the informal sector with economic growth.[9] Between 1987 and 2001, the Indian economy grew at an annual rate of approximately 5 percent; yet the number of households in self-employed and casual labor increased, and households engaged in formal wage and salaried jobs decreased.

Within the category of informal workers, this study focuses on one group — namely casual workers who have to sell their labor as a commodity in a buyers' market. In the Indian context, it is important to qualify the Portes et al. definition of informal workers with a greater emphasis on the lack of protection from the *employer*, and not just the state. As I illustrate below, casual workers in India are indeed fighting for protection from the state. However, it is their employers' continuing lack of responsibility toward their livelihood and welfare that distinguishes them from formal sector workers. Further research is needed to see if this caveat is generalizable to other regional contexts.

## 2. Informal Workers: A Class "*In* Themselves"

In trying to understand the lives of the growing mass of informal workers in India, this study uses a class-analytic approach. Drawing from existing studies, focusing on Western Europe and Latin America, I first incorporate informal workers into the mainstream class structure of India. Doing so highlights the key links between informal workers and capitalist accumulation. Specifically, formal sector accumulation relies heavily on informal workers, because they absorb much of the reproductive costs of formal and informal labor, and they help constrain the expansion of the relatively costly formal sector working class. As a result of their strategic role in the processes of accumulation, class theories predict that informal workers likely have unique interests and interactions with formal sector workers, capital, and the state.

In the early twentieth century, Vladimir Lenin and Rosa Luxemburg asserted that informal workers are an integral part of the working class, rather than a marginal group of temporary workers, in advanced capitalist economies.[10] Recently, Alejandro Portes and Kelly Hoffman explicitly mapped informal workers onto the unique class structure of developing economies during the neoliberal era.[11] As in advanced countries, Portes and Hoffman define capitalists, executives, and professionals as the dominant classes in Latin America. Also similar to advanced countries is Portes and Hoffman's categorization of the formal proletariat as both skilled, salaried white-collar employees, as well as unskilled waged workers with labor contracts. While these classes no doubt hold a disproportionate amount of power and resources, in developing countries they account for only a small proportion of the population. In India, they account for approximately 7 percent of the entire labor force (or 18 percent of the nonagricultural labor force).[12]

Table 1. Informal Workers and Class Structure in India

| Class | Percent of India's nonagricultural labor force* | Percent of India's nonagricultural informal labor force |
|---|---|---|
| Dominant Classes (capitalists, executives, and professionals) | n(18) | — |
| Petty Bourgeoisie/Micro-entrepreneurs or Self-Employed | 45 | 54 |
| Formal Proletariat (skilled and unskilled workers with wage contracts) | j(18) | — |
| Informal Proletariat (casual workers and regular workers in informal enterprises) | 38 | 46 |

*These figures are calculated by the author using India's 55th Round NSS. Currently, informal workers in India can only be calculated in the nonagricultural sectors. In addition, the NSS does not yet allow a distinction between professionals in the dominant classes and those in the formal proletariat. Therefore, percentages for dominant classes and formal proletariat are presented as an unknown percentage (n and j) of the sum total (equal to 18 percent).

The remaining 93 percent of the labor force (or 82 percent of the nonagricultural labor force) in India is comprised of informal workers. While most analyses of class structure in advanced countries do not include informal workers, thereby emphasizing their marginality to the modern economy, Portes and Hoffman add two classes of informal workers to the contemporary class structure of developing economies. In India, the first class of informal workers, called "petty bourgeoisie" or "micro-entrepreneurs" (in India this group is referred to as "the self-employed"), make up 45 percent of the nation's nonagricultural labor force and 54 percent of the nation's nonagricultural informal labor force (see Table 1). As Portes and Hoffman note, in developing countries this class performs the critical "function of linking the modern capitalist economy, led by the three dominant classes, with the mass of informal workers at the bottom. Micro-entrepreneurs organize [informal] labor to produce low-cost goods and services for consumers and low-cost inputs subcontracted by large firms."[13]

The second class of informal workers, called "the informal proletariat," is located at the bottom of the class structure and includes casual workers and regular workers in informal enterprises. In India, this class makes up 38 percent of the nation's nonagricultural labor force, and 46 percent of the nation's nonagricultural informal labor force. These workers lack control of capital and means of production, and they are predominantly unskilled. They have less access to economic or political resources than other classes. That these workers lack formal contracts with an employer renders their work insecure and unregulated by definition; their insecurity, in turn, makes them highly vulnerable to exploitation by the other groups that sit above them in the class structure. This class of informal proletariats is the focus of this article.

Especially significant for those concerned about development is the relative deprivation the informal proletariat faces compared to the formal proletariat in

India. As shown in Table 2 (next page), informal workers have a significantly larger share of illiterates than formal workers; formal workers, in contrast, are more likely to have a graduate education than informal workers. As well, the Provident Fund, India's social security system, covers only 6 percent of informal workers, while nearly 80 percent of formal workers are covered under the same program. Consistent with claims that poverty is becoming increasingly feminized, the share of female workers employed in the informal sector is slightly larger than the share of male workers in the sector.

This depiction of the class structure in developing economies defines the informal proletariat as a separate class-*in*-themselves. Doing so acknowledges the important (and growing) relations between informal workers, formal workers, and modern capital. In addition, it helps scholars identify informal workers' life chances and their unique sources of poverty. Finally, it provides a more accurate depiction of the current social dynamics in developing economies undergoing economic reforms. This study, however, is concerned with the two-step cognitive mediation process that arises *from* class structure: recognizing membership in a class with coherent common interests and acting politically on those interests. In other words, if informal workers are acknowledged as a class-*in*-themselves, how do they organize to improve their livelihoods as a class-*for*-themselves?

## 3. The Dwindling Role of Class in India's Political Mobilization Literature

Surprisingly few studies have examined how the recent changes in employment and class structures have affected the political activities of workers. Until the early 1950s, the Indian labor movement was heralded for its contribution to India's fight for independence.[14] As a testimony of laborers' struggles, values of class equality and progressive laws protecting workers' rights featured prominently in the new government's constitution and institutions. Formally, the new government emphasized collective bargaining as the central method for Indian labor relations, and national unions emerged in every sector to represent workers in front of employers and the state.

By the mid-1950s, however, labor organizations began to split over political power, and the Indian class literature also split on whether or not workers' organizations could ensure substantial gains for their members. Some highlighted the movement's ability to organize with few resources and handle immediate disputes on wages and working conditions as proof of the empowering nature of India's new democracy.[15] Others pointed to the lack of militancy and lax implementation of labor laws as evidence that the labor movement had become a mere disciplinary weapon of the state.[16]

Since the 1980s, the debate on class politics has largely subsided, and scholars increasingly point to the near dissolution of class politics in India.[17] In place of class, Indian scholars are now debating the effectiveness of one-issue, interest-based movements on (among others) women's rights, environment, and development needs[18] or identity-based movements organized along caste, religion, and ethnicity lines.[19] Little consensus has been reached on

Table 2. Education Level and Social Security Coverage by Employment Status (ages >5)

| | Not in Labor Force | Not in Labor Force (%) | Unemployed | Unemployed %) | Employed in Informal Sector | Employed in Informal Sector (%) | Employed in Formal Sector | Employed in Formal Sector (%) |
|---|---|---|---|---|---|---|---|---|
| Illiterate | 152,900,000 | 34.4 | 467,385 | 5.7 | 34,169,363 | 29.8 | 1,625,676 | 6.5 |
| literate below primary | 122,600,000 | 27.6 | 424,715 | 5.2 | 14,384,426 | 12.5 | 1,256,738 | 5.0 |
| Primary | 66,008,255 | 14.9 | 676,078 | 8.2 | 16,356,019 | 14.2 | 1,599,158 | 6.4 |
| Middle | 52,137,411 | 11.7 | 1,679,605 | 20.4 | 20,985,693 | 18.3 | 3,455,788 | 13.8 |
| Secondary | 27,362,937 | 6.2 | 1,825,245 | 22.2 | 13,870,854 | 12.1 | 5,409,274 | 21.7 |
| Higher secondary | 14,631,106 | 3.3 | 1,288,657 | 15.7 | 6,588,301 | 5.7 | 3,715,881 | 14.9 |
| Graduate + | 8,744,497 | 2.0 | 1,859,712 | 22.6 | 8,473,706 | 7.4 | 7,895,521 | 31.6 |
| Total | 444,384,206 | | 8,221,397 | | 114,828,362 | | 24,958,036 | |
| Covered by Provident Fund | | | | | 5,098,336 | 6.2 | 14,604,949 | 79.0 |

*Note:* Calculated by author from *NSS 1999–2000*

the effectiveness of these new movements.[20] Similar trends can be seen in Latin America.[21]

The most common explanation for the supposed demise of class politics in India is that liberalization policies encourage firms to hire informal labor, because it is cheap and flexible and thus helps firms remain competitive in the increasingly liberalized and globalized marketplace.[22] Informal employment, in turn, disperses the site of production through home-based work, complicates employer-employee relationships through multiple subcontracting arrangements, and atomizes labor relationships by eliminating the daily shop-floor gathering of workers. Scholars argue that these changes in structures of production have made it impossible for workers to organize along class lines, which, in turn, has undermined the relevance of traditional class-based organizations.[23]

Implicit in these arguments is a traditional, static model of labor movements. As illustrated in Figure 1, the primary nexus of tension is between the organized formal proletariat and employers, and the state serves as a buffer between the two. The informal proletariat is depicted on the side as an expression of Karl Marx's notion of a "reserve army of labor" — i.e., those who perform odd jobs while waiting to be formally employed.[24] Because informal workers are not viewed as occupying a distinct location in the class structure, they are assumed to have the same interests and goals as formal workers. Only once informal workers are formally employed, so the argument goes, will they become an integral part of the workforce and be able to join the labor struggle to attain those goals.[25] This view of the informal sector has marked labor literature since the early 1900s, thereby limiting most studies to urban formal sector workers and, in some cases, rural peasants.[26]

To the extent that the informal sector has been studied in India, the focus has been on its definition and measurement.[27] Among the few studies that examine the social and political lives of informal workers in India, there is support for the global literature indicating that despite the difficulties, informal workers are organizing politically to improve their conditions.[28] According to the latest round of the NSS (1999–2000) in India, 8 percent of the nation's informal workers in the nonagricultural sectors are unionized.[29] Still, little remains known about the strategies informal workers use to improve their lives.

In contrast to existing studies arguing for the demise of class politics in India, I argue that a more dynamic approach to understanding forms of class-based exploitation and resistance is vital to understanding the conditions under which workers continue to retain or give up power. In particular, I show that the earlier victories of the formal sector labor movement, along with the recent initiation of economic reforms, have ironically pushed the Indian state and capital to increase unprotected employment. However, changes in the structure of production do not necessarily signify the end of all class struggle (and thereby the utility of class analytics). On the contrary, I argue that the circumstances of informal employment have pushed workers to initiate an alternative form of class politics that articulates their unique class-based interests and attempts to improve their basic security.

## 4. Informal Workers: A Class "*For* Themselves"

Using two sets of over three hundred in-depth interviews, one with labor leaders and government officials, and the second with workers in the *bidi*[30] and construction industries, I examine seven informal workers' organizations across three states in India. Six of the organizations are trade unions, registered under the Trade Union Act (1926), and one is a nongovernmental organization (NGO), registered under the Trust and Societies Act. The three cities/states I examined (Mumbai/Maharashtra, Kolkatta/West Bengal, and Chennai/Tamil Nadu) share a deep history in India's labor and independence movement, and they represent the three birthplaces of India's largest trade unions. All 140 workers interviewed are poor women, who are casually employed by a private employer through a chain of subcontractors. The interviews focused solely on women, because over 90 percent of the lowest rung of workers in the tobacco and construction industries is comprised of women contract workers. All interviewees earn between US$ 0.25 and US$ 2.00 per day. At the national level, the tobacco and construction industries represent the most organized among the informal workers' movement.[31]

Contrary to much of the current literature on labor and on social movements, I find that in India informal workers are organizing to improve their livelihoods through state-supported benefits. Using a class analytic approach, I find that the shifts in production structures have pushed informal workers' organizations to make two strategic changes to their mobilization strategies in order to fit the conditions of informal employment and to retain their membership. The first change is to target their demands to the state, rather than the employer, and the second change is to make demands on welfare benefits (such as health and education), rather than workers' rights (such as minimum wage and job security). In the following sections, I summarize findings on the historical evolution of these labor movement changes as the recognized structure of production in two very different informal sector industries (bidi and construction) shifted from a formal to an informal one.

### *Beginning with a Traditional Workers' Struggle against an Employer*

From the 1930s to the early 1970s, the labor movements in the bidi and construction industries focused almost exclusively on formal sector workers, although many of the workers in both industries were informally employed. Employers in both industries had worked hard to avoid the labor laws that the formal labor movement had managed to get in place (such as the 1926 Factories Act for bidi and the 1923 Workmen's Compensation Act for construction). To avoid costly labor regulations, employers hired informal labor by dispersing the workforce into smaller, unregulated units or hiring workers only for short-term tasks.[32] In other words, informality was in part an outcome of capital's strategy to avoid workers' rights legislation. Despite capital's response to traditional class struggles, the labor movement continued to ignore informal workers. Nearly all the workers involved in the early movement were formally employed, literate, skilled men who were recruited by the union at the factory.[33] By 1960,

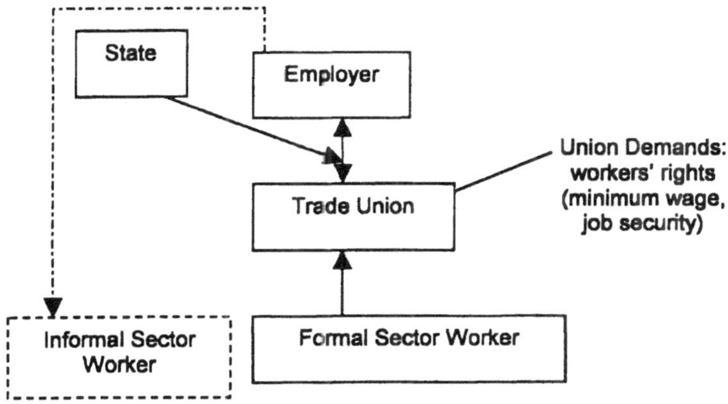


Figure 1. Traditional Labor Movement Model

registered membership in both the construction and bidi unions was 98 percent male.[34] To the extent that unions targeted informal workers at all, unions strove to formalize them. They did not attempt to build a unique class consciousness among the informal proletariat as a class-for-itself.

In their commitment to formal recognition of work from the employer, bidi and construction unions strove to follow the traditional labor movement model depicted in Figure 1. The government was held responsible only for enacting and enforcing laws that held employers accountable to their employees, providing last-resort conciliation services in industrial disputes, and passing protective legislation for certain industries. This model implied a contract between capital and labor where employers formally recognized and provided for their employees, and in return, workers provided their labor for production with minimal strife. Within the unions, leaders focused on educating workers on a class consciousness that viewed provisions from employers as "workers' rights." Because the contract was between labor and capital, the fair returns that workers demanded centered on what employers could provide, such as minimum wages, bonuses, and decent working hours. These provisions were considered sufficient to the broader goals of justice and human dignity. As Ram Ratnagar, general secretary of the All India Bidi and Cigar Workers Federation recalled, "At that time, our main demand was a minimum wage from the employer. We thought everything else could only follow from that."[35] By 1969, nearly 50 percent of all industrial disputes focused on the issue of minimum wages and bonuses.[36]

Unions framed the attaining of these rights as a necessary conflict workers needed to engage in against capital. The first recorded strike against capital in the bidi industry took place one month after the first bidi union was formed in Kerala in 1934. For the next three decades, the strike served as the most popular form of workers' resistance. In 1951 alone, the Government of India reported 120 registered strikes in the bidi industry; hundreds more were said to have taken place on a spontaneous basis.[37] Even when the strikes did not result in

A construction worker carries a basket of stones weighing more than 20 kilos on her head in Hyderabad, India. "In India…employers' continuing lack of responsibility toward [informal workers'] livelihood and welfare distinguishes them from formal sector workers." (ILO/Crozet M., March 2002)

economic gains, they were heralded as a means of bolstering solidarity.[38] In the construction industry, workers also held strikes at worksites to increase wages and bonuses.

To enact protective laws, organized workers sought representation in the government through left-oriented politicians. Therefore, the form of organization was almost always as unions tied to left-wing parties.[39] In 1966, bidi unions' efforts climaxed with the passing of the first national-level legislation to protect bidi workers. The Bidi and Cigar Workers Conditions of Employment Act forced all employers to provide their workers with a minimum wage and work benefits (such as an annual bonus, maternity benefits, social security, and safe working conditions). The passing of this Act was largely due to the collaboration between bidi unions that were tied to left-wing political parties and A.K. Gopalan, then-member of parliament from Kerala's Communist-Marxist Party. Among construction workers, the radical Maoist movement of Naxalites recruited unskilled workers, while guild associations organized skilled workers. Construction unions operated more independently than the bidi unions during this period.

Unions targeting informal workers followed a similar model as those targeting formal workers. In 1962, Sundar Navelkar, one of the earliest female lawyers in India and a member of the Communist Party of India-Marxist-Leninist, started India's first construction workers' union for contract workers in Mumbai, Maharashtra. While the union's focus on informally employed workers was unique for the time, the union's organizing model and membership of literate men mirrored that of formal sector unions. The union fought to enact the National Contract Labor Act, which limited contract labor to "essential" cases and was viewed as a "second-best" option to formal employment. Where contract labor was deemed essential, the Act ensured decent working conditions, which were framed as a "worker's right" and were identical to those sought for formal workers. Provisions included timely payment of wages and the provision of canteens, restrooms, drinking water, and first-aid boxes on the work sites.[40]

By the early 1970s, these movements had succeeded in attaining some protective legislation at the national level.[41] However, these apparent victories soon boomeranged against unionized workers. In order to avoid being regulated by the new acts, employers in both industries hired many more informal workers that fell outside the jurisdiction of the laws. Moreover, unskilled women were increasingly targeted to perform menial tasks, such as carrying bricks and cleaning and mixing cement in construction, and rolling and manufacturing *bidis* in tobacco. This population of unskilled women workers had not been actively involved in the labor movement, they were desperate for employment, and, most importantly, they were willing to work informally, outside the jurisdiction of the laws.[42] Subcontractors were used to veil the employer-employee relationship, and employers were not held responsible for their workers under the new Acts.

As predicted by traditional class literature, the bidi and construction movements became relatively dormant once the labor force overtly shifted from a formal to an informal one. The number of registered industrial disputes continuously fell from a high of thirty-five hundred in 1973 to fewer than seventy-five in 2001. Registered bidi disputes were sporadic between the 1950s and 1970s, but they generally maintained a high level. After 1967, however, they show a marked decline, and from 1973 onward, the Minister of Labor no longer even reported the number. Registered disputes in construction show a rising trend till 1970, after which they steadily declined.[43] The circumstances of informal employment, such as shifting employers and unregistered workers, made it nearly impossible for unions to hold employers accountable to the Acts.

### *Launching an Alternative Struggle against the State*

The setback in workers' organization in India's bidi and construction industries appears to have been temporary, because both movements were revived by the mid-1980s, albeit in new terms. A dynamic class-analytic approach sheds light on explanations for this continued class resistance. To accommodate the shifts in structures of production, the new movement aims to protect workers *within* their informal employment status, rather than trying to transform them into formal sector workers. Moreover, it includes the new labor force of illiterate, unskilled women and men, working on both government and private sector projects. Finally, since employees' workplace can change daily, it identifies and recruits members by going through slums, rather than work sites. To make these changes, informal workers have organized as a unique class-for-itself by shifting its target and demands.

Significantly, informal workers' organizations have had to shift their primary target from the employer to the state. Informal workers operate through subcontractors and often do not even know who their employer is; their work is spatially dispersed in homes and work sheds; and most of them are too frightened to risk losing their jobs by making demands on their employer. Therefore, holding an employer responsible for workers' benefits is difficult. Instead the new movement directs its demands toward the state. The state is viewed as a target that all workers can share.[44] To make demands on the state, informal workers' unions appeal to state responsibilities to *citizens*, rather than to *workers'* rights.

As the following testimony illustrates, even bidi organizations that remain tied to left-wing political parties have altered the movement frame from worker vs. employer to citizen vs. the state. Vajeshwari Bital Iravati, a 55-year-old member of Mumbai's bidi union, has a typical background for women bidi workers in the area. She is a member of the weaver caste. Her family had originally migrated to the state of Maharashtra from the southern state of Andhra Pradesh. Although Vajeshwari grew up in rural Maharashtra, she moved to Mumbai with her husband and in-laws shortly after her marriage thirty-five years ago. In Mumbai, the men in the family got jobs in the textile mills, while the women continued to roll bidis at home. Although the mill work sustained the family for some years, once her husband died, Vajeshwari was responsible for raising their two sons and caring for her elderly in-laws. The mill did not provide any pension. Vajeshwari joined the bidi union shortly after arriving in Mumbai. She learned about the union from the other women with whom she rolled bidis. As a member of the Mumbai Bidi Union, which is affiliated to the Communist Party of India (CPI), Vajeshwari was raised in the traditional class struggle philosophy. She proudly recalled the early days of the bidi struggle when she participated in militant strikes. Despite her traditional labor politics background and experience, however, Vajeshwari's focus has now shifted to targeting the state for her demands. "We always sit outside some parliament building to make sure those fat government officials give us what we need. There is no use in going to the employers. They are all thieves. They don't even admit we work for them. They will just kick us out of our jobs if we ask them for anything. But the government cannot kick us out of the country for making demands!"[45]

Because the new movement has shifted the target from the state to the employer, it has also had to shift its demands to those that the state can provide. Rather than demanding workplace benefits alone, the new movement also demands welfare benefits at home for the entire family. Appeals to the state for these welfare benefits have been operationalized in the form of industry-specific workers' Welfare Boards.[46] The bidi board is implemented by the labor departments of the central and state governments, while the construction board is implemented by the state government alone. Bidi employers (of branded items) must contribute Rs. 2 per one thousand bidis to the welfare board, and construction employers must contribute 1 percent of the costs of each construction project that exceeds Rs. 1 million. Workers pay Rs. 25 per year to become members of a Board, and the central and state governments make varying contributions (depending on the industry, year, and state politics). The Bidi Board's annual income is estimated to be Rs. 1 billion, and worker membership is approximately 4 million. Construction Boards' income and membership varies by state. To date, Tamil Nadu and Kerala have fully implemented their Boards, and Delhi, Pondicherry, Haryana, and Madhya Pradesh have initiated theirs. In 2005, Tamil Nadu's Construction Board had 630,000 members.

In return for their membership contribution, informal workers receive benefits, such as education scholarships, neighborhood-based health care clinics, grants for daughters' weddings, houses in women's names, funeral expenses, and pensions. The central and state government use unions to ensure that all members are indeed workers.[47] Benefits are thus extended to workers, *regardless of who their employer is.* In Tamil Nadu, the Construction Board spent Rs. 39 million in benefits in 2003.[48] In 2001, the Bidi Board spent approximately Rs. 560 million throughout India. Nearly 80 percent of this amount was used to build health care clinics and provide education scholarships for workers' children. By 2002 the Board had provided identity cards to nearly 4 million workers and had built four new hospitals with 160 beds and 210 dispensaries and respiratory clinics designed especially for bidi workers. The hospitals and dispensaries are all located in the heart of the slums and villages, where the majority of bidi workers live.[49]

The most publicly lauded success of the Bidi Welfare Board has been the housing projects created for bidi workers. The state and central governments contribute Rs. 40,000 toward the construction of a one-room kitchen tenement plus a courtyard, and each worker must contribute the remaining costs (approximately Rs. 10,000). Land is donated from unused government land, and developers are allowed to sell remaining portions of the land for commercial use. Each home is formally owned by the woman bidi worker. In March 2004, the president of India, A.P.J. Abdul Kalam, inaugurated a project that would construct ten thousand homes in Shoalpur, Maharashtra. Uttam Khobragade, chief executive officer of the Maharashtra State Housing and Area Development Authority, wrote, "[This] is a wonderful experiment executed by the collective efforts of the poor."[50] In 2003, Tamil Nadu's state government initiated the same project in its state.

Since the mid-1990s, both construction and bidi workers' struggles in India have shifted away from holding strikes against capital, and focused instead on pressuring the government to create and implement these welfare boards. Welfare boards do not ensure the structural changes necessary to eradicate social injustices, nor do they represent a perfect substitution for worker demands (such as minimum wages and job security). Worker and welfare demands would ideally be met in conjunction with one another, and indeed some informal workers' unions are continuing both struggles simultaneously. At the moment, however, India's informal workers are attaining more success in mobilizing members and attaining state attention based on their welfare demands. Employers do not resist the contributions they must make to welfare boards as much as they resist paying minimum wages; states are increasingly implementing welfare boards, as they are repealing laws on labor protection; and informal workers are more willing to make welfare demands on the state than worker rights demands on the employer.

To ensure proper implementation of welfare boards, informal workers in both industries have held multiple demonstrations and hunger strikes in front of politicians (not judges or civil servants). Unlike the earlier movements, workers ensure that production is not disrupted during their rallies. Rather, it is the work of the politicians that is disrupted. Ramakant Patkar, general secretary of the CITU Mumbai Bidi Union, recalled with great pride a rally he led of thirty-five hundred bidi workers in front of the Parliament, "We rolled our bidis outside all day. Finally, the labor minister and the housing minister come out to

Making *bidi* cigarettes at home, in the village of Puttige. Research shows that in India "informal workers *are* organizing to improve their livelihoods through state-supported benefits." (ILO/Crozet M., March 2002)

speak with us. This gave the ladies a lot of confidence. They offered to get us tea, but I warned them not to make these ladies' heads hotter than they already were!"[51]

The tone of the new movement is nonviolent, framed as a bargain between the citizen and the state. Although leaders of the earlier movements critique this strategy as a tacit approval of employers' exploitation, the members and leaders of the new movements view the welfare-oriented struggle as strong as, and even more appealing than, the violent struggles of the past. Geeta, founder and head of the Tamil Nadu Construction Union, recalled her union's efforts with pride: "We gathered thousands of angry workers outside his [the labor minister's] door. We were immediately arrested and spent twelve days in jail. But we were so happy we had made him scared and angry."[52] Leaders and participants of the new movement expressed this shift in attitude as their only alternative, given the new structures of production. They argue that if they stop production in order to protest, they will not only forfeit their already low incomes, but they will also risk being fired.

This model of a welfare-oriented movement targeting the state spread across construction and bidi workers' organizations throughout the country in the 1980s and 1990s. In 1979, in response to government inaction to increasing labor vulnerability, a group of informal construction workers in Tamil Nadu formed the Tamil Nadu Construction Workers Union (TNCWU),[53] which has been heralded in recent media as the forerunner of a new informal workers' movement.[54] TNCWU has organized labor activists from across the country to pressure the Central Government to require all states to implement the Construction Workers Welfare Board. They have held nationwide rallies in front of government offices and have worked to incorporate their interests into politicians' election manifestos. In 1989, they submitted a petition with the signatures of four hundred thousand construction workers from across the nation demanding the protective legislations. Unlike the earlier union movements, which were tied to left-wing political parties, the revived national construction workers' campaign is lauded for transcending political and ideological affiliations. Most construction workers' organizations today are independent of political parties, and they hold the state, regardless of their party, responsible for workers' well-being.[55] On 19 August 1996, then-prime minister H.D. Deve

Gowda enacted the Building and Other Construction Workers' Welfare Cess Act, which called on each state to create and implement its own Construction Workers' Welfare Board.[56] The announcement received substantial media coverage, as it was the first action of this kind.[57]

In the case of bidi, organized workers pushed to enact a Bidi Welfare Board during the 1960s. At that time the aim was to provide workers who were formally employed with additional welfare provisions.[58] In 1976, the Government of India passed the Bidi Workers Welfare Cess and Fund Act.[59] However, by 1979, the collection of the cess designed to fund the welfare board was stopped. Bidi unions did not focus much on ensuring the implementation of the Welfare Act, but rather, concentrated on first trying to implement the Bidi Conditions Act, which aimed to ensure that employers formally recognize and protect bidi workers.[60]

During the 1980s and 1990s, however, bidi unions revived their struggle to pressure state governments to re-implement the Welfare Boards for informally employed bidi workers, regardless of the Conditions Act. The struggles included widely publicized rallies in front of the offices of labor ministers at both the state and national levels, as well as marches through city centers.[61] As a result of the struggles, the cess collection (which the earlier labor movement had not focused on) was resumed on 22 May 1987. In addition, the Bidi Welfare Fund Act was amended to make the failure to issue worker identity cards to bidi workers an offense under the Act. Finally the revised Act made family welfare one of its primary objectives.[62]

### *A New Informal Workers' Identity*

The strategic changes that informal workers' organizations have made in order to survive have had an important impact on organization members' class identities. This identity articulates the unique interests faced by informal workers in their specific class location. The informal worker's identity is based on work status, not income or occupation. To be a member of an informal workers' organization and a Welfare Board, and to attain the welfare benefits outlined above (i.e., health care services, education scholarships, pensions, and housing), one must prove her/his status as an informal worker to the union and the government.[63] Once proof is provided, informal workers attain an identity card. Forty percent of the respondents in this study who had received this worker identity card said it was one of the most important benefits they had received from the organization. The identity card ensures informal workers' eligibility to receive the welfare benefits.

However, workers appreciated the card, even if they had not yet received any direct welfare benefits from it, because they claimed that attaining state acknowledgment of their membership in the working class (even when the employer refused such acknowledgment) legitimated them as worthy citizens. This legitimation in turn allowed them to make citizen demands. Like formal workers, informal workers in India do not own their own means of production. Unlike formal workers, however, informal workers operate outside state jurisdiction, and they are building an identity that connects them to the state through their social consumption needs. Significantly, their emerging identity simultaneously asserts their informality *and* their position within the working class. Their identity is not expressed as an antithesis to capital. The importance of an official acknowledgment of their work status, even when it is unskilled and informal, was expressed by workers as a means to social legitimacy, especially when their other identities (such as caste and gender) tend to demote them on the social hierarchy. In other words, being a worker legitimates people as active participants in the social contract between the state and citizen.

Take Jyotsna Bhoya, a member of Kolkatta's Communist Construction Union, for example. Jyotsna's mother and father were construction workers who had migrated to West Bengal from the neighboring state of Bihar before she was born. Because her family moved from site to site, and she is a member of the lowest caste in Hindu society, Jyotsna did not attend school and is illiterate. At the age of thirteen, she was married to a family of sweepers. She is now twenty-eight years old and a mother of four girls; she has no sons. At the age of seventeen, Jyotsna began working as a construction worker because her husband's income was not enough to sustain the growing family. Each day, Jyotsna commutes four hours on the train by herself to find work in the city. In order to complete her work shift, she must ride the train before dawn and after sunset. As a young, lower-caste, illiterate, Bihari migrant woman, traveling alone at odd hours, Jyotsna is incredibly vulnerable to abuse. Four years ago, a fellow worker convinced her to join the union, because they promised to "empower" her.[64] The most empowering benefit Jyotsna felt she had received from the union has been the identity card. "With this card, I don't feel scared walking home from work at night. If the police stop me, I can show them that I am a construction worker, and not a prostitute or some wasted woman," says Jyotsna.[65]

For Badhrunisa, a member of Chennai's Bidi Union, the worker identity card legitimates her as a vital part of modern, urban society. Badhrunisa is thirty-two years old, illiterate, and Muslim. Badhrunisa was born into a bidi-making family and began rolling bidis by her mother's side when she was seven years old. When she was twenty, she married and gave birth to a daughter the following year. Shortly after her daughter's birth, her husband left her. Today she lives with her mother and her 12-year-old daughter. Like many of her neighbors, Badhrunisa's most important goal in life is to educate her daughter. Still, however, she needs to rely on her daughter's help in rolling bidis as soon as her daughter returns home from school. Living in an all-female home, Badhrunisa must constantly face the charges that she was a "bad wife" because she could not keep her husband happy or bear any sons; a "bad daughter" because she could not help to keep her father alive; and a "bad mother" because her daughter is still working in "the dirty bidi profession." Five years ago, Badhrunisa joined the union because they helped connect her to a new bidi contractor. Badhrunisa was adamant that she "did not join the union to fight." "I don't want to fight," she told me. The biggest benefit of the union for Badhrunisa has been the identity card. "This card proves that I am a *good* worker. I show it at the municipal office, when I have to ask for water. I show it when I register my daughter at the school. I show it at the bidi workers' hospital so I can get help faster than at the

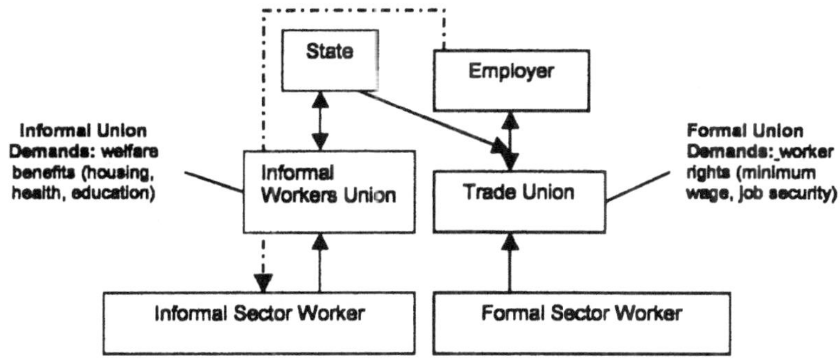


Figure 2. Alternative Labor Movement Model among Informal Workers.

corporation hospital. With this card everyone knows I work."[66] To Badhurnisa, a government-issued card that proves she is a worker arms her with an identity of legitimacy that she would otherwise have lost by joining the informal sector. Although her wages are not enough to meet her reproduction needs, being a "legitimate" member of society allows her to demand at least some of her basic consumption needs.

These changes in the labor movement among informal workers can help us adjust the traditional labor movement model that India's early unions relied on. As outlined in Figure 2, the new model provides a parallel structure to the traditional formal sector labor movement in which informal workers are also organizing into class-based entities. While they continue to engage in economic activities outside the jurisdiction of the state (just as they did under the traditional model), their organized demands negotiate directly with the state. While the employer continues to serve as the primary target of formal sector workers' movements, the employer remains outside the direct interaction of informal workers' movements. The focus of demands among informal workers has shifted from workers' rights to welfare demands at home and for the family.

## 5. Conclusions

These findings reassert class as an important analytical tool with which to examine continuing differences in life chances and resistance against exploitation, especially in developing countries. Policies that transfer the economy from public to private control (liberalization) and policies that integrate one economy with another through increased free trade and foreign direct investment (economic globalization) alter the structures of production. Such alterations in structures of production necessarily redefine class structures, class relations, and class interests.

Based on this dynamic understanding of class structures and interests, this study offers an alternative labor movement model to explain current forms of political activity among the majority of the world's workers. The alternative model tested in this study, using in-depth interviews of labor leaders and organization members in two Indian industries (bidi and construction), incorporates the informal sector as an active participant in capitalist growth. Informal workers occupy their own position in the class structure (as a class-in-themselves), and therefore have unique interests. Despite scholars' claims to the contrary, this study finds that informal workers identify, articulate, and demand these unique interests. Class remains an organizing and mobilizing principle for these workers as their access to resources, their relationship with other classes, and the structures of production within which they operate influence how they organize as a class-in-themselves.

The alternative model presented in this study also illuminates changing relations between capital, labor, and the state. In India, the victories of formal workers' struggles resulted in increased legislation on labor protection; formal workers ensured that employers were held responsible for their workers' rights. Ironically, such protection of formal workers pushed employers to rely more heavily on unprotected informal workers. Recently, the state has supported capital's reliance on informal labor. This study shows that informal workers, in turn, are forcing the state, rather than the employer, to decommodify their labor power. Fully commoditized labor is inseparable from the ways the commodity is treated. If there is no demand for labor power, there is no return to the living bearer of labor power and in the end no claim on subsistence. Capital is no longer being held responsible for this dilemma. Therefore, informal workers in India are trying to hold the state responsible for meeting their basic, social consumption needs, ***regardless*** of their informal labor status, by demanding welfare benefits. In other words, if the state will not ensure a wage that will allow poor workers to meet the costs of their social reproduction, then the state must directly ensure that such reproduction is possible. Acknowledging and understanding the development of these interests is vital to ensuring an adequate response from policy-makers and scholars.

The informal workers' movement is now at a critical juncture in terms of its future growth. On the one hand, the movement could grow to shape the state's role in workers' lives across all sectors of the economy. On the other hand, the movement could fall backward into a scenario where the state continues to extend its responsibilities to its workers, but in an ad hoc manner that eventually mirrors traditional patron-client relations. Further research into the sustainability of informal workers' movements and the conditions for their success in a liberalization context is essential to understanding the myriad of problems arising in the implementation of state benefits for workers and differences in organizational structures.

❑

# 5. Middle-Class Activism and the Politics of the Informal Working Class

## A Perspective on Class Relations and Civil Society in Indian Cities

John Harriss

"Politics is a dirty river." — *Civil society activist, a former banker*

"Only the poor agitate; the rich operate." — *Civil society activist, a former Indian Administrative Service officer*

IN THIS ARTICLE I AIM TO DO TWO THINGS. I want, first, to contribute to understanding of class relationships in metropolitan cities of India, and secondly, and, relatedly, to show how essential it is to take account of these relationships in analyzing "civil society." The latter is of course a quintessentially contested concept, both in general and in particular regard to India, but in the way it has come to be used in quite a wide range of contemporary writing, and in policy practice, it is treated as a social sphere outside the state and market institutions, in which people come together, as equal rights-bearing citizens, on a voluntary basis, and may engage in deliberative action in addressing public problems. This is not a straw man conceptually and it remains hugely influential in a lot of thinking about contemporary politics and so it seems to me that it is important to examine how civil society, thus conceived, is affected by class relationships. The article draws on comparative research that I have done over the last several years, with colleagues, on "Rights, Representation and the Poor" in Latin America (in the cities of São Paulo and Mexico City) and in India. Our main research was in Delhi, but I also draw extensively on ethnographic studies of "civil society" in Bangalore and in Chennai. I believe that our research represents one of the first attempts to study civil society systematically — certainly in Indian cities. The literature on civil society is burgeoning, but much of it, if it is not primarily theoretical, depends heavily upon anecdotal evidence or upon case studies of particular organizations or movements. The research involved (in Delhi as in São Paulo and Mexico City) large-scale sample surveys of individual citizens (with around 1400 respondents in each city), enquiring into different dimensions of political participation, associational activity, and citizen-state relations; and surveys, based necessarily on snowball sampling,[1] of civil and social organizations.[2] Through these "associational surveys" we sought to map the civil society space in each city (including in this case also Bangalore and Chennai, as well as the other three cities).

## Class Relationships and the City

While the structural opposition between capital and labor may be seen as being fundamental in social and political reproduction in capitalist societies, there is equally no doubt that actually existing class relationships are almost infinitely more complicated. In the context of India's cities the "capitalist class" includes an enormously wide range of actors from big business and large national and international institutions to a numerous and diverse set of owners of small capitals; while "labor" or the "working class" is no less diverse, divided as it is between the progressively smaller fraction — relatively, certainly, and perhaps absolutely so, too — that is employed in organized or formal enterprises, and the very much larger workforce in unorganized enterprises or employed on an informal, casual basis. There remain large numbers of petty producers. And then there is the "middle class," which is no more susceptible of precise definition in the Indian context than it is anywhere else in the world, but which surely includes increasing numbers of highly paid professional people, managers and executives, white collar workers, and intellectuals — and the mass of petty traders and producers, as well — and which is certainly of ever increasing significance though its actual size and precise boundaries are very hard to determine.[3] Here I am especially concerned with the middle class, and with the numerically preponderant fraction of the labor class that I refer to as the "informal working class" (to distinguish it from the numerically much smaller organized fraction in formal employment).

In these complex circumstances there is a great deal to recommend the analytical procedure advocated by Satish Deshpande, who proposes, rather than an empirical description of the middle class, three hypothetical definitions "to think with': the middle class is the class that articulates the hegemony of the ruling bloc — in the senses both of "giving voice to" and of linking or connecting (here especially the relations between the ruling bloc and the rest of society); it is the class that is most dependent on cultural capital; and it is an increasingly differentiated class — its elite fraction specializing in the production of ideologies and its mass fraction engaging in "the exemplary consumption of these ideologies, thus investing them with social legitimacy."[4] In this essay I mean to refer (descriptively) to those disposing of significant cultural capital — which may consist of particular types of *identities* (in terms of caste, community, or region) and *competences* (educational, linguistic, or other social skills — usually including a facility in English) — and who have some property or relatively well-paid salaried or professional employment, and who are consequently generally somewhat better off than the majority of people in Indian society.

The category of the "informal working class," comparably, refers to working people who are "subaltern" (rather than "articulators of the hegemony of the ruling bloc') and who do not dispose of significant cultural capital, and who also lack the advantage of protection through regulation by the state of their terms of employment or occupation. In the Indian context this means that they come disproportionately from the historically lower castes, with limited or no property, depending on casual labor incomes or incomes from self-employment in petty businesses and who are consequently generally poorer, not necessarily in terms of income but certainly of vulnerability. I have previously described this fraction of the labor class as the "working poor," referring by this term to "large numbers of people who make their livings as casual workers — literally drawers of water and hewers of wood in some cases; as petty traders or petty producers or artisans; or as short-term wage workers in an enormously diverse range of productive and commercial activities,"[5] and distinguishing such workers from those in permanent wage work who may, in some circumstances at least, be described as the "labor aristocracy." In a somewhat similar way, Nandini Gooptu, in her work on North Indian cities in the late colonial period, refers to the "urban poor" rather than to the "working class," so as to "encompass various urban occupational groups and to highlight the diversity of their employment relations" and "to draw attention to vital aspects of urban experience, other than work, that determines the nature of politics."[6] These are perhaps good reasons for questioning the use of the term "working class," because this expression has tended to be taken as referring to those in permanent wage work, who have commonly been organized by trade unions. On reflection, however, I have come to think that it is as important in the context of Indian cities as it is in that of the United States to emphasize in our terminology the class relations that determine the practices and the circumstances of the large numbers of people who are being referred to. As Alice O'Connor argues with reference to the United States the use of the expression "working poor" "offers a substitute language, of deviance and deprivation, for the language of inequality."[7] In relation to policy the term helps to attribute their "welfare" to the characteristics of individuals, and to draw attention away from the political economy of poverty. There remains, however, good reason for distinguishing between those working people in permanent, protected wage work, and others, and it is for this reason that I use the term "informal working class." The possibility that it is important, too, to distinguish between those who are informal employees and those who work in their own tiny "businesses," remains, but as research such as my own, or Gooptu's, shows, there is a great deal of commonality in the everyday experience of those who are "informal" workers.

References to the importance of cultural capital in these "definitions to think with" draw attention to the intersections of "class" and "caste" that are no less significant in urban than they are in rural India. There continues to be an important overlap between being part of the middle class, as I have suggested that we

Diamond cutting workshop. In India's cities "labor" or the "working class" is diverse and divided between the progressively smaller fraction in organized enterprises and the larger workforce employed on a casual basis. (AMRC/Sanjiv Pandita)

may think about it, and coming from higher-ranking caste backgrounds. Those from lower caste backgrounds are still likely to find it more difficult to break into the middle class, in terms of occupations, even when they may possess the requirements in terms, say, of education. This is a point that comes out, for instance, quite strongly in recent studies of how people get jobs in the IT sector — the industry that has by now become the overarching symbol of middle-class India. Various sources speak of the intense competition between firms for IT-trained employees (as indeed there is for experienced and skilled IT professionals), and the impression is sometimes given that there is a sellers' market for those with IT knowledge and skills to offer in the market place. But in a PhD dissertation based on field research in Bangalore, Nisbett has shown convincingly just how uncertain employment is in the IT industry; how the industry is stratified and how difficult it is for someone to move up from the more basic jobs; and — most significantly — how important social and cultural capital are in the ways in which people secure jobs.[8] The kinds of interpersonal skills that employers look for, for example, and that are probed in candidates for jobs through aptitude tests, are much more likely to be found in young people coming from higher caste families. It is widely held that the industry is meritocratic and that people get jobs through a combination of competence and merit. Nisbett shows that "merit" is socially constructed. The sons of first generation factory workers such as those whom he knows from amongst a group of friends in a cybercafe where he worked are unlikely to be successful in securing the "good jobs" in the industry because they lack the social skills and connections of their peers from higher caste families. There may be greater equality of opportunity in this industry than in the "old economy" — though even this is not sure — but there is certainly not equality of agency between those competing for jobs.

In what follows I want to describe the social and especially the political relationships between the urban middle class and the informal working class in the social sphere or space that I shall label, initially, as that of civil society. These relationships are actually very significant in the definition of the "middle class" and a critical dimension of the reproduction of class relationships. They also show up, very clearly I believe, the limitations of a view of civil society that abstracts it from the field of class relations — such as appears in some contemporary arguments about the political potentials of civil organization. I begin, however, with some observations on the character of citizen-state relations in India, drawing on survey findings from Delhi — in comparison with those from São Paulo and Mexico City — that tell us quite a lot about the quality of citizenship and how it varies across society.

## Citizens and their Relations with the State

Through surveys of individual citizens in the cities we studied we aimed to investigate political participation along three dimensions. In addition to studying electoral participation we also examined participation in the activities of associations, and participation in efforts to address significant public problems — following in this the classic work of Verba, Schlozman, and Brady on the United States, in which they argue that political participation (as "activity that is intended to or has the consequence of affecting, either directly or indirectly, government action") should be understood as including "much...non-electoral activity [that] takes place outside official channels. This includes a vast number of official contacts and communications with government officials as well as a large volume of informal, problem-solving activity among friends and neighbors in local communities."[9] The capacities of individuals to activate government action to address concrete problems that affect their well-being represent a constitutive dimension of citizenship, and differences between societies and social groups in this respect carry major implications for the quality and scope of citizenship. What sort of access do people have to officials, and on what terms? And how does this vary across social hierarchies?

We asked our respondents about the salience for them of a range of public problems that are important for well-being: access to health care (a social right in each of the cities we studied); access to basic needs (which may be claimed as an economic and social right); violence and crime (freedom from which is a basic civil right); access to basic urban services (public goods); and air pollution (as an issue affecting the health environment that has latterly become politically significant). In all three cities we established that at least four out of these five problems were either significant or major problems for the great majority of people. And it was usually the case that they held the government to be the principal agency with responsibility for acting upon these problems, neither market actors nor civil society organizations. It was very striking, for instance, that in spite of liberal market reforms and moves towards privatization of services in

Table 1: Share of Problem-Solving Efforts by Channel (in percentages)

| | Delhi | São Paulo | Mexico City |
|---|---|---|---|
| Government | 37.0 | 54.0 | 33.0 |
| Court | 1.2 | 3.2 | 4.0 |
| Party | 29.0 | 4.0 | 9.0 |
| Patron | 8.0 | 6.0 | 3.0 |
| Demonstration | 8.0 | 8.0 | 7.0 |
| Self-Help | 16.0 | 20.0 | 42.0 |
| Petition | No data on freq | 5.0 | 2.0 |
| Total | 100 | 100 | 100 |

each of the cities, citizens still held the state responsible for urban public services (79 percent in São Paulo, 76 percent in Mexico City, and as many as 91 percent in Delhi). We then asked people about whether or not they had been involved, over the five years up to the time of the interviews, in any efforts to try to solve any one of these public problems, distinguishing between direct approach to government officials (whether in local or central government), action through the courts, an approach through a political party, an approach through a local "big man" or patron, participation in public protest or claim-making through demonstrating or joining in a petition, and finally problem-solving on their own through participation in collective self-help. We asked, too, about the ways in which people had taken up these different problem solving actions — whether on their own, or with others such as neighbors, or with the support of an organization of some kind. Most interesting and significant differences appeared between cities, reflecting upon the quality of citizenship in each of them.

In Delhi more than half of the population, according to our sample estimates, have attempted some action to try to solve problems, though those who live in slum areas (*jhuggi jhopris*), and who are prominent amongst the informal working class of the city, are significantly more likely to have been involved in problem solving than others.[10] People rarely try to problem solve alone, however (only 7 percent of problem-solving instances), and overwhelmingly take action of whatever kind with friends and neighbors — a pattern that is in striking contrast with what is observed in São Paulo where people much more commonly try to problem solve alone (48 percent of problem-solving instances).[11] Organizations of any kind, on the other hand, were little involved in Delhi citizens' problem-solving activities (12 percent of instances — a frequency less than half that of São Paulo and a third less than in Mexico City[12]). Those that were involved were mostly neighborhood associations, in efforts at self-provisioning. Nongovernmental organizations (NGOs) were hardly ever mentioned (only five citations).

What is most striking about the actions of citizens in Delhi with regard to the state, in the course of efforts at solving public problems, by comparison with both São Paulo and Mexico City, is (1) that it appears possible that a higher proportion of them (53 percent, by comparison with 45 percent in Mexico City and only 35 percent in São Paulo) use a combination of methods of problem solving; and (2) more clearly, that the approach to problem solving of many more of

Table 2: Share of Individual Problem Solvers in Each Category of Citizen-State Relations (in percentages)

| Relation to State | Delhi | Sao Paulo | Mexico City |
|---|---|---|---|
| Direct | 20 | 33 | 22 |
| Brokered | 12 | 4 | 4 |
| Contentious | 4 | 19 | 4 |
| Detached | 12 | 11 | 25 |
| | | | |
| Direct — Mediated — Contentious | 35 | 20 | 12 |
| Detached + others | 18 | 15 | 33 |
| Total | 100 | 100 | 100 |

them, than of the citizens of either of the Latin American cities, is mediated or brokered by political parties (especially) and by "big men" or patrons (while we also know from ethnographic observation that the big men in Delhi, notably the *pradhans* of slum areas, are usually connected with one or other of the major parties).

São Paulo clearly stands out for the importance of direct approach to government (and we know also that when Paulistas go to government they are likely to go about it on their own); Mexico City stands out for the importance of collective self-provisioning; and Delhi (where we also know that problem solving is usually done with others) for the much greater importance of political parties and patrons in problem-solving efforts than in the two Latin American cities).

The different ways of going about public problem solving that we have distinguished suggest different forms of citizen-state relationships:[13] direct approach to government, or taking legal action, may be considered as indicating a ***direct*** relationship of citizens to the state; taking action through parties or patrons seems to reflect the fact that citizen-state relationships are ***brokered;*** action by means of demonstration or petitioning indicates a ***contentious*** relationship with the state; while problem solving through collective self-help would seem to show a ***detached*** relationship between citizens and the state. In terms of these concepts of citizen-state relationships Delhi compares with São Paulo and with Mexico City as follows:

Overall, in Delhi citizens have mediated (or "brokered') and direct relationships to the state, and a notably high level of combinations. The brokered relation with the state is very much more significant than it is in either Latin American city. Those who problem solve through parties and patrons together with those who combine these approaches with direct approach to government constitute altogether 32 percent of problem solvers. The patterns of problem solving activity are also differentiated across social hierarchies: poorer people with low levels of education, and those in informal employment — and some others who suffer from particular disadvantage such as women and Muslims — are relatively more likely to try to solve problems through political parties, through participation in demonstrations or (in the case of women and Muslims) through big men. Wealthier people, generally, when they do engage in problem solving activity, and those who are more educated tend to go directly to government, to take legal action, or to engage in self-provisioning. They are less likely to go to political parties, and much less likely to take part in political demonstrations, or to go to big men. These patterns also obtain amongst permanent, formal (sector) employees. The "fit" between these patterns and social classes is of course far from being exact, but it is fair to conclude that people from the middle class are more likely to have a direct relationship with the state, whilst those of the informal working class are more likely to relate to the state via the brokerage of political parties.

Children employed to do home-based *jari* work (the application of gold and silver thread in fine textiles). (Courtesy: Ravi Agarwal, from *Down and Out: Labouring under Global Capitalism*, Jan Breman and N. Das, Oxford, 2000).

What then accounts for the much greater importance of the mediation of citizen-state relations through brokerage by political parties in Delhi than is the case in Latin American cities? Why are parties involved in mediating the relationships especially of informal working-class people with the state? A number of factors may be distinguished. The relatively high incidence of problem-solving activity across the city population — and amongst people from jhuggi jhopris in particular, the frequency of combinations of different approaches to problem solving by individual citizens in Delhi, and the relatively low level of direct citizenship (and we also know that when they do go directly to government people in Delhi very often go with others rather than going on their own, as they do in São Paulo) reflects both the widespread failure of the local state to satisfy people's needs and its relative inaccessibility to them. Slum dwellers, in jhuggi jhopris, may be relatively more active problem solvers than other citizens, but it appears that their chances of getting things done by government are not very good, and ethnographic observation shows that local officials frequently disregard them. by Slum dwellers are disproportionately from lower castes and they are at a disadvantage in their interactions with officials who are commonly from higher castes. Generally speaking, according to ethnographic evidence,[14] poorer, less well-educated and lower-status people (with little cultural capital) have a tough time of it in India when they go to a government office — and it is not surprising that they go if they can with others or accompanied by some influential person, or with a "fixer" who knows the ropes.[15] Our data also show that it is those with little or no education who are most disposed to going about problem solving through the brokerage of political parties. These observations recall, in fact, the distinction made by Chatterjee between "civil society" and "political society" (which he defines idiosyncratically). His point is this: "Most of the inhabitants of India are only tenuously...rights-bearing citizens in the sense imagined by the constitution. They are not, therefore, proper members of civil society and are not regarded as such by the institutions of the state."[16] People like those of the informal working class of Delhi relate to the state (as they do to many NGOs, too) as defined "populations" — such as that of "slum dwellers" — which are the targets of policy and to be controlled by the state. The people who are thus defined take action that is quite often technically illegal — such as squatting on public land or stealing electricity — and in so doing effectively make claims upon the state for the realization of what they believe to be their rights to welfare. This is what Chatterjee refers to as "political society." The "denizens" (as they may be called — the word means "inhabitants" — to distinguish them from the "rights-bearing citizens') of this political society are in fact also more active in party politics in Delhi than are middle class people[17] — as they are generally in India.[18] Political parties increasingly mobilize their electoral support from the informal working class, often — in Delhi — operating through local influentials, the *pradhans*. Party politics, generally, is oriented toward the denizens of political society, rather than the middle class citizens of civil society.

I turn now to consider patterns of participation in civil and social organizations. The differences between middle-class people and those of the informal working class are sharply apparent, and I want to suggest that activism in civil society is both a significant dimension of "being middle class" and of class relationships.

## Patterns of Participation in "Civil Society"

Evidence shows that participation in associational activities (presumptively, "civil society") in Indian cities is heavily skewed toward those people with higher incomes and higher levels of education. Whereas we found in Delhi that poorer and sometimes also less well educated people are more active in political life, and that poorer people (especially those who have some education) are more active problem solvers, the same is not true of associational activity. If we take associational activism as an indicator of political participation then we find a strong tendency for wealthier and particularly more educated people to be involved, clearly calling into question the popular notion that poor working people are able to secure effective representation or "empowerment" through participation in associations in civil society.[19] Those from the informal working class are much less prominent in these social networks than are the usually wealthier and more educated people from the middle class.

The most telling feature of the associational space in Bangalore, and in Chennai — the two cities about which I can draw on ethnography — is the sharp stratification of organizations.[20] On the one hand there are organizations like (in Bangalore) the Public Affairs Centre (PAC), CIVIC (Citizens Voluntary Initiative for the City), and Janaagraha that are distinctly elitist, run by upper-middle class-people (often those with strong corporate ties and sometimes formerly Non-Resident Indians [NRIs]) that even geographically are clearly confined to upper and middle-class neighborhoods. These are organizations that adopt the formal language of "citizenship" and speak of (and work on) participation in budgeting, and of transparency and accountability in local government. Many of these organizations are run with large budgets, drawn partly at least from overseas funders, with a high degree of genuine professionalism. Their attempts, however, at establishing a broad popular base for themselves have not really materialized. On the other hand there are some organizations that typically originate with or are focused on the informal working class, that mobilize and organize people to make demands upon the state, such as KKNSS (Karnataka Kolageri Nivasigala Samyuktha Sanghatana), a federation of slum dwellers' associations, and Womens Voice. The focus of their work is typically the slums and much of their effort is directed at securing basic rights for the people, making the important connection between rights to somewhere to live and rights to a livelihood.

These two types of organizations engage with government in very different ways. The former have adopted the paradigm of "public-private partnership" and champion the notion of "collaborative change." The idea is that "synergy" between citizens and government is essential to bring about change. The Bangalore Agenda Task Force is a case in point (and there are similarities with the Bhagidari Scheme of the Delhi Government, which sets up "partnerships" between residents' welfare associations and the government). Constituted by the Government of Karnataka in 2000, its "single-minded mission is to modernize Bangalore by the end of 2004" through "public-private partnership with Corporates, Stakeholders and the Citizens." Members of this Task Force are clearly drawn from the upper strata of civil society organizations and movements as well as the corporate giants of Bangalore (like Infosys, the company that is the icon of the Indian software industry). Its links with "Citizens" seem similarly skewed in favor of the elite. Its articulation of a citizen-centered approach does not appear to have any place for the poor people from the informal working class, and efforts supposedly aimed at poor people may be criticized for their tokenism. A common complaint, for instance, is that the Pay and Use Toilets that have been built, through the BATF, though of better quality, have in many instances replaced free toilets, and it is strongly felt by poor people that the former should have been set up in addition to the latter.

Mass movements such as the KKNSS, on the other hand, have consciously adopted "protest" and see their methods as being successful in protecting the rights of the poor and the marginalized. "Partnership" with the state is inconceivable to most of these organizations, and the way they seek to obtain political representation is usually through entering into mainstream politics. Several do see the capture of political power as the logical conclusion of their struggle, enabling them to bring about genuinely pro-poor and pro-labor policies. The "partnership" mode, however, seems to have underlined the disinterest of a whole stratum of civil society organizations, some of them claiming to represent the interests of the poor, in engagement in the political process.

The question then arises as to who the "citizen" is in these supposedly "citizen participatory" efforts, and who constitutes the "private" in Bangalore's Public-Private Partnerships (PPPs). It appears that in Bangalore alongside stratification in civil society organizations there is also a dualism that distinguishes "citizens" from "denizens" (inhabitants, who may be "done unto"), and that a technocratic associational elite defines citizenship in particular ways. Networks among civil society organizations tend to form within the realm of either "citizens" or "denizens," rarely straddling both. Decentralization of urban governance in Karnataka, meanwhile, has been undermined by the State government through the control that it has arrogated to itself over urban planning and real estate; and this has left little possibility for most of the informal working class to exercise any influence at all over decisions that have a great influence on their lives.[21] It is only the elite fraction of the voluntary sector with its corporate links that finds any representation in the political arena. Our evidence suggests that "citizen participation" actually has very little space for the informal working class, who are rather "denizens." This is partly the outcome of the path and policies adopted by the State government with its stated goal of making Bangalore among the world's best cities — reaching which goal seems often to involve confrontation with people from the informal working class.

A similar pattern of differentiation amongst organizations appears in Chennai, where I found almost discrete networks of organizations located, respectively, in the relatively affluent, distinctly middle-class south of the city, and in the north — which is historically where the old working class of the city lived and worked, and where there are now large numbers of informal workers, very many of them Dalits. The cluster, mainly of advocacy or service associations located in South Chennai, is organized and led in the main by Brahmin professionals, with overlapping sets of trustees, also mostly Brahmins, and including former senior civil servants, prominent lawyers and other professional people; while the other significant cluster of civil associations, and including service providers as well as advocacy NGOs, and also mobilizational movements, that is located geographically in North Chennai is organized and led especially by Christians (mainly Catholics) — no less middle-class activists, but from a different, less wealthy, less-propertied fraction of the middle class.[22] There is a definite distancing between the two networks of organizations. Many in the North Chennai set identify strongly with Dalits and there is resistance amongst them to Brahmin dominance — even though this may exist alongside grudging respect for the work done by some of their organizations.

The North Chennai network has a close set of connections with mobilizational movements, including the unions and the women's movements, and the Tamil Nadu Slum Dwellers' Rights Movement. There is a significant difference, therefore, between the South Chennai Brahmin cluster of associations and the dominantly Christian cluster because the latter includes organizations that actually work *with* people in poor parts of the city, as well as the relatively few social associations or movements in which poorer people are active participants — those organizations that may be described as being *of* informal working-class people. The former, Brahmin cluster, does not include such organizations. Some of the associations within the Brahmin cluster are concerned with problems relating to citizenship and to problems of governance — such as the deepening of decentralized government — that surely affect and are of relevance to the informal working class, but they principally address middle-class interests. Exnora International — an internationally celebrated environmental NGO movement — provides an important example that makes the point. I see no reason to doubt that the leadership of Exnora does wish to extend the work of the organization into slums and poorer parts of the city, and that it takes very seriously its stated mission of "taking back governance" (to, by, or on the part of) ordinary citizens. But the organization has its origins in the idea that for India to become truly developed public cleanliness has to be improved — a classic concern of the middle classes, not only in India, and associated elsewhere, and sometimes in Chennai, with slum clearance campaigns that are intended to modernize and to "beautify" cities. The concern — as with the organizations that are part of the Bangalore Agenda Task Force — is with "Roads, rather than public transport; garbage and pollution, rather than public housing; mosquitoes and public toilets rather than public health."[23] Nair continues (writing of Bangalore, but the point applies as well to Chennai):

> Other studies...of how different sections of the city prioritise their municipal problems reveal altogether different concerns: they include, importantly, concerns about the availability of water, the existence of job opportunities in poor neighbourhoods, and an overwhelming anxiety to claim citizenship and voting rights by getting onto the voters' lists. The last was seen in many cases as critical to the survival of the poorest groups in the city, as politics is often the only resource in a system which may deny the benefits of policy decisions or legal remedies to the poor.[24]

Note the convergence with our findings in Delhi on citizen-state relations.

The North Chennai Christian network, however, includes not only organizations that serve poor people of the informal working class, like the service-providing NGOs, but also mobilizational movements — the most notable of them actually being women's organizations. The Penn Urimai Iyyakkam, in particular, though started initially by four middle-class women — a teacher of physics, two other academics, and a lawyer — is an organization of poor women. A group from Penn Urimai with whom I met included two women with no education at all, one with education to ninth standard and one with Secondary School Leaving Certificate (SSLC). The husband of one is a day laborer, and that of another, a watchman. The other two were victims of domestic violence and had been deserted by their husbands. They are all members of the Committee of an organization with about seven thousand members in Chennai and ten thousand in the state that aims to fight for women's rights, campaigns on violence against women, provides legal aid and counseling services, and — most importantly, for those women with whom I spoke — fights to secure housing rights and basic services for women living in slums. Penn Urimai is a constituent member of the Tamil Nadu Slum Dwellers' Rights Movement, and both through this formal connection, and through the central involvement in both associations of the same leading women's rights campaigners, it is also closely connected with the mobilization of informal sector workers by the Nirman Mazdoor Panchayat Sangh (the construction workers' union, founded in 1979) and now with the more recently formed Unorganised Workers' Federation. The Federation links unions of informal workers: domestic workers, construction workers, scavengers, tailors, gem

Ragpickers specializing in fabric, in the slums of the Srinivaspuri area of Delhi. "Middle-class members of residents' associations commonly regard hawkers or ragpickers…, who may visit their neighborhoods, with deep suspicion or outright hostility." (ILO/Crozet M. 2002)

cutters, vendors, agricultural laborers, handloom weavers and, latterly, fish workers, and (reportedly) it joins together about one lakh (100,000) people across Tamil Nadu. Its objectives are to campaign for the rights of unorganized sector workers — including those that have been formally legislated for already by the Government of Tamil Nadu, but not fully implemented — and against globalization (on the grounds that liberalization and globalization harm the livelihoods of poor workers).[25] The close links of these organizations — the women's rights movement and those for unorganized workers, depending partly on their overlapping leadership — reflect their common position that housing rights and rights to livelihood are intimately connected.

The priorities of these movements of the informal working class are clearly different from those of the advocacy associations of South Chennai, or of the numerous residents' welfare associations found in middle-class residential areas, in apartment blocks, and the increasing numbers of condominiums — and their modes of action are also very clearly contrasted. These are all associations of those who may be described as "consumer-citizens" — the hyphenated term that is preferred by one of the South Chennai advocacy associations, on the grounds that the term "consumer" emphasizes the principle of accountability. In practice, however, the "consumer" side of the concept seems the weightier one. When the association called a meeting in a large public hall in Chennai on matters relating to terms of access to cable TV the hall was packed to overflowing; when it called a similar meeting on public space in the city, hardly ten people turned up.[26] It seems to be the case that the rights of citizens are evoked for consumer assertion rather than the other way round. The residents' welfare associations, similarly, increasingly mobilize around matters of consumption (deals on cable TV are one example) rather than over public services — unsurprisingly, given the steadily increasing resort on the part of the middle classes to private services, and their withdrawal from engagement with local government. The relations of these civil organizations with people from the informal working class in their settlements in the city are ambivalent. On the one hand the members of residents' welfare associations may be encouraged to dispense patronage, through such activities as collecting old clothes, or old school textbooks, and supplying them as gifts, or occasionally through programs of "adoption" of particular slum settlements. The Ladies' Clubs set up by some residents' associations may be eager to help the "poor women" of neighboring slums, but they certainly do not welcome those women as members of their clubs. Alongside this paternalistic mode of action, on the other hand, the middle-class members of residents' associations commonly regard hawkers or ragpickers, for instance, who may visit their neighborhoods with deep suspicion or outright hostility. The middle classes and the informal working class in Indian cities come into relationships with each other especially over living space, and over related issues having to do with the occupations of informal workers — and much middle-class action, thinly veiled by patronage, can fairly be seen as being aimed at extending control over their lower-class neighbors.

The women's movements — so unlike the "Ladies' Clubs" — appear to supply the backbone of the mobilizations of informal workers in Chennai.[27] In addition to the Penn Urimai Iyyakam, there are in different slum areas of the city groups organized by Mahila Milan (the women's organization described by Arjun Appadurai as one of the three constituents of the coalition in Mumbai that he argues has had an important impact in creating a "culture of aspiration' amongst poor people there.[28] More significantly, and sometimes allied with Penn Urimai Iyyakkam, there is the CPM-linked All-India Democratic Women's Association (AIDWA). AIDWA has 460,000 members in the state, and 66,000 in Chennai, including 45,000 in North Madras and 21,000 in South Madras. (By way of comparison CPM reportedly has 90,000 members in the state, including 11,000 women). Eighty to 90 percent of the AIDWA membership is described as being of poor and working class women — in North Chennai almost entirely of working women, while in South Chennai only about half the membership is of working women. The local leadership in North Chennai, certainly amongst those whom I was able to meet, including one municipal councillor, is constituted by women from amongst the informal working class.

The numbers of women who are organized by Penn Urimai, AIDWA, and Mahila Milan seem to far outweigh the numbers of men from the informal working class, living in slum areas, who are involved in such mobilizational movements. All those involved in the Slum Dwellers' Rights Movement spoke of the difficulty of holding together local organizations of people in slum areas, either because of their politicization by competing political parties, or because of the buying off of leaders by landlords. Exactly as Janaki Nair has said of Bangalore, therefore, politics "is often the only resource in a system which may deny the benefits of policy decisions or legal remedies to the poor."[29]

## Conclusions: Middle-Class Activism and Working Poor People's Politics

The word "activist" is used very commonly in conversations with and about middle-class people in India's cities. Someone, for example, who runs a well-endowed organization promoting music, dance, and drama, might well describe herself as a "cultural activist." Why is it that some middle-class people feel such a need to use this term? It seems possible that as middle-class people have either failed to take on roles in political leadership, or have vacated the sphere of politics — as they have done according to the electoral studies that have demonstrated their declining political participation — so they have increasingly found in civil society the domain for their self-assertion. Activism in civil society is a part of what it means to be "middle class" — or at least in the elite fraction of the middle class, as Deshpande has described it, that specializes in the production of ideologies and articulates the ruling bloc with the rest of society. In other words, this elite fraction of the middle class mediates the relations of the power holders in Indian society with the mass of the people, through the sorts of activities that were described above. Such middle class people have responded to their impotence in the political sphere by devoting their energies to activism in civil society, and in doing so de-valorize party political activity in the manner of the former banker, now noted civil society "activist," whom I have quoted in the first epigraph to this paper as having described politics as a "dirty river."[30] As I have argued their preferred mode of action emphasizes rational problem solving rather than democracy. This observation recalls Rueschmeyer, Stephens, and Stephens's finding concerning the ambivalence of the middle class in regard to democratization in their comparative analysis of democratic transitions.[31]

In Delhi, Bangalore, and Chennai people from the middle classes dominate the sphere of civil and social associations. Even those associations in which numbers of informal workers are mobilized, like Penn Urimai in Chenai, or the KKNSS in Bangalore, have been established by middle-class people, though they may now have leaders from amongst the poor. There is nothing at all surprising in this observation. "Civil society" is the arena for middle-class activism and assertion; and to a significant extent the middle classes engage in such activism whilst people of the informal working class engage in politics. As the activist cited in the second epigraph above put it, the rich *operate* whilst the poor *agitate* — though it should be added that they agitate relatively rarely and then in a rather fragmented way.

Of course, there are many middle-class people who are not activists, and who rather retreat from any kind of engagement in the public sphere into personalized consumption, in the manner that is deplored by Pavan Varma in his polemic about *The Great Indian Middle Class*.[32] The activists do come disproportionately from upper-caste groups that are still imbued with values of service, and in practice their activities are often perceived as reflecting paternalism, and the perpetuation of hierarchy (in the manner that was true of their forebears in the colonial period, as Watt has explained[33]).

There is one set of associations, including advocacy NGOs and certain service and advocacy NGOs, as well as large numbers of local and residents' associations, that uses the language of consumer-citizenship and addresses the interests principally of middle-class citizens. These associations commonly enter into implicit or explicit partnerships with government (as the Municipal Commissioner for Chennai claimed happens in that city, and as certainly happens in the Bhagidari Scheme in Delhi). But the associations can be effective in acting as public watchdogs, monitoring and checking the actions of government. Their engagement in politics, however, is of the "anti-politics" kind, involving the attempt to find rational solutions — outside "the dirty river" — to what are defined as key public problems that have to be addressed in the process of modernizing society. When they do address the needs of informal working-class people then they are liable, like their predecessors in the colonial period when they sought to "uplift" the Depressed Classes, to be seen as imposing brahmanical values.[34]

There is then another set of associations, including some other of the advocacy NGOs — those that use the language of human rights rather than of citizenship, as well as service providers, that addresses the needs of people from the informal working class. These associations, however, serve these people, rather than being *of* them, and there is a sense in which, partly through the performances in which they engage, they often seem to treat the people for whom they work as "denizens" rather than as citizens — as people "to be done unto," through "dispensing drops of charity" (as one association puts it, in its brochure) rather than as people endowed with the rights and responsibilities of citizenship. Such civil associations also frequently work with government, and draw part of their funding from government sources. Some of them may be very effective in supplying services — in health care for instance — and either meet needs that are not being met by the state, or supply those needs more effectively than does the state. But they too are engaged in a kind of "anti-politics."

The activist whom I quoted in the first epigraph in this article believes in the possibility and the fact of a "new politics" beyond what he describes as "the dirty river" of politics. The "new politics" that he and others believes to be emerging is based in life-spaces and is built up around local associations, replacing the "old politics" of political parties and the social movements associated with them. The ideologists of the World Bank referred implicitly to such a politics when they wrote in the *World Development Report* of 1997:

> In most societies...citizens seek representation of their interests beyond the ballot as taxpayers, as users of public services, and ***increasingly as clients or members of NGOs and voluntary associations.*** Against a backdrop of competing social demands, rising expectations and variable government performance, these expressions of voice and participation are on the rise.[35]

These trends are clearly in evidence in India's cities — but, it seems very clear, they are largely exclusive in regard to the informal working class, except sometimes as clients for services that are provided by some civil organizations. As a matter of fact — and contrary to what the World Bank seems to suppose — rather few of the organizations I have mapped in Delhi, Chennai, and Bangalore are membership organizations (17 percent in Delhi). The extent to which the vibrant associational activity of Delhi, Bangalore, or Chennai provides for "voice and participation" on the part of the informal working class is very limited. The context of civil society organization in class relationships is conveniently ignored by many of the protagonists of "new politics."

Those from the informal working class, on the other hand, "have politics," in the sense that in order to claim rights as citizens they very frequently have to do so through the mediation or brokerage of political parties. This is not to say that civil society actors have not sometimes been very successful in bringing the problems of informal workers and their families to attention — and even in bringing about action to address these problems. This is true of some of the organizations that I have described in Chennai, or of a number of the well-organized rights-based campaigns in India, like those that are mobilized around the Right to Food and the Right to Employment, the Peoples' Health Movement, the Campaign for the Right to Education, and the Campaign for the Right to Information. But they also are not engaged in mass mobilization, and are not "social movements" in the accepted sense of this term. They are more or less effective campaigning and lobbying organizations usually centered around particular NGOs. And as Neera Chandhoke asks, "[C]an all this substitute for the activity we call politics?...do civil society actors actually represent people?" She worries that what all this activity connotes is "the collapse of the idea that ordinary men and women are capable of appropriating the political initiative."[36] The evidence that I have presented suggests, I think, that she is right to be worried, not only in regard to "global civil society" (the subject of her essay) but also in regard to civil society in general. Middle-class activists, as I have argued, tend to prefer technocratic, problem-solving approaches. Working poor people, our evidence shows, may be excluded through the "new politics," and progressively denied the possibility of engaging in politics as self-realization. There are now more channels for influencing government (and thereby securing representation) — established as a result of civil society activism — but those who can avail themselves of the opportunities offered by organizing in civil society tend (unsurprisingly) to be the better educated and relatively wealthy. The paradox that increasing opportunities for participation may actually increase political inequality stands opposed to the claims of the protagonists of "new politics" who tend to ignore the class-differentiated character of the civil society space.

The potential and the possibility of politics, Chandhoke argues, involves "activity that is empowering inasmuch as, when ordinary people engage in political activity they acquire agency, they recover selfhood, and they earn self-confidence."[37] This is what is taking place in those few organizations that I have described as organizations of informal workers for-themselves — which seem often to be dominated by women, and that link struggles for women's rights (against domestic violence for notable instance), struggles for living space (slum dwellers' rights movements) and struggles for rights to welfare of unorganized workers. These struggles are — as Rina Agarwala also argues in her article in this volume — directed at the state, and are about claiming rights as citizens, rather than being about wages and directed against capital.[38]

The commitment of many poorer people in India to the democratic idea, through all the manifest imperfections of the political parties and their leaders, and in spite of the failures of democracy in regard to the solution of their problems of livelihood and well-being, demonstrates their rational recognition of the potentials of politics. The vision of participation that is suggested in the statement that I quoted from *WDR 1997*, by contrast, reflects a very stunted view of the meaning of "representation" because it reduces politics to a marketplace of buyers (people are presented as customers or clients rather than as citizens) and sellers. It is in this sense that the World Bank discourse, and that of some of the other protagonists of new politics, is anti-political.

ACKNOWLEDGMENTS: I am grateful to the editors, Ron Herring and Rina Agarwala, for their careful and stimulating comments on earlier drafts of this article, and to my LSE colleague Chris Fuller for his customarily helpful remarks. My colleagues are Peter Houtzager at IDS, Sussex; Adrian Gurza Lavalle from CEBRAP in São Paulo; Neera Chandhoke from Delhi University; K. Nagaraj from the Madras Institute of Development Studies; and Ms. Sudha Narayanan, now at Cornell — who conducted, extremely well, the study of civil organizations in Bangalore to which I refer. I am very grateful to them all.

❑

# 6. Why Did "Operation Cremate Monsanto" Fail?

## Science and Class in India's Great Terminator-Technology Hoax

**Ronald J. Herring**

"Pushed into deepening debt and penury by Monsanto-Mahyco and other genetic-engineering multinationals, the introduction of Bt cotton heralds the death of thousands of farmers....High costs of cultivation and low returns have trapped Indian peasants in a debt trap from which they have no other escape but to take their lives." — Vandana Shiva (2006, 86)

FAILURE OF PROTEST MOVEMENTS IS COMMON, no matter how worthy the cause. Struggles to gain women's suffrage, to abolish slavery, or to end colonial rule took decades. We learn much about politics and society from the success and failure of these movements. This essay examines the failure of a particular episode of protest against genetic engineering that received global attention — the battle over India's first officially approved genetically modified organism (GMO), Bt cotton.[1] This particular failure suggests what is lost in the move away from class analysis in Indic studies, for both analysts of social movements and for the movements themselves.

Activists who claim to speak for Indian farmers have taken diametrically opposed positions, for and against genetic engineering.[2] Before any transgenic crop can be approved for cultivation, elaborate biosafety testing is required, in line with international norms of the Cartagena Protocol on Biosafety of the Convention on Biological Diversity. A transgenic cotton with the generic designation "Bt" for the transgene it carried, taken from a common soil bacterium, promised to reduce farmers' dependence on purchased pesticides and increase harvests by controlling the worst predator on Indian cotton: the bollworm. "Operation Cremate Monsanto" opposed even the testing of transgenic cotton, and attempted through direct action to prevent the trials. The movement was national, and to some extent international, though the first manifestations were in the state of Karnataka.[3] Protests were held, test crops were burned in the fields, public tribunals (*bij panchayat*) were staged, courts were moved. Opposition was constructed in terms of threats: threats to national independence, in the form of dominance of agriculture by multinational corporations; threats to farmers, in the form of bondage to monopoly seed corporations; threats to nature, in the form of "biological pollution" [horizontal gene flow]; threats to human health, in the form of undiscovered allergens. The recuperative opposites were posed in terms of universal valents: biodiversity over biological reductionism; self-reliance in place of subordination to foreign market power; safety over uncertainty and risk; the natural over the unnatural.[4]

Operation Cremate Monsanto was launched in 1998; it shared ideology, symbols, tactics, and normative critique with similar movements throughout the world.[5] Public intellectuals and numerous nongovernmental organizations (NGOs) attempted to alter public understandings of genetic engineering and to stop its introduction to India. The movement had international backing: Greenpeace, in particular, as well as Via Campesina and other networks opposed to both globalization and genetic engineering, which were conjoined through the mechanism of multinational corporations' control of transgenic seeds. It is difficult to know who or how many the coalition represented. The Karnataka Rajya Raitha Sangha (Karnataka State Farmers' Organization, or KRRS) that launched the operation claimed a membership in the millions but proved unable to mobilize significant electoral support. The Andhra Pradesh Coalition in Defence of Diversity claims to be a coalition of 140 civil-society organizations.[6] Numerous other organizations — some ephemeral, some peripheral — add their endorsements to movement demands, such as a moratorium on transgenic plants in India. The most prominent spokesperson is Vandana Shiva of Navdanya, itself a coalition that convenes subnational organizations. Devinder Sharma has been a major spokesperson, representing an "independent collective" in New Delhi, the Forum for Biotechnology and Food Security. The movement waxes and wanes, regionally and over time, and has no coherent structure; it is a moving target for analysis. Nevertheless, the sum total of anti-transgenic activities bears enough commonalities to be analyzed collectively. Organizations promoting the same technology that the suicide-seed coalition seeks to prevent from being tested in India have the same problem of assessing membership and representation: some are intermittent coalitions of farmers' organizations — e.g., the Kisan [peasant] Co-ordinating Committee — and others are major regional farmers' organizations with a continuing political presence and significant following and some clout — e.g., the Shetkari Sanghatana [Agriculturalist Association]. On both sides, social-movement organizations represented in this episode are typically not membership organizations, and there is a great deal of overlap among them. Yet it is clear that more recognized activists, both internationally and within India, have been oppositional; this loose confederation of opponents of genetically engineered organisms is what I call the suicide-seed coalition, for reasons that will become apparent.

Despite intermittent victories in delaying approval of transgenic cotton, the movement failed to stop the spread of Monsanto's technology. Even before the Government of India (GOI) approved the Mahyco-Monsanto hybrids for cultivation in March 2002, farmers were growing Bt cotton from unapproved sources, with Monsanto's transgene, beneath the radar screen of firm and state. Bt cotton was not officially for sale until the cropping season of 2002-2003; by 2003, the area under official Bt hybrids came to 230,000 acres; in 2004 this area expanded to 1,213,359 acres and to 3,212,300 acres by 2005. The NGO ISAAA estimates official Bt plantings on 7,907,200 acres in the 2006 planting season. Even by official data, the rate of adoption is very steep, as in China.[7] But ISAAA's estimate, like the GOI's, counts only official seeds — i.e., varieties vetted by the Genetic Engineering Approval Committee in Delhi on biosafety grounds. No one knows the actual area under what I have called "stealth seeds," but ISAAA estimated 2.5 million hectares in 2005: i.e., almost twice the area under official seeds at that time.[8] The officially reported area has from the beginning lagged behind the actual transgenic area. The main and undisputed point is that official seeds are spreading to more farmers and acres and the unofficial seeds have become a cottage industry, especially in Gujarat.[9]

Estimates of illegal planting areas are understandably imprecise. Jayaraman cites "industry sources" as estimating that more than half the transgenic cotton in India comes from illegal varieties;[10] my discussions with Gujarati seed producers and farmers suggest a much higher figure for that state. Data from Navbharat Seeds indicate that on an all-India basis, about 34 percent of the cottonseed packets sold are transgenic, of which 9 percent are legal and 25 percent illegal. The ratio is highest in the North Zone (Punjab, Haryana, Rajasthan): 107,000 packets of legal transgenic seeds to 1,170,000 illegal packets, together accounting for about a third of cotton acreage.[11] These estimates apply only to packaged and branded stealth seeds, and do not include F2 seeds saved by farmers for replanting. The reason for more rapid adoption of illegal over legal transgenic cotton is both price and better adaptation to local conditions: new varieties are produced by hybridizing the transgenic with a local variety that grows especially well.[12]

Though it is widely accepted that the cultivars into which the Bt trait was officially inserted were not the best, Mahyco-Monsanto Biotech (MMB) has been successful in selling their three approved Bollgard hybrids. Sales in 2004–05 totaled Rs. 166.4 crores, an increase of 207 percent over the previous year. Moreover, MMB has licensed their technology to the dominant domestic cottonseed firms of India, at very steep rates. As of June 2006 there were forty-four officially approved Bt cotton hybrids containing the first Monsanto-Mahyco event (the Cry1Ac gene, known as event BG-I). An additional technology from Monsanto-Mahyco was incorporated into seven more approved Bt cotton hybrids. These hybrids contain stacked Cry X genes (Cry I Ac and Cry 2 Ab, known as Event MON 15985 or BG-II). Contrary to the frequent assumption of monopoly, approval has also been secured for four Bt cotton hybrids containing Cry1Ac gene, known as Event-1, from the indigenous firm JK Seeds (IIT Kharagpur, India). Finally, a technology from the public sector in China is incorporated into three Bt cotton hybrids: fusion genes (Cry 1Ab and Cry Ac), known as the GFM event, in collaboration with the Indian firm Nath Seeds.[13] Rather than being kept out of India, Monsanto's specific Bt cotton technology has spread commercially, and has been indigenized, naturalized, and made into something of a cottage industry.[14] Monsanto's Cry1Ac technology has been joined by a newer Monsanto transgenic event, and by transgenic cottons developed in China and India.

Rather than asking why there is such a sharp adoption curve of both small and large farmers, and commercial seed firms, across all cotton areas of India, activists continue to declare "the failure of Bt cotton." Vandana Shiva and Afsar Jafri declared more generally the "Failure of GMOs in India," with sections entitled: "Bt cotton failed in India; Bt cotton does not give higher yields; Bt cotton does not increase farmers' income."[15] Why then do farmers not only buy the seeds, but sometimes save and replant them, and cross them into new Bt hybrids? Why do capitalist firms buy expensive licenses to produce a failed technology?

## Property, Patents, and Power: Cultural Urban Bias Confronts Bharat

Opposition to transgenics could involve a claim that the technology does not work, that there are serious ecological risks involved in adoption, or that whether it works or not, is safe or not, biotechnology enables corporate power over farmers. In the movement framing in India, all these claims have been made. If it is Monsanto that needs cremating, property logically comes first; they brought the technology. One wonders what kind of response would have confronted Bt cotton had the technology come first from China or an indigenous Indian firm — as it has subsequently. But in the event, Bt cotton *was* linked to multinational capital. Patents assumed extraordinary power in the movement discourse: to crush nations and farmers. Shiva has provided the main frames for the connection between globalization and transgenics: patents provided the mechanism for "the control of agriculture by multinational corporations.[16] In a typical formulation, the Deccan Development Society study of Bt cotton concluded that "a handful of corporations…[are] using intellectual property rights (IPRs) as tools to exploit farmers."[17] Shiva, the dominant theoretician of opposition, took a stronger line; in a call to mobilize a *bija yatra* (seed march), she defined the objective in opposition to "Seeds of Suicide, Seeds of Slavery, Seeds of Despair." Her explanation for this somewhat counterintuitive linkage was that "Farmers' suicides are concentrated in the regions where corporations like Monsanto have established a seed monopoly, selling costly and unreliable hybrid and GM seeds like Bt. Cotton."[18]

Monopoly is a strong claim about property, particularly in India, where there was no patent protection for Monsanto's seeds, nor anyone else's. But the power of the multinational exceeded even that of a monopolist. In an essay entitled "Practicing Earth Democracy," Shiva wrote: "Patents of life are a total control system….A system in which seed has become a corporate monopoly, a system in which a few companies control the seed supply is in effect a system of slavery for farmers."[19] Shiva et al. wrote in their 1999 article in the prominent Indian social-science journal *Economic and Political Weekly* that "the promotion of genetic engineering by corporations like Monsanto can only be based on dictatorial, distorted and coercive methods." Moreover, "genetic engineering in

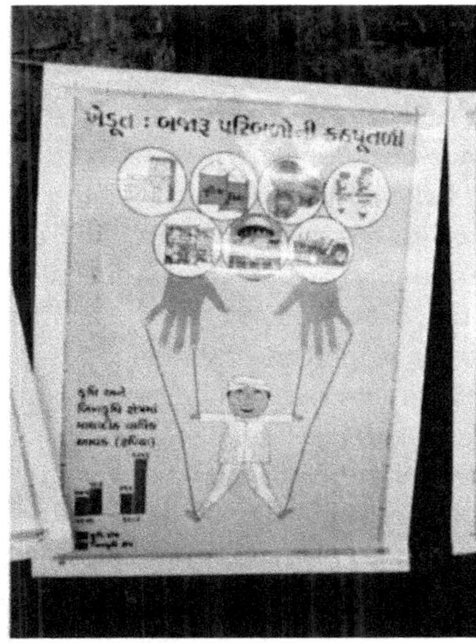

(Left) Package of "illegal" Bt seeds. Studies indicated that "more than half the transgenic cotton in India comes from illegal varieties." (Right) Poster suggesting that nongovernmental organizations fall into the trap of paternalistically regarding Indian farmers as puppets rather than agents "negotiating new technology." (Ronald J. Herring)

agriculture must necessarily be anti-nature and anti-people."[20] In a market economy, it is difficult to conjure the mechanisms through which dictatorial or coercive powers could be imposed on millions of individual choices about cottonseeds.

At the same time that these claims dominated news about Monsanto, Indian farmers were growing transgenic cotton with Monsanto's technology transferred through underground channels and developed by a small Indian firm in Ahmedabad, Gujarat: Navbharat Seeds. The full story of underground seeds is not known, though we do know that at least one farmer — Shankarikoppa Mahalingappa — deserted the KRRS because he found by simple experiment that the suicide-seed rhetoric was a hoax: he got very good germination rates from Bt seeds secreted away from field trials in Haveri.[21] Far from constituting a monopoly, Monsanto's seeds were still undergoing field trials for biosafety and unavailable for purchase while farmers were growing Bt cotton with Navbharat's seeds and their underground offspring, now called "variants" or "indigenous Bt." Once the Bt technology had been naturalized and appropriated, farmers in Gujarat became engaged in what Anil Gupta has informally called "the greatest participatory plant-breeding experiment in human history," making and remaking transgenic hybrid cotton varieties.[22] The common characterization of this vigorous rural anarcho-capitalism is "cottage industry."

There is no space in the cottage-industry scenario — which is not disputed — for dictatorial power, coercion, or even monopoly. This specific error could arise because Indian organizations were parroting a European discourse on transgenics — that is, were victims of coalitional discursive hegemony in a hierarchical system of knowledge. Coalitions seek to keep strands together, even when there are contradictions across strands: if you are against globalization, you are against biotechnology. But for this construction to be accepted in India, activists had to make a radical discursive leap: farmers are assumed to have no capacity as active agents, but merely constitute passive victims. If that is so, the prior question is: Why should farmers be less able to take advantage of leaky global intellectual property rights (IPRs) than are people in other sectors? "Piracy" of computer software, for example, is rampant. Aggregate data from *The Economist* indicate that of business software in use in China, 92 percent is pirated; in Vietnam, 92 percent; in Ukraine, 91 percent, In Indonesia, 88 percent; Russia, 87 percent and so on.[23] Few people of my generation have paid for all the software we use. The phenomenon is general. In his book *Illicit : How Smugglers, Traffickers and Copycats Are Hijacking the Global Economy*, the editor of *Foreign Policy*, Moises Naim, argues that commonly observed illegal transactions are not isolated pockets of deviance, but are integrated with major currents of politics and economics on a global scale. Property systems are vulnerable to the agency of those who would create niches outside the scope and under the radar of states and firms. Why should the same dynamics that operate on the streets of Beijing and Delhi not apply to biotechnology in rural Bharat?

The suicide-seed coalition's assumption that farmers were hapless before the powers of corporate property illustrates a key weakness of elite interpretation of rural dynamics: correlates of class distance. This particular case manifests a deep cultural bias: urban people are capable of deploying something like "weapons of the weak" against global intellectual property regimes quite effectively: software, music, films, pharmaceuticals; but in rural areas, intellectual property will somehow overwhelm the rural Volk, who otherwise are held to possess superior knowledge and wisdom. Denigration of "the peasantry" has historically defined farmers as a class — culturally, politically, and economically inferior to those sectors of society that dominate them. The assumption of patent power (especially at a time that India allowed no patents on plants) can be understood only as an outcome of overlapping forces: ignorance of agronomy (the "terminator-technology" hoax discussed below), cultural denigration of rural people, or conformity to a discourse of global coalitions to which activists subscribe.

The argument that Bt cotton technology failed requires one to believe that neither capitalist seed firms nor cotton farmers in India possess simple market rationality; that extraordinary leap of logic is not only unsupportable, but curious from a political point of view. What could opposition political forces gain from misrepresenting farmer experiences? Official Bt seeds were certainly more expensive than alternatives, but the spread of the technology suggests — as many farmers say directly — that the extra cost is more than compensated by additional income. Mahyco-Monsanto announced in 2006 significant price reductions for technology fees to licensees, but the price differential remained. There were many alternatives, however, both Bt and non-Bt at different price points. That there was choice seemed of no importance to the discourse of coercion and control. The linchpin of class analytics — property — in Operation Cremate Monsanto and its successor movement was at no point an empirical puzzle, but rather a postulate, without reference to struggles over various strands of property claims in the bundle we call ownership. The role of agency in contesting and constructing property disappeared beneath this unexamined postulate.

At the same time the suicide-seed coalition was mobilizing against monopoly and dependence, farmers were making a cottage industry of Monsanto's transgenic technology, sans Monsanto. Simultaneously, several global trends were pointing away from monopoly and coercion and toward a more nuanced construction of property in biotechnology. First, there was a rising tide of research in public sectors of low-income countries, especially China, where Bt cotton was rapidly adopted on an average farm size even smaller than India's.[24] The Chinese version of Bt cotton, in collaboration with the Indian firm Nath Seeds, has now been approved for cultivation in India. Second, "humanitarian use transfers" from commercial intellectual property to common property have been pioneered, first in the case of Golden Rice; the Gates Foundation grant of $25 million for bio-fortification signaled more to come. Finally, it was increasingly evident that multinational corporations (MNCs) were unable to enforce their property claims on transgenic seeds in agriculture, beginning with Monsanto's failure in Argentina in 1995, then in Brazil 1997–2005.[25] Seed police are hard to come by in the villages. The real world was presenting an array of local anarcho-capitalisms, public-sector developmental statism, and private-sector philanthropy in agricultural biotechnology. An empirical and critical view of property would have avoided the assumption of monopoly. Part of the undergirding of this assumption was bad science: "terminator technology."

## Science: The Great Terminator-Technology Hoax

Property figured prominently in a second strand of oppositional discourse: Monsanto was held to own the patent on a so-called "terminator gene." Monsanto flatly denied this claim. There does exist a patent for what biologists call gene use restriction technology (GURT), but it is not held by Monsanto and has not been incorporated into any commercial crops. The name terminator — and the alarm in India — originated with the Rural Advancement Foundation International (RAFI) of Canada. The terminator was said to permit engineering of plants that could not produce viable seeds, forcing farmers to return each season to buy new seeds — generating a biological dependence of farmers on firms unmatched by customary arrangements. RAFI rhetorically linked terminator technology to "suicide seeds": seeds could not be saved by farmers because they were engineered to be sterile.[26] Dependency and the cash nexus would replace the venerable cycle of "self-organizing" agriculture.[27] This construction — linking multinational capital, globalization, and the cultural abomination of suicide seeds — proved powerful and durable. Monsanto was large, American, and carried heavy historical baggage. Clubbed together with Dow Chemical, which together "brought us Bhopal and Vietnam," Monsanto was accused of planning to "unleash genetic catastrophes."[28]

The global discourse against transgenics assigned the terminator a dual role. First, seeds that terminated tied farmers to corporate monopoly. Second, the very idea of terminator seeds placed the technology itself squarely in the realm of the unnatural: a bio-cultural abomination. The terminator story was not only tenacious in India, but spread throughout the world in knowledge about India. The most unsettling construction was that terminator genes would escape and make all plants sterile. It takes only a little common sense to see the fallacy in sterile seeds mating, and across species at that. More obviously, since Monsanto's hybrids under testing had been back-crossed into local cultivars, there were at least six generations of Bt cottons in India at time of the field tests: it would be difficult to manage six generations of seeds from terminators.[29]

From the farmers' point of view, Monsanto enjoyed a privileged market position in 2002–2003 because of Delhi's biosafety regulations, not property. Transgenic alternatives considered superior by many farmers — Navbharat 151 and its local variants — were ruled illegal for failing to receive the approval of Delhi's regulatory system; when these were taken off the market for a time, farmers especially in Gujarat turned to saving and planting transgenic F2 seeds. When Delhi discovered the underground seeds, and ordered Gujarat to destroy the crop in 2001, farmers rose up and defended their cotton fields. Delhi backed down. Maharashtra quickly followed Gujarat in promising its farmers access to the very popular Bt technology. In both cases, counter-mobilization by farmers was decisive.

Suicide seeds took on a darker connotation with publicity about suicides by debt-ridden farmers — most notably in Warangal district, Andhra Pradesh, in 1998. Vandana Shiva and colleagues produced in 2000 a volume *Seeds of Suicide*, "dedicated to the farmers of India who committed suicide." Deepening dependence on hybrid seeds of multinationals — variously called "seeds of death" or "suicide seeds" — did not distinguish transgenic seeds from other hybrids; nevertheless, field trials of transgenic cotton in 1998 were explicitly linked to terminator technology and farmer suicides.[30] Monsanto's marketing director for India responded that the farmers' suicides had nothing to do with Monsanto, but ironically might have been prevented by its technology. With transgenic cotton, Monsanto argued, farmers would have had less debt from pesticide purchase and less loss of yield — less poverty, fewer suicides.[31] Glenn Stone correctly argued that "India is a key battle line in the global war over GM [genetically modified] crops, and both sides interpret the Warangal suicides as supporting their position."[32] But at this time, no Monsanto seeds were commercially available, and would not be until 2002.

The narrative of terminator technology and suicide seeds carried great power, in India as abroad.[33] How much activists knew about its truth is uncertain. Shiva et al. wrote in 1999 that the Bt seeds "are in an ecological sense terminator, which terminates biodiversity...." And: "The freedom of the seeds [is] simultaneously a resistance against monopolies...like Monsanto and a regeneration of agriculture....The seeds of suicide need to be replaced by the seeds of prosperity." Suman Sahai, leader of Gene Campaign, wrote in India's most prestigious journal of social science: "Trials of a genetically altered cotton variety (Bt cotton) conducted by the American company Monsanto have provided the trigger because Monsanto also happens to own the terminator technology." Jackie Assayag, repeats this conventional wisdom long after its decisive disconfirmation in the fields of India, in a book ironically subtitled *Perspectives from Below.*[34]

As the terminator hoax suggests, much of the anti-transgenic discourse takes an instrumental view of science; science ceases to be a method of inquiry with particular canons for truth claims and becomes instead a political weapon or artifact of power. It is argued that science underlay colonial rule in an instrumental fashion.[35] Part of the constructivist worldview is that knowledges are plural, with science having no particular advantage over other claims. Moreover, the instrumental view of science enables constructions such as "Western science" and "imperialist science" and "totalitarian science."[36] P.V. Satheesh of the Deccan Development Society talks of "corporate science," and adds a darker implication. In his response to a critique of NGO studies of Bt cotton as "unscientific," he responded to the author: "Bravo Dr Shantharam, you have done a yeoman service to your masters but on the day of judgement in a future not so far away, scientists like you will be remembered as 'Enemies of the People.'"[37] Suspicion of science as a system of knowledge figures prominently in critiques of biotechnology. Devinder Sharma, a major publicist of opposition to Bt technology in India explained his skepticism well:

> Scientific research is rigged, alarming evidence of health dangers are covered up, and intense political pressure silences the sane voice of dissidents. Distortions, omissions, cover-ups and bribes are used to promote an unhealthy and risky technology, and that too with the "pious" intention of increasing productivity and thereby, eradicating hunger.[38]

The movement's view of farmers seems to have precluded their understanding of biotechnology. The subtitle of Vandana Shiva's *Biopiracy: The Plunder of Nature and Knowledge* is telling: *The Plunder of Nature and Knowledge* presents a world in which biological value resides in the South, clever biopirates in the North. The Bt cotton episode presented precisely the opposite directionality.

Though the CEO of Navbharat Seeds denies it, much of the world views his incorporation of Monsanto's Bt technology in India as ingenious plant breeding based on unauthorized appropriation of the Cry1Ac transgene. Sharad Joshi, leader of the pro-Bt farmers' movement Shetkari Sanghatana, dubbed Dr. D.B. Desai, CEO of Navbharat Seeds, "Robin Hood." It was Dr. Desai's transgenic hybrid NB151 that became the stock for farmer-bred "indigenous Bt," especially in Gujarat. When a BBC story portrayed the farmers of Gujarat as clever pirates of Monsanto's intellectual property, Vandana Shiva's Research Foundation for Science Technology and Environment responded: "This rumour about piracy is initiated by Monsanto whose Bt cotton has totally failed throughout the length and breadth of the country and to divert attention of the public and policy makers from the failure of its genetically engineered seeds, Monsanto is trying to focus on the outstanding success as unjust and illegal of an indigenously bred cotton variety."[39] Indian official science determined that the "indigenous" label was accurate, and constituted a crime, not for violation of a nonexistent patent, but for commercializing a hybrid that had not been approved through national procedures for biosafety testing.[40] This Robin Hood was not accused of violating property law, but rather biosafety regulations.

Intellectual property is especially subject to "Robin Hood" tactics — but this position requires a construction of farmers as agents, not hapless objects. There is no reason in biology or empirics to posit inability of rural people to join the global anarcho-capitalism fueled in part by the unauthorized appropriation of intellectual property. The assumption that biopiracy can flow in only one direction is patently false, but does indicate a deep cultural disposition. This final observation suggests another weakness in the campaign that seems diagnostic: the denigration in theory and practice of science as a form of vetting knowledge claims.

Rejection of Enlightenment values by well-educated people is a global phenomenon, as prominent in Washington, D.C., as in Delhi. Yet the devaluation of science as knowledge does not float randomly above class position. The postmodern and constructivist stance on multiple knowledges is affordable by some classes, but not others. Indeed, this privilege of disbelief creates class antagonisms. Farmers as a class, because of their position in production, and the pressures of reproducing farm livelihoods, are driven to science of necessity. They cannot afford ideology: rather, an empirical pragmatism is rooted in, and necessary for, their material life. The same constraints do not apply to activists; indeed, controversy is their mode of production. Protests from Monsanto that there were no terminators in India, nor anywhere else; that Bt cotton certainly contained no such thing; and that the company did not have a patent on any such gene were simply ignored. Evidence was available had movement spokespersons been interested in obtaining it. But what would be their interest in so doing?

## Class Interests in Genetic Engineering

The most powerful factor in the spread of technology opposed by the suicide-seed coalition was the material interest of cotton farmers. As in China and other countries, Bt cotton technology is adopted by farmers because they believe it reduces input costs, improves insect management, and thereby raises farmer incomes.[41] The more farmers are dependent on pesticides for bollworm management, the greater the attraction of Bt technology. The technology is, unlike many agrarian changes, scale neutral; there are no significant size or scale distinctions differentiating access for size-classes of farmers — in contrast, say, to a tractor or tube well. Indian cotton farms are small, though somewhat larger than those in China. Unless one assumes farmers incapable of calculating their interests, the suicide-seed construction was bound to fail as a mobilizing trope for agrarian movements. Despite its powerful cultural resonance, that narrative ran counter to the experiential base of farmers, who know what grows well in their fields and what does not. Any movement claiming to represent farmers should be able by investigation and consultation uncover these essential agroeconomic and biological facts. Farmers' material interests preclude behavior driven by ideology. The material conditions for reproducing movement leaders are not tethered to crop success or failure, and correspondingly their interests have no necessary connection to empirical consequences.

The most serious empirical question about class interests is that of the most vulnerable class in rural India, but it is a question lost in the rhetoric of terminator technology. The most obdurate rural poverty is that of landless workers who must find wage employment on whatever crops need labor. They are put at risk by crop choice, but have no voice. What is a livelihood for the laborer is a cost for the farmer. In high-wage agriculture, labor-saving technologies are profitable and will be attractive to rational cultivators. Reduction in aggregate demand for labor under many agrarian conditions either destroys livelihoods or puts downward pressure on wage rates or both. Moreover, the rural poor who depend on casual wage labor for a livelihood are frequently those cumulatively disadvantaged across dimensions of social stratification: women, depressed castes, ethnic minorities, migrants. Bt cotton adoption means that laborers could lose work applying pesticides. Are wage losses in chemical applications compensated by more harvest labor if yields increase, and by safer ground water and less exposure to toxins? If net wages are lost, but health improves, a difficult trade-off arises. This trade-off depends on variations in wage systems: for example, when wages are based on weight harvested — rather than a daily sum — income increases with yield and ease of harvest, as sometimes occurs in Bt cotton.[42] Moreover, whatever the effect on demand for spraying labor, protection from crop loss has implications: there are no harvesting wages if crops are destroyed by bollworms. It was only fields of Bt cotton that survived the "bollworm rampage" of 2001 in Gujarat.[43] To the extent that transgenics reduce the risk of crop failure, they reduce risks for the landless poor, as well as farmers.

Other interests in genetic engineering are quite straightforward: industry would prefer less regulation and faster approval of new varieties.[44] The developmental state supports transgenic development, noting that China already has already seized the lead in this expanding sector.[45] Pesticide companies are opposed to Bt technology as it reduces use of their product. Rumors of pesticide firm funding of opposition groups are quite persistent in India, but evidence is illusive.[46] Though opponents prefer to cast Bt technology as being more important to big farmers, the technology seems to be scale-neutral both theoretically and empirically. There would seem to be no reason for differential class advantages in seed use among farmers given the affordable alternatives and absence of scale effects.

But then what can citizens make of the avalanche of reports claiming "failure of Bt cotton in India?" It is a complicated question, and much is unknown. Accounts of failure come from NGOs opposed to Bt cotton; most come from Andhra Pradesh, not from Gujarat. Sometimes their studies produce rather implausible conclusions that are picked up by the press:

> [I]n North Telengana region, the net income from Bt varieties was five times less than the yield from local non-Bt varieties. In Southern Telengana, the income from Monsanto's Bt crop was nearly seven times less

than what was obtained from the indigenous non-Bt cotton varieties, demonstrating the resounding failure of the Monsanto variety.[47]

Yield and income get mixed in odd ways, as do cultivars and traits: Bt is a trait, not a variety of cotton. Characteristics such as staple length and sensitivity to wilt are attributed to addition of a trait that has no biological connection to these phenotypic variations. Studies illustrating failure seldom are transparent about sampling frames and methodology.[48]

Much of the failure literature, especially that promulgated by the Deccan Development Society, comes from Andhra Pradesh. Is it possible that what has become the dominant technology and a cottage industry in Gujarat fails in Andhra for reasons of soil, climate, or general agronomic variation?

What do adoption rates tell us? In the ISAAA (International Service for the Acquisition of Agri-biotech Applications) data, adoption of Bt technology has been more rapid in Andhra than in other states: a gain of 250 percent from 2004 to 2005. It was in Andhra that the state government, evidently from political pressure, requested refusal of reauthorization of MMB varieties: local seed companies have licensed the technology and now sell their own Bt cotton brands with less competition. The rate of change in cultivation of Bt varieties varies quite a bit across states, but is everywhere increasing. Interestingly enough, Gujarat shows the smallest increase, 15.4 percent. The reason is almost certainly that the unofficial Bt varieties are so well established in Gujarat. They are certainly cheaper than MMBL versions and many farmers hold them to be agronomically superior.[49] Glenn Stone, who has done detailed field work in Andhra Pradesh, and in fact in Warangal district, reports that farmers are adopting Bt cotton seeds with such alacrity that he can legitimately write of "more than innovation adoption, more than a tipping point: it was a craze." Stone believes this craze is based on poor knowledge of agronomy; Bt cotton has resulted in the "de-skilling" of farmers.[50]

This dispute cannot be settled here. But it is useful to point out that opponents fail to distinguish Bt technology from specific cultivars. Bt confers a trait; some hybrids with this trait do better than others, as there are vast agronomic differences across Indian cotton terrain: varieties that work well in one region, district, farm, or even field, may fare less well in the next. Farmers know this; many who claim to represent them do not. Ecological variability is why Indian farmers grow hundreds of cultivars of cotton, many of which now have incorporated Bt technology. There is great variation in performance of cotton cultivars, both Bt and non-Bt. Reasons for variance are not always discernable, either by farmers or researchers, since there are many unmeasured variables in complex interactions, including local climate, soil chemistry, pest variance, water timing, and nutrients. These variables, and their interaction, vary every season: MECH 184 does well for some farmers in some years, but experiences wilting in years of inadequate, early moisture. This agronomic characteristic is true of the cultivar with or without the Bt trait. Nevertheless, some farmers find better yields with MECH 184 than with other MECH varieties or even Navbharat variants. Second, spurious seeds are pervasive: some varieties sold as Bt are not; some farmers honestly but mistakenly believe their Bt crop has failed. There are adverts in Indian newspapers for underground seeds: there is no way for farmers to verify the quality of these seeds. One reason many farmers prefer Mahyco-Monsanto seeds to the farmer-bred "variants" (Viraat, Rakshak, Maharakshak, Agni, Luxmi, etc.) is that Mahyco has a reputation for reliable seed quality. Third, there are demands for financial compensation from Mahyco-Monsanto and the government for Bt crop failure; there is a material incentive to claim poor results. Fourth, poor performance of some Mahyco-Monsanto hybrids is attributed to the technology. Actually, the MMLB hybrids are clearly not the best germplasm for insertion of the Bt gene: many farmers seem to prefer Navbharat and other varieties, legal and illegal. New firms vigorously entered the market as licensees of MMLBs technology, but with different cultivars. Finally, and most importantly, none of the claims of failure compare two isogenic varieties, one with and one without the Bt gene, to assure control of varietal characteristics.[51] Rather, all disadvantageous variance across over time and space — which will be extreme in India — is attributed to the Bt gene, constructing a biological absurdity. The Cry1Ac gene codes for a single protein; there is no reason for production of that protein — lethal to Lepidoptera — to cause staples to shorten or leaves to wilt.

The most careful controlled study I have seen in of Mahyco-Monsanto Bollgard MECH-162 compared to the isogenic non-Bt MECH 162 and a conventional hybrid. This study used a participatory field trial to test meaningfully paired hybrids with and without integrated pest management (IPM). Consistent with other studies, Bt plants required half the sprayings of other plants, and experienced less bollworm infestation. With IPM, the Bt variety recorded a yield of 7.1 q/ha and a net return of Rs. 10,507/ha. Damage to fruiting bodies was much less with Bt plants, which would account for the premium some Bt farmers receive for their lint in the market. The authors concluded: "Bt Mech-162 used in an IPM mode resulted in highest yields and economic gains to the farmers; pesticide consumption was also reduced."[52] Bt technology and improved agro-ecological practices, rather than being incompatible, each contributed to superior outcomes. The most sustainable solution turned out to be new germplasm with traditional means of cultivation.

Claims about the biological and agroeconomic failure of Bt technology are difficult to sustain; that the claims persist is puzzling. It is hard to see a strategic advantage in claiming that "Bt cotton has failed," or that the seeds are "genocidal." Measures of success and behavioral indicators are hard to ignore. It is not surprising that opposition has continued with the frame of ecological uncertainty: that Bt cotton will "terminate biodiversity." Since there is no way of disproving a negative — that something will not happen — this strategy for stopping transgenics by raising anxiety surely stands a better chance than representation of biotechnology as a death threat to farmers. Indeed, the science on horizontal gene flow ("biological pollution") is incomplete. Keeping uncertainty alive is clearly in the interest of all who have livelihoods as brokers in the global coalition against biotechnology. Tethering the campaign to distal threats ("destruction of biodiversity," for instance) prevents any decisive confrontation with facts, and rests on anxiety about the unknown, which is inexhaustible.

Given the lack of definitive knowledge, and anxiety, the interest of most citizens is rooted in caution. Indeed, one could argue that there is no advantage whatsoever to most Indians in Bt cotton, at least before it was discovered that pesticide levels in bottled water and soft drinks had reached alarming levels.

## Brokerage, Cultural Capital, and Authenticity Rents

This account of the failure of Operation Cremate Monsanto has stressed the incompatibility between the interests of farmers and the perceptions of farmer interests by activists. The cognitive screen of leaders seemed impermeable to confounding information. Why would activists continue to declare the failure of a technology that was spreading?

Social movement theorists consider "framing" to be of central importance in explaining outcomes.[53] Framing presents both opportunities and dangers for movements. Framing necessarily involves condensation symbols and simplification, especially of issues involving scientific complexity. Effective framing, through necessary for dramaturgical purposes of activism, frequently uses metaphors or scenarios that create or raise anxiety — "Frankenfood" as a framing of what many consider to be ordinary nutrition represents a classic case in point. Conditions of high anxiety and low information enhance the power of symbolic politics[54] on which social movements feed. To present a rather stark divergence of interests in framing, India in 2003, following Zambia and Zimbabwe in 2002, rejected food aid because the food contained some transgenic grains that North American parents feed their children every day. Coding this food dangerous — or in the African case "poison" — has no consequences at all for some class positions, possibly quite a bit for others. One's class position determines to a great extent whether this coding is of consequence or not, or how much latitude there is for mistakes.[55]

Activists attempt to form broad coalitions; the size and diversity of these coalitions is to match the size and diversity of the threat.[56] Globalization has produced global networks for mobilization against globalization. Joining global coalitions presents unique opportunities for national- or local-level groups, as is well recognized, but may also less obviously create risks for social movement organizations (SMOs).[57] International NGOs such as Greenpeace can link protest sites, symbols, and tactics, and can sometimes provide vital resources for movements. But scaling up to the global level may detach movement leaders from rank-and-file activists, undermine internal democracy, fracture broad social coalitions, and demobilize grassroots activists.[58] Additional resources become available, but movement toward the global core creates potential conflicts with representation of the peripheral base. If nothing else, conflicts of language and culture become more glaring, as was certainly the case with Operation Cremate Monsanto.[59] Yet it is the representational claim of a social base that legitimates movement leaders and makes them useful to coalitions.

Interaction with far-from-local policies and institutions inevitably changes the terrain on which strategic calculations about representation and tactics are made. Making linkages between two or more sites of contention by intermediary agents or organizations is called brokerage. Brokerage often entails the construction of new organizational forms or institutional channels that allow protest to shift from a local to a national or even transnational scale.[60] Brokerage may be a first step in transforming amorphous or spontaneous forms of social mobilization into more institutionalized patterns of political representation. Coalitions functionally require brokers; brokerage commands resource flows. New connections enabled by both globalization and protests against globalization produce brokerage positions. These are not randomly distributed, but depend on skill sets and cultural capital not universally available. Erik Olin Wright posits "expertise" or "knowledge" as dimensions of class standing in highly differentiated contemporary societies.[61] Knowing how to run a listserv is a valuable asset, as is being able to read, write, and speak in English. International politics and the cultural capital of India's metropolitan middle class match up well.

Brokers deal with factors removed from the common experience of the social base; they live in a different strategic and cultural environment. This cleavage is particularly evident when knowledge differentials are large, and thus the cognitive mediation of interest more decisive. Even in the most literate of societies, for example, few citizens can independently access the technical issues necessary to determine their interests in genetic engineering. Technical expertise is unevenly distributed globally across societies, and on the ground in social movements; the gulf between metropolitan elites and those they claim to represent may well be yawning. Who speaks for the poor? For the farmer? For indigenous authenticity? For national interest? Metropolitan elites can make these strategic claims only by alliance (partnership is the preferred terminology) with "stake-holders." Authentic brokers are critical, as coalitions speak for those anonymous stake-holders who cannot easily speak for themselves.

Who is authentic? Authenticity is a function of national subaltern status and individual ethnicity. Authentic critiques must come "from below,"[62] not from above. Global difference and global coalitions permit cultural capital to be converted into what we might call authenticity rents. A rent is a return on capital, whether physical in the case of a landlord or positional as in the case of "bureaucratic rents." Cultural capital is a necessary condition to access the metropolitan core of international coalitions; authenticity conveys authority to speak for others without that cultural capital. Continuing the "GMO controversy" preserves positions for brokers: mediators, protagonists, and participatory facilitators. There is no normative denigration in this conclusion: just as "tribals" are allowed certain latitude in environmental protection normatively to preserve their subsistence routines, metropolitan members of the NGO industry create and preserve livelihoods from niches enabled by brokerage: cultural capital augmented by indigeneity.[63] To expect otherwise is to misunderstand the most basic insights of class analysis.

The availability of authenticity rents is vastly expanded in global settings. Ram Guha wrote in his provocative *EPW Perspectives* piece (22–29 March 2003), "The Ones Who Stayed Behind," that a parallel trend has appeared in scholarship: "In the eyes of their American colleagues, the diasporic scholar has come to 'represent' India much as the Vietnamese or Ukrainian emigré represents Vietnam or the Ukraine." Guha argues that this outcome is "doubly unfortunate, because post-structuralism and cultural studies are trends of dubious intellectual worth, and because its South Asian proponents belong overwhelmingly to the upper class." Guha believes that cashing in on this cultural capital has advantaged many scholars from the subcontinent in North American and European markets but at the cost of impenetrable and irrelevant work.[64] Sharing one strand of the style of scholarship critiqued by Guha, suicide-seed activists have been unconstrained in their discourse by any tethering to fact. Their discourse about India has fed heavily on the global movement against genetic engineering.

Representations of India, in turn, feed the global discourse on the horrors of biotechnology: "40,000 Indian farmers commit suicide" has became a staple of the global argument against GMOs (though curiously the number does not change, even as there are more suicides every week) as did the death of thousands of sheep from eating Bt cotton leaves.[65] At the UN Meeting of the Parties to the Convention on Biological Diversity, in March of 2006, in Curitiba, Vandana Shiva — always described as a scientist and recipient of the Right Livelihood Award (Alternative Nobel Prize) — summarized a common theme in her writings:

> These seeds kill biodiversity, farmers, and people's freedom — for example, Monsanto's Bt cotton, which has already pushed thousands of Indian farmers into debt, despair, and death. Bt cotton is based on what has been dubbed "Terminator Technology," which makes genetically engineered plants produce sterile seeds....High costs of cultivation and low returns from genetically modified seeds have trapped Indian peasants in considerable debt from which they are escaping by taking their lives. More than 40,000 farmers have committed suicide over the past decade in India — although the more accurate term would be homicide, or genocide.[66]

These are the same seeds that were once only "suicidal." Simultaneously, a new international movement to "Ban Terminator" has emerged, and quickly attracted endorsements from hundreds of organizations worldwide; the Deccan Development Society is one of eighteen Indian NGOs to sign on.[67] There is some irony in Indian organizations' petitioning against the emergence of the terminator, the reality of which they have deployed dramaturgically for eight years.

The movement against biotechnology continues to misrecognize the nature of biology and property in biotechnology, and the agency of rural people negotiating new technology. What difference does this make? This misreading — which has been largely hegemonic among NGOs visibly active on the issue[68] — undermines the potential of a broad and viable political coalition to seek environmental integrity, agricultural improvement, and social justice under threatening conditions of agriculture in India, exacerbated by globalization, rigged markets, and global warming.

## Interests, Politics, and Movement Failure

Social movements opposing government policy frequently fail; causes of failure are multiple, complex, and overdetermined. Asymmetries of power are often decisive. Operation Cremate Monsanto failed in an open political system in which the mobilization of farmers and rural people is both permitted and common, courts were accessible, the press was attentive to controversy. Farmers who adopted Bt cotton believe they are reducing toxification of soil, water, and people by using the technology, and simultaneously reducing expenditures on pesticides and thus the risk of indebtedness. Because these outcomes are inconceivable to the suicide-seed coalition, they could not represent farmers. Their movement to stop Bt technology failed because of overlapping misconstructions: of farmers' interests and behavior; of the biology of biotechnology; of the empirics of intellectual property on the ground; of the rationality and agency of farmers. How could these tactical errors be consistent with the interests of intelligent, articulate, and dedicated activist leadership?

Risks of global coalitions for activists locally are that (a) a global discourse replaces discourse rooted in local conditions, empirically validated; (b) authenticity substitutes for knowledge as a source of legitimacy; and (c) external support, premised on conditions a and b above — i.e., incorporation of the global discourse and displaying authenticity — substitutes for legitimation based on democratic methods within movements and an understanding of interests on the ground. These dynamics are similar to those stressed in the literature on "political substitution effect" in foreign aid and ethnic conflict: regimes that come to depend on external props fail to generate internal support by addressing emergent cleavages in society.[69] The danger for activist movements is that ideology as a cognitive screen replaces empiricism; interests are deduced from global discourses, not science on the ground. Moreover, there are externalities of framing: delegitimization of a broad coalition for environmental integrity and social justice, for example, may result from one egregious strand of inaccurate framing. The divorce of the anti-biotechnology movement from the base it claimed lay not only in different class interests, but in the selection pressure that those interests have exerted on authoritative knowledge. Appropriation of knowledge is not random. The interests of those whose assets are connectivity and rhetorical skill are not tied to any empirical process. Campaign politics selected for junk science over real science, discursive consistency over empirical investigation. Material constraints on Indian cotton farmers operate in the reverse direction: close margins necessitate an empirical and pragmatic approach to technology; the margin for error is small, as recent tragedies have illustrated.[70]

What is most surprising is that cognitive screens between interest and action proved impermeable. Only consonant information penetrated the screen. The screen itself was constructed with inadequate attention to choice and agency, too much structural determination. The global discourse of lumping GMOs into one giant political category defies both biology and the interests of farmers. Hostility to science became part of the screen because of the reality of asymmetric control of genetic engineering resources in 1998. The possibilities of Bt cottons from India and India-China firms and from creative Indian farmers was simply not admissible, but are now realities. Biotechnology is particularly susceptible to cognitive screens for those alarmed by claims and counterclaims. Is food aid from the United States really "poison"? If so, even the hungriest person may rationally avoid it; the interest calculation is simple once the mediation is in place. If not, how does one calculate the risk? Is the risk worse than malnutrition? Interests in genetic engineering are demonstrably contingent, malleable, and situational, and they are filtered through cognitive screens that admit of less nomothetic solidity than the interests of deductive structural accounts.

Globalization seldom produces the clear and monolithic results portrayed in political rhetoric. Interests are difficult for ordinary people to calculate, whether from ecological threats of transgenic organisms or monetarist orthodoxy as the solution to economic crisis; perception of interests is brokered by both cognitive rules of thumb and reliance on trusted intermediaries in civil society, such as political parties, NGOs, and advocacy networks. The indeterminacy of critical knowledge — and the related authority of science — empower articulate intermediaries, however misinformed. Pinstrup-Andersen and Schiøler argue that "too many well-to-do individuals and groups from Europe and North America have taken an unacceptably paternalistic position, claiming to represent the interests of the developing countries and to know what is best for the poor within these countries." The "almost silent majority" of people are not heard in international forums.[71] The problem for activists is one of scaling up. With scaling up comes the potential loss of legitimacy in the base and increasing dependence on cognitive screens that are not widely shared. The organizational imperative creates a cultural disconnect. The leader of the farmer's organization at the core of Operation Cremate Monsanto, the KRRS, was Professor Nanjundaswamy; he did own land, and could be called a farmer, but tellingly was called by the title Professor.[72]

The literature on "new social movements" is a European literature, but so too is much of the anti-transgenic story. One insight of that literature is the connection to "post-materialist values." That is, movements around issues not involving class interests — the "old social movements" of labor and peasants, for example — are enabled by material prosperity. These are movements of people who have solved the subsistence problem. Jung nicely summarizes:

> Scholars of the new social movement theory identified these movements as."new" in that they represented a post-materialist and universalistic critique of modernity and modernization by challenging institutionalized patterns of technical, economic, and political rationality without falling back upon established institutional arrangements such as political parties.[73]

Post-materialist is hardly a descriptor one would use even for "shining" India. Nevertheless, class differentiation within India has long produced class positions that float above concern with the brute compulsions of economic facts. This material base, as well as the cultural capital so entailed, permit hostility to modernization unsupportable on a two-acre farm. Indian cotton growers face difficult odds, from adverse agronomics to rigged global markets. Though the WTO has ruled against the United States on illegal subsidies for cotton, low and inconsistent yields will continue to threaten subsistence on Indian cotton farms. Some help with the humble but often devastating problem of bollworms made Bt technology attractive, despite the brilliant dramaturgy and articulate rhetoric of Operation Cremate Monsanto.

Much of the world picked up the terminator-technology and suicide-seed story of biotechnology in Indian agriculture, especially in otherwise progressive fora. That Indian nationals were successful in diffusing this hoax about India illustrates the power of authenticity. The deep irony is that the hoax was born on a website in Canada, now defunct. The discursive distortion is bounced back to India via authoritative books about India published in London[74] — or New York. Inside this resonance chamber there are no constraints, only mutual reinforcement.

ACKNOWLEDGMENTS: Derived from "What's Left Out When the Left Goes Discursive? Science, Property and Transgenics in India." Princeton University, 21 April 2005. Helpful commentaries at Princeton included those of Zia Mian, Karen McGuinness, Atul Kohli, Smitu Kothari, Vivek Chibber, Patrick Heller, and Rina Agarwala; Devparna Roy, Anil Gupta, Vikas Chandak, Shanthu Shantaram, and D.B. Desai aided me significantly as well.

❑

# 7. Hegemonic Aspirations

## New Middle Class Politics and India's Democracy in Comparative Perspective

Leela Fernandes and Patrick Heller

STUDIES OF CONTEMPORARY INDIAN POLITICS have traditionally been dominated by a narrative of Indian exceptionalism. Indian politics, according to such exceptionalist arguments, has been characterized by the politics of cultural identity such as caste, religion, and ethnicity rather than the politics of class.[1] Such arguments have overlooked the salience of class analytics for an adequate understanding of the workings of democratic politics in India today. This article seeks to move beyond the conceptual limitations of exceptionalism in two ways. First, we locate the politics of India's democracy within the framework of comparative class analytics. Second, our analysis moves away from an opposition between the politics of class and the politics of caste, religion, and region.

The comparative literature identifies two democratic paths to substantive democracy. The classic liberal trajectory is associated with a strong and hegemonic bourgeoisie and the social democratic trajectory (and its more redistributive outcomes) has been linked to the formation and organization of a cohesive working class.[2] The bourgeoisie in India has never achieved hegemonic status,[3] and working class formation has been weak and fragmented. Instead, any account of distributive politics in India must bring the middle class into focus. Not only has this class played a critical role in managing the ruling bloc (which includes the bourgeoisie and landed interests), but it has also been an important actor in its own right. If social scientists largely neglected or underestimated the role of the middle class during the Nehruvian period of state developmentalism, the middle class today is routinely inflated into an amorphous mass defined by its own worldview or consumption patterns.[4]

In this article, we ground our analysis of middle class politics in two arguments. The first is that the middle class, and in particular the dominant fraction of the middle class, plays a central role in the politics of hegemony. These hegemonic politics are played out both as attempts to coordinate the interests of the dominant classes and to forge internal unity within the highly diverse fragments of the middle class. But rather than producing the classical pattern of liberal hegemony (in which the ruling bloc actively elicits the consent of subordinate classes) in the Indian context these projects have been marked by middle class illiberalism, and most notably a distancing from lower classes. Second, we argue that the well-known difficulties of defining the middle class can be overcome in part by focusing on the specific class practices through which it reproduces itself.[5] Because the middle class derives its power from cultural and educational capital, it actively engages in hoarding and leveraging its accumulated privileges and in reproducing social distinctions.[6] In the Indian context this implies that caste and other cultural attributes (most notably command of English) become critical assets in the continuous struggles that define class fractions. Sociocultural inequalities and identities (such as those based on caste and language) are an integral part of the process of middle class formation. The result as we will argue is that patterns of middle class illiberalism are strongly shaped by such inequalities and exclusions.

We develop both these arguments through an exploration of the rise of India's new middle class (NMC) in the context of policies of economic liberalization. The past two decades have witnessed a significant reconfiguration of class forces marked in particular by the ascendance of a NMC that is conventionally portrayed as the natural carrier of India's intensified embrace of economic liberalization. Public commentators, media images, and academic analyses have depicted this NMC as a consumer-based group benefiting from economic reforms. This narrative not only naturalizes and oversimplifies the NMC relationship to liberalization (and implicitly modernization) but also exaggerates and essentializes its internal coherence. We argue that the NMC is a tangible and significant phenomenon, but one whose boundaries are constantly being defined and tested. Further, we contend that the contours of the NMC can be grasped only as a *class-in-practice,* that is, as a class defined by its politics and the everyday practices through which it reproduces its privileged position. This conceptualization moves away from a static opposition between structural and political/cultural/ideological processes. While theoretical and comparative works have attempted to move beyond such oppositions, conceptions of class in India have often implicitly reproduced such dichotomies. Studies of the middle class, for example, have alternated between purely culturalist definitions and economistic measures based on income and occupations.[7]

At a macro level, the NMC has been forged at the intersection of liberalization and a political context marked by organized political challenges from below, that is, the increased political assertiveness of other backward castes that Yogendra Yadev has dubbed the "the second democratic upsurge."[8] The hegemonic aspirations of the NMC have taken the form of a politics of reaction, blending market liberalism and political and social illiberalism. On the one hand, the dominant fraction of the NMC projects itself as the central agent in India's drive to open and modernize its market economy. On the other hand, significant segments of the middle class have played a key role in the rise of Hindu nationalism. The ideological and social basis of Hindutva is far too historically complex to be simply equated with the NMC. Yet the consolidation of Hindutva as a political movement marked both by the rise of the Bharatiya Janata Party (BJP) and the Congress Party's periodic attempts at courting a Hindu nationalist vote[9] cannot be explained without reference to the political reconfiguration of the middle class. From its fairly limited traditional support base in trading castes, the appeal of Hindu nationalism has spread rapidly into the ranks of the broader middle class over the past two decades. We argue that Hindu nationalism has resonated with large sections of the Hindu middle class because its doctrines of nationalism and cultural essentialism provide an ideological frame for NMC self-assertion as well as a political response to newly mobilized lower class constituencies and their varied claims for incorporation.[10]

It is this relational dynamic that underscores both the limitations of the hegemonic project that the NMC attempts to represent and the inherent contradictions of middle class politics. Both the unifying discourse of Hindutva and the modernist NMC claims are belied by exclusionary social practices through which the middle class constitutes itself. In the next section we explore the politics of Hindu nationalism as a more general expression of middle class reaction.[11] In the following sections we analyze a range of practices through which the fractions of the NMC deploy, combine, and convert cultural and social capital to leverage their privileges in the new economy. We point in particular to the importance of inequalities such as caste and language in fields such as education and urban space to illustrate such exclusionary practices. Through this analysis we seek to demonstrate the mechanisms and strategies of capital conversion involved in the process of NMC formation while simultaneously pointing to the historical durability and structured nature of class inequality.

## India's New Middle Class: A Theoretical and Comparative Perspective

The middle class has always been a category that defies definition. In the Indian context, the particularities of India's developmental trajectory and the sheer heterogeneity of cultural and social formations make the middle class an even more elusive object of analysis. Yet no class has been more central to India's fortunes than the middle class, and any understanding of the post-liberalization period calls for coming to terms with how this class is being transformed even as it is being preserved. Conventional class categories that posit a relatively unmediated relation between structural position and politics, between economic interests and ideology, are clearly inadequate to the task. What is required instead is a set of class analytics that give greater attention to the actual mechanisms through which structure and agency are linked. This set of analytics must in particular shed light on three problematics. First, rather than impute political and social forms from an economic position, it is essential to explain how the economic and political interests of the NMC have in fact been aligned. Second, because classes are forged rather than given, we can only speak of a class as a historical agent if we can demonstrate that for all its diversity of material and social interests the NMC has some political cohesion. Third, and directly following this last point, it is necessary to explain the actual practices through which this class differentiates itself from other classes and through which its internal fractions are defined.

Both structurally and historically, the middle class occupies an intermediary position that has discomfited conventional class analysis. Because it does not occupy either of the categorical and binary structural positions of the bourgeoisie or the working class (productive assets vs. no productive assets) analysts have assigned the middle class a "contradictory class location"[12] and emphasized the liminal and contingent nature of its interests. With the understanding that class boundaries are constructed and contested, we would broadly identify the middle class as the class of people whose economic opportunities are not derived primarily from property (the bourgeoisie) but rather from other power-conferring resources such as organizational authority or possession of scarce occupational skills. In contrast to the working class whose labor is reduced to the commodity form, the segments of the middle class who earn a wage or a salary have skills that are specific to their class position (and not as such readily accessible to the working class) and have the capacity to reproduce the relative scarcity of those skills either by securing institutional sanction (legal recognition of credentials and administered returns to scare skills) or otherwise hoarding the skill through social networks and gatekeeping. Given the centrality of cultural and educational capital to the middle class, its fortunes are very much dependent on the outcome of what Bourdieu calls classification struggles.[13] The petty bourgeoisie, that is, small property owners (including independent farmers) and merchants, do not fit this definition neatly. However, since their property is rarely sufficient to provide material support for the next generation, the class practices of the petty bourgeoisie often mimic those of the middle class proper. More specifically, precisely because this fraction has some economic capital, it is in a position to acquire educational and cultural capital.

Though it is not our purpose to map the complexities of the middle class, it is useful to delineate three basic strata within the Indian middle class. The dominant fraction consists of those with advanced professional credentials or accumulated cultural capital who occupy positions of recognized authority in various fields and organizations and whose interests are closely aligned with the bourgeoisie. The petty bourgeoisie is a middle category enjoying some material independence, but nonetheless aspiring to dominant fraction status and thus most often engaged in emulating the practices of the dominant fraction. This fraction includes small business owners, merchants, and rich farmers. The third, and the most numerous, are the subordinate middle class fraction of salaried workers who have some educational capital, but do not occupy positions of significant authority over other workers. This fraction includes middle- and lower-level employees that include public and private sector clerical staff and office workers, and various low-authority professions such as teachers and nurses.

The NMC is not "new" in terms of its social composition (that is, new entrants to the middle class). Rather its newness is characterized by the ways in which this fraction has sought to redefine middle class identity through the language of liberalization. This dominant fraction presents itself as the social group that embodies the benefits and virtues of liberalization. This process is most visible in new consumption practices and public discourses in the English-speaking media (for instance, most starkly evident in a growing public assertiveness and debate on the nature of the Indian middle class).[14] The self-assertion of this dominant fraction interacts in complex ways with the other middle class fractions and the broader social differentiation that actually characterizes the Indian middle classes. At one level, the cultural and social barriers between the subordinate and the dominant fraction are significant, and are aggressively enforced by the dominant fraction. At another level, this NMC identity also becomes a standard against which the aspirations of other fractions of the middle classes are measured. In this respect, to treat the ambiguity of the term "middle class" as a mere definitional problem for scholarly analysis would be to miss the productive political significance that this ambiguity holds for the middle classes. Such ambiguities allow the NMC, as bearer of the liberal ethos of opportunity and mobility, to hold out the promise of inclusion to other aspiring social segments even as it reconstitutes the subtle hierarchies and exclusions that anchor its class position. Thus while NMC identity is shaped by a fairly narrow segment of the middle classes, the implications of this identity are much broader. Insofar as the dominant fraction plays the leading ideological role in the politics of hegemony, most of this article focuses on the agency of this fraction.

From a historical perspective, to understand the politics of India's NMC — and specifically to explore the affinities between market liberalism and sociopolitical illiberalism that this social group represents — we have to begin, as Corbridge and Harriss do, by examining the crisis of the Nehruvian modernist project.[15] The ruling bloc represented by the Congress substituted a passive revolution for a classic bourgeois revolution.[16] In the absence of a hegemonic bourgeoisie that could go it alone, planning and incremental reforms replaced a full-blown assault on the old dominant classes and a thorough transformation of property relations. This placed the dominant fraction of the middle class, which had already accumulated significant educational and cultural capital in the colonial period, in a strategic position. As is often the case in peripheral economies, the middle class came to play an inordinately large and influential role given the functional requirements of extended state management (both in terms of state-directed industrialization and social reform) and the heightened political-ideological tasks of securing legitimacy in a socially diverse and fragmented liberal electoral democracy. Among others, Kaviraj and Bardhan concluded that the Nehruvian middle class (the "bureaucratic-managerial-intellectual" elite for Kothari and the "professional class" for Bardhan) played a central, distinct, and self-expanding role in the dominant class coalition of the Nehru period.[17]

From this pivotal role, the middle class developed distinctive political claims that elevated their class interests to the universal interest and laid claim to a leading role within the ruling hegemonic bloc within the newly founded Indian nation. Drawing on its historical leadership during the nationalist movement in the nineteenth and early twentieth centuries, the middle class claimed for itself the twin pillars of Nehruvian legitimation — secular nationalism and techno-

A gated community in Bardoligam, India, for village landowners. "No class has been more central to India's fortunes than the middle class and any understanding of the post-liberalization period calls for coming to terms with how this class is being transformed even as it is being preserved." (Courtesy: Jan Breman, *The Poverty Regime in Village India*, Oxford University Press, 2007)

cratic management. With its emphasis on rationality, meritocracy, and progress, the ideological project had hegemonic pretensions in Gramsci's sense that it sought to construct "an organic passage from the other classes into their own, i.e., to enlarge their class sphere 'technically' and ideologically," in contrast to the conception of "a closed caste" that marks traditional ruling classes.[18] However, though this ideological project was successful in terms of nation building, the Nehruvian ruling bloc never successfully consolidated hegemonic power on three counts. First, even as its organic intellectuals forged a coherent ruling ideology of constitutionalism, high modernism, and developmentalism, it could not build and sustain a lasting material compact with subordinate classes. Patronage was substituted for redistribution, labor incorporation was limited to a small segment of the working class, and agrarian reform — with notable regional exceptions — was never fully carried through. Second, the imperatives of managing an unruly dominant class coalition precluded precisely the economic-transformative projects — and most notably the disciplining of capital — that would have created the material base for hegemony. Indeed, as the dominant proprietary class whose specific capitals — organizational authority and credentials — depended directly on the state, the middle class was centrally complicit in fueling — and as Bardhan emphasizes, managing — the conflictive rent-seeking interests that inhibited capitalist transformation.[19] Third, and most critical to understanding the politics of the NMC, the very political logic of the passive revolution — to contain social conflict — proved impossible in the context of electoral democracy.[20]

The effects and failures of the developmental state and the competitive logic of mobilization eventually triggered new social claims from below, and in turn new state responses. If the Nehruvian state failed in its transformative projective, its interventions nonetheless had molecular effects that with time have eaten away at dominant-landed caste orders.[21] Not only did the grip of local elites weaken, but new political entrepreneurs emerged both from outside the middle class as well as from new aspirants and entrants to middle class status from subordinated caste groups. These political entrepreneurs mobilized a range of subordinate groups.[22] The Congress-dominated state that followed the Nehruvian period oscillated between attempts at incorporating these groups into rent-seeking politics (the politics of "votebanks" in the language of Indian politics), on the one hand, and exclusionary measures that catered to dominant upper caste middle class fractions, on the other. The most extreme examples of the latter dynamics of exclusion was Indira Gandhi's Emergency, which received, at least initially, widespread support from the middle class.[23] In fact, many of the contemporary NMC practices that attempt to produce an exclusionary civic culture cleansed of the urban poor (a point we turn to below) were prefigured in Sanjay Gandhi's use of authoritarian state practices to cleanse squatter settlements through forced demolitions.

These failures, however, should not detract from our central point. The middle class not only occupied a key functional position in the ruling bloc, but it has also played a decisive ideological role. Thus, if in economic terms the middle class pursued its narrow self-interest through rent-seeking, in ideological and political terms the middle class claimed to represent the national interest as the visible agents of the Nehruvian ideology of developmentalism.[24] Our analysis seeks to further develop an understanding of the broader political implications that this middle class "assertion without consolidation" of hegemony holds for an understanding of democratic politics in India. This role has, we argue, both continued and been transformed with the rise of a NMC identity in the post-liberalization period.

The continuity lies in the intermediary role of the middle class and the specific logic of its class practices. First, as Satish Deshpande has argued, "the middle class is the class that *articulates* the hegemony of the ruling bloc."[25] Second, as we show in the next section, the middle class continues to secure its position through the strategic deployment of social and cultural capital. The change lies in the scope and the logic of the hegemonic project. The focal point of middle class structural power (especially the dominant fraction) has shifted not only from the state to the market, but also from playing an auxiliary role in the market to playing a leading role. India is unique in the periphery in having integrated itself into the global economy through global sourcing of services.[26] With the rapid rise of the information economy and the shift in the valorization process of capital from production to innovation, design, branding, coordination, and other knowledge-intensive functions, a pattern clearly reflected in the service-intensive composition of growth in the Indian economy, the dominant fraction of the middle class occupies a strategic position in India's new economy. This shift in the material base of the economy (which affects both the bourgeoisie and the NMC) coupled with the rapid realignment of organized political forces over the past two decades, has given rise to an entirely new infrastructure and discourse of hegemony. With the proliferation of satellite television and the expansion of the advertising industry, the media have come to play a much more prominent role in shaping identities. Television and advertising images have produced an NMC identity that is associated with consumption practices of commodities made available through market liberalization. These images differ significantly from earlier decades in the Nehruvian period (particularly given the state control of the television in this period) when the scope of television and advertising was much narrower and public images were associated more with state advertising campaigns for policies such as family planning.

The political project of the NMC represents an opportune alliance of market-oriented commercial and professional interests eager to exploit new market opportunities and socially conservative elements protecting a range of status privileges. The later element clearly corresponds to the dominant fraction, while the former roughly aligns with the petty bourgeoisie and the subordinate fraction, two fractions eager to preserve and leverage the social and cultural advantages they hold over subordinate groups. These fractions most clearly started to merge politically in the reaction to Mandal as upper caste groups came together to oppose extending reservations to OBCS (Other Backward Castes).[27] There have been of course significant regional variations,[28] but by the early nineties a new alignment of middle class fractions had clearly emerged. Yogendra Yadev and his colleagues summarized this logic in their analysis of poll data from the 1999 13th Lok Sabha election. Noting that the BJP represented the formation of a new social bloc, they commented:

> The new social bloc is formed by the convergence of traditional caste-community differences and class distinctions. It may be an exaggeration to say that the BJP represents the rebellion of the elite, but it is nevertheless true that its rise to political power has been accompanied by the emergence of a new social group that is defined by an overlap of social and economic privileges.[29]

Indeed, this reflects a central trait of the middle class. Since its power does not derive primarily from property but rather from education and cultural capital, it is particularly dependent on the need to protect status privileges. These dynamics have contributed to the intersection between middle class politics and the agenda of Hindutva.

The middle class' flirtation with Hindu nationalism has a long political trajectory reaching as far back as Hindu revivalist movements during the colonial period to the more recent — but critical — formation of the Vishva Hindu Parishad (VHP). As others have argued, the Sangh Parivar's carefully constructed Hindutva ideology is symptomatic of middle class conservatism.[30] This conservatism is not an essential quality, but rather a relational and contingent one. The embrace of Hindu nationalism most clearly represents a defensive response to the growing independence and assertiveness of lower classes that began with the decline of the Congress's electoral dominance. Long contained and subdued within the Congress Party's passive revolution, the second democratic upsurge has mobilized new claimants to modernity and new modes of claim making. In response, the Congress resorted to periodic strategies of appeasing Hindu nationalist sentiment and played a role in the early dynamics of the Hindu nationalist movement in the 1980s. In both its timing and normative substance (family, order, hierarchy) the rise of Hindu nationalism is also quite clearly a response to the rapid socioeconomic change that has accompanied the transition from state developmentalism to liberalization. Indeed, when viewed comparatively the Indian case appears to replicate a pattern familiar to comparativists — social and economic disruption feeds directly into the traditional sources of middle class conservatism: preoccupation with cultural purity, order, stability, and discipline, inflected most notably by status anxieties.

Comparative political scientists and sociologists have long acknowledged the critical political role that middle classes play in great transformations. If Eric Wright can place the middle class in a contradictory class location, we argue that its historical role is inherently contradictory. Historically, middle classes have been notoriously fickle vis-à-vis democracy. If middle classes helped usher in formal democracy, rejecting the status privileges of pre-democratic orders, they have also drawn the line at empowering those that would threaten their own privileges. And as Polanyi has emphasized, under certain historical conditions, market liberalism and political illiberalism find each other, typically through the agency of the middle class. In his magisterial comparative study of interwar Europe, Gregory Luebbert provides a configurational picture of middle class politics.[31] Luebbert explains the liberal, social democratic, and fascist trajectories of the period by linking each to a specific class configuration defined in terms of both a general balance of class forces and the degree of organizational coherency of different classes. The key trigger in all cases is the entry of the masses into politics with the expansion of universal suffrage and the labor movement. Luebbert shows that where middle class internal consolidation occurred at an early state (England, France, and Switzerland), the middle class was able to preempt more autonomous and militant forms of working class organization that emerged elsewhere in Europe by making selective concessions to labor. The resulting ***liberal hegemony*** allowed for a strengthening of democracy and capitalism, but at the expense of a more assertive and independent working class. On the other hand, when modernizing, market-oriented middle classes were internally divided, the response to a rising working class was an opportunistic alliance with conservative elements, be it the Roman Catholic Church or the family peasantry (Italy, Germany, and Spain). This alliance of town and country, one might add, was made possible by the success with which urban-based middle classes were able to nurture mass bases of support by tapping into paternalistic, hierarchical, and militarist traditions and social structures.[32] Latin Americanists have painted a similar picture of middle class reaction. When corporatist structures proved inadequate to the task of containing the working class, the bourgeoisie, with significant support from urban middle classes, restricted or simply dismantled democratic institutions. Diane Davis has recently provided a new perspective on how we understand middle class support for authoritarian growth regimes by showing how the South Korean developmental state was rooted in an alliance between technocratic elites and the middle class, including the rural middle class.[33]

For all the complexity of these configurations, a few points can be distilled. First, as the key intermediate class of modern capitalism, the middle class is pivotal to political outcomes and can support reaction or revolution. To paraphrase Brecht, it's not the working class, but the middle class that is radical. Second, depending on the conjuncture, a well-formed middle class can coordinate its interest with subordinate classes as in cases of liberal hegemony, or it can side with reaction. The later response is crucially conditioned by the internal cohesion of the middle class and by what alliances it can make. In this conjunctural moment, politics and ideology take center stage, and any analysis must take note not only of the organizational forms of middle class politics (such as its control of civil society, and of political parties) but also of the specific historical forms, social identities, and ideas that middle class politics can seize upon.

In contrast to the cases of authoritarian (or democratizing) states in Latin America and interwar Europe, India represents a stable liberal democracy. An analysis of middle class politics in India nonetheless helps highlight the effects that a conjunctural reconfiguration of class forces has on the substantive nature of democracy. In the Nehruvian period, the middle classes cast themselves through the mantle of the nationalist movement and as the leaders of state-led developmentalism. In the current period of market liberalization, the dominant fraction has faced new challenges in producing a unified identity for both the middle classes and for the nation. The complexities and crosscutting pressures of political allegiances split by caste, religion, and class has called forth a NMC politics, and most notably a new disposition toward democratic institutions. If Indian democracy has assuredly crossed an irreversible threshold of consolidation (in Linz and Stepan, electoral democracy is "the only game in town"[34]) NMC politics today are fundamentally reshaping and restricting democratic practices and norms.

We argue that the politics of the NMC has taken an illiberal turn not because the middle classes are essentially reactionary or drawn toward Hindu nationalism. Rather Hindutva provided a mechanism for the NMC to incorporate the subordinated middle class fractions within a unified nationalist project. Specifically, the cultural politics of Hindutva provided a unifying political frame that did not disrupt the dominant NMC interests in the benefits of liberalization or its interests in reproducing existing hierarchies such as caste and language. While Hindutva has intersected with the political imperatives of the NMC, *both* religious nationalist and secular forms of illiberalism have enabled the NMC to manage its paradoxical need to produce order and unity amongst its fractions, on the one hand, while preserving its dominance through the reproduction of hierarchy and exclusion, on the other. The rise of the Hindutva movement and the crisis of the Nehruvian project provided a political opportunity for the NMC to reassert itself at a time when the middle classes increasingly began to view the Congress as a party that had been seized by subordinated groups such as the OBCS and Muslims.[35]

## Political Illiberalism and the New Middle Class

The forging of the NMC represents a reworking of the role of the middle class and the ideology it articulates for the ruling hegemonic bloc. The project is both transformative and grounded. The transformative element elevates the middle class as the carrier of India's modernizing aspirations. It is the project of globalization, technological mastery, competitiveness, and striving, and it is manifested in the rhetoric of newness. But such a project falls short on two counts. First, it has only a limited capacity for forging unity within the middle class. Only some segments of the middle class have fully benefited from globalization and the lower segments of the middle class — the subordinate fraction — find themselves in a much more precarious position, including those in the public sector whose interests are directly threatened by liberalization.[36] It is thus not surprising that local strategies of groups such as the Shiv Sena and the Rashtriya Swayamsevak Sangh (RSS) family organizations have often successfully tapped lower middle class frustrations particularly when it comes to unemployment. To take just one example, the recent Hindutva agenda of the Shiv Sena should not obscure the fact that the Sena's initial rise to power was based on anti-migrant (South Indian) sentiments of unemployed lower middle classes in Maharashtra. Similar "sons of soil" movements have emerged in other regions.[37] Second, in a country of India's inequality and diversity such a transformative project necessarily fails the hegemonic test of eliciting consent from below. The BJP appears to have maximized its electoral support at a quarter of the population. Pragmatically then, the middle class articulates hegemony — that is, tries to extend support beyond its dominant fraction — through a more culturally grounded ideology that takes the general form of a nationalist-organicist ideology. This is characterized first and foremost by the construction of an organic whole — created through juxtapositions to demonized others — and asserted through an essentialized cultural unity that misrecognizes internal differences of class and other social cleavages.

At first view, Hindutva and liberalization would seem to be odd bedfellows. Yet as we have seen, the marriage of a conservative ideology with the market is the historical norm when a liberal hegemonic project is foreclosed. The Indian middle class is itself enormously diverse, and under the impetus of accelerated globalized consumption, subject to increasing fragmentation. Indeed, survey findings show that white-collar workers and BJP supporters have mixed views of liberalization (in no small part because large swaths of the middle class remain dependent on state employment or subsidies) and yet as Sridharan notes still support the BJP because of "class identification and aspiration."[38] The consumer sovereignty so often portrayed as the marker of the middle class rests on a social logic that reproduces and intensifies social differentiation (for example, by associating consumption practices with differences of caste, class, and language) and has limited socially integrative capacity. Hence the attraction of an essentialized culture that identifies common roots in traditional and familiar structures of family, community, and religiosity. [39] This construction of middle class identity serves a dual purpose: even as it forges a cohesive middle class identity rooted in a singular identity, it simultaneously denies the salience of caste/class/communal cleavages and the social reality of pervasive inequality.[40]

The intersection between middle class politics and this particular form of political illiberalism can been seen in the concrete practices of the Hindutva movement. Here the Sangh Parivar has played a critical role in systematizing, packaging, and diffusing the new identity and the boundaries of exclusion. On the one hand, the standardization and centralization of the many "small traditions" of a plural Hinduism into a sanctioned, authorized narrative of a single Great Tradition of Hinduism has been the work of the VHP. On the other hand, against liberalism, organicism secures a cultural core by denouncing pluralization as a form of vulgarization. Specifically the edification of Hinduness and its association with education, self-discipline, and moral rectitude is portrayed as threatened, and indeed polluted, by the encroachment of Muslims and untouchables on the public domain.[41] Hindutva becomes then not only an act of unification, but also one of purification in response to the plebianization of culture, space, and politics of the second upsurge.[42] And it is precisely through this kind of ideological production of difference that a class can be imagined: "an immediate adherence, at the deepest level of the habitus, to the tastes and distastes, sympathies and aversions, fantasies and phobias which, more than declared opinions, forge the unconscious unity of a class."[43] The different fractions of the middle class are thus drawn together through juxtapositions to others and new imagineries of a shared civilization that reaffirm core cultural values. Such practices have been most acutely represented by new visual practices such as the screening of television productions like the Ramayana and by strong Hindu nationalist discourses surrounding India's successful nuclear tests.[44] Finally, the selective appropriation of global culture — technology and science, but not Western values or tastes, "computer chips not potato chips" — glorifies the universal significance and modernity of Indian culture while preserving its essential heritage. The seemingly contradictory impulses of exclusionary nationalism and globalization (from Ram Rajya to "India Shining") are reconciled by affirming the essential and inviolate character of Indian civilization. This fusing of core values and progress provides a basis for integration in a rapidly changing world and provides comfort and even a rallying point to conservative lower middle classes.

The marriage of market liberalism and political illiberalism that characterizes NMC politics is not limited to the politics of Hindutva — it also takes the form of an antipolitics. This form of antipolitics constitutes a form of social illiberalism as it allows a naturalization of "the market" to enable the reproduction of various forms of socioeconomic inequality. The rise of market liberalism, as Polanyi showed, is marked by the liberal myth of the spontaneous and self-regulating market.[45] In India, the English-language media, market research firms, iconized businessmen and pro-liberalization politicians[46] have all actively produced, per Bourdieu, neoliberalism as *doxa*, "as an economic and political orthodoxy so universally imposed and unanimously accepted that it seems beyond the reach of discussion and contestation."[47] Liberalization is routinely presented as a natural, apolitical process of unleashing the power of the market and diminishing the role of the state. This doxa in turn construes all forms of distributive politics as not only inimical to the efficiency of the market, but as venal and self-interested. In an economy where 93 percent of the labor force is in the unorganized sector, the business press and multilaterals routinely denounce unions and labor laws for overprotecting workers. Meanwhile, the NMC supports privatization of education despite the fact the large segments of the middle classes depend on public education (state funded higher education has been a significant support of the middle classes) and the fact that primary and secondary school education has lagged behind in quality and access for most of the postindependence period.[48] And at a time when the World Bank recently found that 47 percent of Indian children are underweight, the public food distribution system has been rolled back.[49] The breathless abandon with which the English-language media trumpets India's growth is accompanied by increasing disdain for the role of the state and politics and a high modernist impulse (fed by multilaterals) to insulate necessary social and economic policy in the hands of technocrats (i.e., economists) far from the messy world of politics. This form of antipolitics has had significant implications for the substantive workings of democratic politics. As new actors (from previously subordinated groups such as the lower castes) have entered political society and claimed the unredeemed normative claims of a constitutional democracy (e.g., equality of treatment, basic rights), the middle class has increasingly debased politics and the new lower class/caste politicians as dirty, dishonest, corrupt, criminal, and vulgar.

While, the BJP electoral defeat in 2004 clearly signals the limits of the Hindutva hegemonic project, there have nevertheless been important shifts in national political culture and in the dynamics of democratic practice. While much of the commentary on the BJP has focused on the electoral arena, Hindutva is first and foremost a social movement operating in the interstices of civil society, and here its effects remain profound.[50] The Sangh Parivar has sponsored or captured a vast array of organizations including schools, women's self-help groups, cooperatives, labor unions, and neighborhood associations. This has not only lead to the communalization of civil society, but also to new forms of clientelism and the reaffirmation of patriarchal authority and caste hierarchies.

This fragmentation and verticalization of associational life strikes at the heart of the pluralism and associational autonomy that anchor the normative ideal of democratic life. We are reminded once again that much as associational life can promote horizontal ties, it can also become the conduit through which reactionary elites or authoritarian regimes mobilize support. The effects of the communalization of civil society have been profound. Interpreting polling data collected by Center for the Study of Developing Societies (CSDS) during the 2004 election, Datar notes that even as pundits were interpreting the election as a vote for secular politics, the data underscored how much "public debate and opinion has undergone a change in the last decade or so. There has been a shifting of the middle ground of the debate in favour of majoritarian sentiments."[51] Datar goes on to report that "more people had heard about the Godhra incident than about the massacres that followed."[52] And the survey data also revealed that near two thirds majorities believe that each community should have its own family law (66 percent), that intercommunity marriage should be banned (63 percent), and that there should be a ban on religious conversions (65 percent).

## The New Middle Class and the Durability of Caste

While we have analyzed the intersections between middle class politics and the Hindutva movement, the NMC is not reducible to the politics of Hindutva. The politics of NMC illiberalism is also characterized by the production and reproduction of social hierarchies and distinctions that are produced through everyday micro-level practices.

We draw here on Bourdieu's analysis of how class structures are constantly reproduced through an "economy of practices."[53] Our purpose is not to provide a comprehensive analysis of the logic of class practices in India, but rather to provide some illustrations on how a focus on class practices brings back the critical insights of class analysis in a context where class formation remains in flux and where the traditional anchors of class analysis — property and the wage labor form — are not nearly as institutionalized an in advanced capitalist societies. This lack of institutionalization of social property relations — most obviously manifest is the sheer size of the informal sector (93 percent of the workforce) and the importance of informal networks in all factors markets — heightens the significance of the array of practices through which middle class fractions deploy their respective capitals.

Bourdieu's treatment of class is based on the three related concepts of the habitus, the field, and capital. Habitus is the intimate social context in which individuals acquire certain skills, demeanors, cultural competences, and dispositions. The field is the formal or informal setting (a profession, a discipline, a subsystem) in which different capitals are deployed and valorized. Economic, social, and cultural capital are specific assets that reside in individuals and classes. Class fractions accumulate, combine, and convert their capitals in order to maintain and/or improve their social position. The struggle to accumulate and deploy capitals is situational and relational — it takes place in a specific field that is governed by its own rules, laws, and recognized competencies, and in strategic orientation to other social groups.

A first observation is the manifest relevance of habitus in the Indian context to shaping life chances. Due to the continuing practice of caste endogamy, primary socialization in India still confers very significant intergenerational transfers of individual dispositions and competencies. By the same token, caste — which in every respect is simply one of the more manifest and codified expressions of habitus — remains a powerful source for reproducing difference. Just how deeply inscribed caste remains in the cultural competencies and dispositions of individuals is revealed by an experiment conducted by Hoff and Pandey:

> Children from different castes were asked to complete simple exercises, such as solving a maze, with real monetary incentives contingent on performance. The key result of the experiment is that low-caste children perform on par with high-caste children when their caste is not publicly

announced by the experimenter but significantly worse when it is made public.[54]

When understood as an expression of habitus, caste is no longer a premodern identity — an ascribed subjectivity destined to be swept aside by modernity — but rather a mechanism through which the continuous struggle between classes to reproduce their respective bundles of capital is organized. To borrow Charles Tilly's language, caste is a categorical inequality that helps to do the organizational work of reducing the transaction costs associated with the joining or deployment of resources.[55]

We emphasize the role of the habitus in shaping class practices for three reasons. First, it helps expose the static treatment that definitions of the NMC invariably produce. Whether the emphasis is on its new occupational structure or new patterns of consumption, a focus on these dependent variables masks the host of practices through which these outcomes are generated (and constantly reconfigured). Second, in contrast to conventional economic sociology that gives embeddedness of economic activity an almost benign (the social capital literature) or functional character ("the non-contractual elements of the contract") an *economy of practices* gives central place to power (and specifically the initial distribution of resources) and to the strategic actions through which the borders and contours of classes are maintained. Third, recognizing the role of habitus not only links cultural practices to material outcomes, but also explodes the tradition/modernity dichotomy. Even as the NMC vociferously celebrates the status equality of a market society, its many fractions actively deploy caste, community, and kinship to defend their social position.

A focus on the practices of producing and deploying cultural distinctions helps explain two observable paradoxes. The first and the clearest, is that even as liberalization unleashes the discourses of merit, ability, achievement, and mobility and the world is said to become flatter, the fractions of the NMC deploy their positional assets with ever greater assiduousness and the logic of class struggle relentlessly delivers inequality. Contrary to the "commonsense" middle class wisdom that caste matters less in urban areas, a careful analysis of the latest round of National Sample Survey Organization (NSSO) data found that caste inequalities are more pronounced in urban than in rural areas.[56] A second paradox points to the difference between classes. Much of the commentary on subordinate politics has focused on the explosion of identity-based mobilization and the increasing saliency of caste, leaving the impression that it is the subordinated groups that have brought caste back in. Narratives of a modernizing India portray everyday caste practices of exclusion and endogamy as relics of "backward areas," the poor and the uneducated. The first assertion of course glosses over the obvious caste agenda of the BJP; the second assertion raises an interesting empirical question: which class has the greater volume of distinctions to deploy and the greatest interest in leveraging those distinctions? As Bourdieu argues, if the tastes and preferences of the lower classes are a function of necessity, the tastes and preferences of the dominant class are carefully cultivated as sources of power.

## Class in Practice: Language, Caste, and Education

The concept of habitus draws attention to the intersecting forms of social capital and hierarchies that NMC power is built on. Historically produced forms of inequalities such as caste, language, and religion shape the resources, practices, and identities of the post-liberalization NMC in significant and enduring ways. Such historically produced social distinctions have provided particular social segments with varying forms of resources that they have attempted to use to preserve or raise their social standing. Historical continuities underline the significance of both temporality and agency in the reproduction of what seem like immutable social structures. If the habitus explains the stock resources that the NMC disposes of, the concept of field and of capitals explains the changes in the practices and strategies of the NMC. We examine this dynamic through the example of the way in which education serves as a central field for the conversion of resources of caste and language.

Human capital, rather than property, has long been the asset specific to India's middle class. The acquisition of an English education represented a primary means for entry to the colonial middle class, a new elite social group that was emerging distinct from and in an uneasy relationship both with traditional elites as well as with other less privileged segments of the middle classes, particularly the vernacular, lower middle classes. The very first claims made on modern education in colonial India were cast in terms of the universalist, rationalist, enlightenment discourse of the British state. However, as Chopra points out, "the educational field in colonial India was also shaped at the moment of its inception by a majoritarian — Hindu, specifically Brahmanical and upper-caste, middle class and above, educated, English-speaking — discourse...that clearly represented and privileged the interests of certain social groups, those who formed the vanguard of the nationalist movement."[57]

When India became independent, 55 percent of the members of the provisional parliament were urban professionals.[58] The conception of education that emerged in India was carefully aligned with middle class cultural capital. Higher education in the medium of English rather than primary education was emphasized, and the substantive focus on science and technology directly serviced the various segments of the middle class. The credentialization of the highest state offices (IAS) on the basis of broad, liberal, and classical education guaranteed that the state nobility would be upper caste. The myriad of cultural capital selection mechanisms that govern access to quality higher education in any class society are compounded by caste and the exclusivity of English. The educational field in India represents a prototypical instance of opportunity hoarding. Myron Weiner has carefully documented how the attitudes and dispositions of upper caste bureaucrats and politicians are directly responsible for India's failure to universalize quality education.[59] In the Nehruvian period, the tension between the egalitarian promise of democracy and the practices of educational inequality were in part resolved by simply equating middle class interest with the national interest. "[T]his [educational] privilege has been sanctioned and endorsed by the state in the *name of the nation* since scientific and technological education have been historically understood as leading to economic prosperity as well as social progress."[60] The rapid proliferation of private schools and in particular the mushrooming of a multitiered system of private engineering and medical colleges marks a new stage in the composition of the middle class.

The question of access to education, specifically English-language education, has continued to shape NMC formation in ways that are distinctive to post-liberalization India. The acquisition of English-language skills represents a critical means that various segments of the middle class use to preserve or gain access to NMC membership. Meanwhile, this link between language and middle class formation has been intensified by globalization as an expanding private sector and global processes of outsourcing have consolidated the importance of English language skills. Segments of the middle classes that have historically had access to English-language education have been poised to convert this capital into new forms of mobility in a liberalizing labor market.

Such NMC strategies of social capital accumulation and conversion have been further complicated as the politics of caste has intersected with language and education. The OBC challenge to upper caste dominance in higher education has triggered a classic conversion strategy.[61] As the grip of the middle class on tertiary public education has been loosened by the second democratic upsurge, and as liberalization has devalorized some fields (Indian Administrative Service (IAS; public enterprises) and valorized new fields (IT, marketing, financial services, commercial law) marginal educational advantage is now being secured in the market (including abroad), and the value of a public education is being downgraded. The growth of the service sector, and of specific niches within that sector that have accompanied liberalization, have changed the conversion rate between economic, cultural and educational capital.[62] The premium on technical education has increased, as has the premium on English, especially de-indigenized English. Domestically, middle class fractions mobilize all their social and cultural capital to secure access to the best schools, including schools abroad that carry a particularly high return on cultural capital.[63] They also, as Kapur has recently shown, have fully leveraged the mobility and fungibility of their capital assets to a historically unprecedented degree by migrating.[64]

The exclusivity of this strategy is clear: only 1.3 percent of surveyed households in India have immediate family abroad, yet one in four urban households reports global networks, and while rural areas have almost no ties abroad, the richest rural households are more likely to have ties abroad than poor rural households. Kapur also estimates that fully 70 percent of the Asian-Indian population in the United States is high caste. The compounding effects of capitals is finally reflected in Kapur's finding that those with tertiary education are 42 times more likely to migrate than those with primary education.[65]

If the global economy does indeed mark a shift from territoriality and place to networks and flows[66] and from production to branding,[67] then the differential distribution of cultural and social capital between classes in India portends a hardening of social exclusions. This trend is underlined by preliminary evidence of the continued salience of caste inequality in shaping NMC employment. While there has been a significant shift in the caste composition of the

Stall of a merchant near the dam of the Haji Ali mosque, Mumbai. The central role the new middle class plays in the politics of hegemony is marked by "middle class illiberalism" and most notably by a distancing from India's lower classes. (ILO/Crozet M. 2002)

middle classes,[68] caste continues to play a central role in shaping the NMC. The reliance of subordinated caste groups on state policies and state employment in gaining access to middle class membership has consolidated the upper caste composition of middle class private sector employment that is associated with the NMC.[69]

## The Local Politics of Democracy

A practice-oriented approach to the politics of the NMC exposes the extent to which politics in India is being reconstituted far beyond the realm of formal electoral politics. Studies of electoral politics in India point to a reduced role for the middle class in favor of subordinate social groups. Levels of middle class electoral participation in recent elections have been relatively low.[70] Meanwhile, the discursive and organizational field of politics has shifted dramatically with the upsurge of groups such as the OBCS.[71] However, the political significance of the NMC lies in a range of local political practices that operate below the surface of electoral politics. Consider the case of local conflicts over urban space. Metropolitan cities have witnessed growing political conflicts over public space. Local state governments, middle class organizations, and the urban poor have increasingly been battling over scarce urban space and corresponding models of urban development. The growth of civic organizations represents an emerging trend in which the NMC has begun to assert an autonomous form of agency as it has sought to defend its interests against groups such as hawkers (street vendors) and slumdwellers.

Local spatial practices are an instance of a broader range of strategies, associational activities, and everyday politics that shape middle class civic culture. Such practices exemplify a broader pattern in which civic life in contemporary India is reconstituted through the intensification of social exclusions and hierarchies. Examples of local spatial practices include the case of "beautification" projects undertaken by middle class civic organizations and local state officials in cities such as Mumbai, Bangalore, Delhi, and Calcutta and middle class citizen drives to remove street vendors from local neighborhoods and public city spaces.[72] In such cases, though middle class demands are made through representative claims of citizenship, they in effect represent class projects of spatial purification. For instance, middle class activity in the form of such "citizen's groups" and media representations of such issues have largely produced a construction of hawkers as a threat to the civic culture of the middle classes.[73] These discourses have focused on the "hawker menace" as a threat to a wide array of middle class interests, including inconvenience, sanitation, fears of social disorder, and the threat of declining real estate prices for residential areas marked for relocating hawkers. Such associational activity begins to provide specific organizational mechanisms for the political representation of the NMC. Several middle class and residents and citizens associations have put forth legal challenges to zoning plans in order to prevent hawkers being relocated to their neighborhoods. These practices represent a growing set of middle class demands on the state that are being exerted outside the realm of electoral politics and party politics.[74]

Such local examples reveal micro tactics that hint at much broader changes in how the NMC engages the state and its strategic response to the increasing political assertiveness of subaltern groups. Increased lower class electoral participation and independent political organization (most notably the rise of the Bahujan Samaj Party [BSP]) has translated into a much greater presence within the state itself. Representation of Scheduled Classes (SCs) in Class I category positions in the federal bureaucracy grew from 0.53 percent in 1953 to 10.77 percent in 2000.[75] As the social composition of the state has expanded, however, its powers have eroded. Not only has the boundary of allocative power shifted with liberalization from state to market, but the public sector has been downsized and the share of organized sector employment — that is, forms of employment within the purview of state protection and regulation — has fallen.

This hollowing of public authority has also been accompanied by what might be called a de-representation of politics, as the middle class has shifted its political practices from representative structures to making representations through civil society structures. Solomon and Bhuvaneshari make a similar argument for Bangalore (the poster child of the Earth-Is-Flat discourse). As land has become scarcer and more valued, municipal governance structures have been centralized and the mode of intermediation has shifted in favor of middle class interests. In what they describe as *governance via circuits*, "hi-tech firms lobby the State government levels and interact with powerful parastatal institutions to access land and high quality infrastructure. The richer groups in planned neighborhoods of South Bangalore press the government via senior bureaucrats to rid their streets of accumulated garbage.[76] In sum, social capital (in Bourdieu's sense of the term) displaces representation.

## Conclusion

This article has used a relational and comparative class-analytic approach to understand both the politics of India's NMC and the impact that this *class-in-practice* has had on the substantive nature of India's democracy. As is true of many developing economies, the middle class has played a critical role in Indian politics, most notably in forging the ideology of the dominant bloc. The fragmented nature of dominant classes in India and an arrested economic transformation that has failed to incorporate the lower classes (the passive revolution) has precluded a classic path of liberal hegemony. Instead, we have argued that patterns of middle class illiberalism have set significant limits on the workings of substantive democracy in India. We have focused in particular on the ways in which the politics of this class have both intersected with the politics of Hindu nationalism, on the one hand, and with ideological support for liberalization, on the other. If a great deal of attention has been devoted in the literature to analyzing how the rise and limits of Hindutva has played out in Indian politics, less attention has been paid to the ways in which Hindutva embodies the illiberal politics of the middle classes. This form of middle class reaction, situated at the confluence of accelerated marketization and rising lower class demands, represents a conjunctural pattern of comparative significance. We have also argued that these illiberal politics also take varying forms that rest on the reproduction of social inequalities such as language and caste in secular spaces such as education and urban space. Caste and religion are not essentialized or exceptional characteristics of India's middle classes — they are forms of inequality and differentiation that typify middle class politics and practices.

Our argument of course is not that the Indian middle class is intrinsically illiberal. Our purpose rather has been to analyze broad national patterns that emerge at particular historical conjunctures. However, as we have noted earlier, the regionalization of Indian politics means that there are important variations that depart from the configurational patterns we have outlined and present alternative possibilities for middle class politics. Having said this, the politics of India's NMC holds broader implications that transcend local variations. Viewed comparatively, an analysis of middle class illiberalism provides an important caution in the face of public discourses on the NMC both in India and globally that are rife with a rhetorical celebration of the cultural and economic ascendancy of this class. Given the crosscutting strains that high levels of political mobilization and demands on the state place on Indian democracy, the nature of middle class responses is a crucial force that will continue to shape the nature and direction of democratic politics. This force has resurfaced most recently, as proposed caste reservations in educational institutions have once again woven together middle class interests and anxieties, caste politics and inequalities, and (inadequate) state responses in a passionate debate on the substantive direction of Indian politics.[77] Regardless of the specific outcome at hand, the politics of the NMC is certain to influence this political context through a dynamic set of class politics that belie conventional narratives of Indian exceptionalism.

❑

# Notes

## *Introduction*

1. Deaton and Drèze 2002.
2. NSSO 2001.
3. Members of the People's Guerrilla Army, Peoples War Group (PWG), Maoists Communist Center (MCC), of India (Maoist), and the Communist Party of India (Marxist-Leninist) Janashakti are called ultra-leftists or Naxals, after the 1967 agrarian uprising in Naxalbari, West Bengal, which was sparked by landlord abuses of tribals. Singh's comments in GOI 2006.
4. Gupta 2004.
5. Kalyvas 2006, 211.
6. Elster 1985, 331.
7. Ibid., 325.
8. Wright 1997, 10.
9. Paul Krugman (2006, A19) noted: "So what's our bitter partisan divide really about? In two words: class warfare." For an argument that politics in the United States follows class coalitions that either fatten the rich or attempt mild distribution, see Phillips 1990.
10. Ost 2005, 19.
11. See Corbridge and Harriss 2000, 143–72, and passim; Herring and Mohan 2001.
12. On early analyses of how India's urban workers' movements reflected the strength of the nation's democracy, see Fisher 1961; Kennedy 1958. On early official agrarian class diagnosis for policy in India, see Herring and Edwards 1983, 17–49; 153–79; Herring 1983, 17–49; 153–79.
13. Tilly 1995.
14. Agarwala 2006
15. Chibber 2006. On the assault on science, see Nanda 2003. On the postmodern move in history in particular, see Richard Eaton's "(Re)imag(in)ing Otherness: A Postmortem for the Postmodern in India," in Eaton 2000; see also Hutnyk 2003.
16. Drèze and Sen 1996, Chap. 1; Harriss 2001.
17. Stiglitz 2002.
18. Bardhan 2001; Bardhan and Rudra 2003; Guha 2001. See also, Chibber 2003 on left failure politically.
19. Sombart 1976.
20. For example, see Tilly and Tarrow 2006, 57–67.
21. Even under the "Islamic socialist" regime of Zulfikar Ali Bhutto. See Candland 2007.
22. John 2005; Basu and Kohli 1998.
23. Gail Omvedt's *Reinventing revolution* (1993) is tellingly subtitled "New Social Movements and the Socialist Tradition in India." On material interests in ethnic politics, see Herring and Esman 2001; Chandra 2004.
24. Harriss 2006a.
25. Ibid.
26. Herring 2006.
27. Becker 1976.
28. Elster 1985.

29. Wade (1988) offers an example of how careful attention to material forces and rational decisions by farmers explain some interesting puzzles in water and land control in South India, to his satisfaction, controlling for cultural variables.
30. Herring 2003b.
31. See Elster 1985, 335–41 for a detailed discussion on this point. There is a parallel to gender studies: tables showing numbers of males and females in various occupations do not tell us much about gendered relationships on the job or in society generally.
32. An excellent treatment of the "qualitative-quantitative" divide, and synthetic methods, is Kanbur 2003.
33. Chibber 2006.
34. Wright 1997, 1.
35. On useful distinctions among these concepts, though somewhat different from the text, see Wright 1997, chaps. 1, 2, 10.
36. Fernandes and Heller 2006.
37. Wright 1997.
38. Scott (1985) comes very close to this position. Much of the resurrection and celebration of "local knowledge" likewise assumed inherently superior *Volk* information and wisdom.
39. See Teitelbaum 2006 for the worker's dilemma in choosing between well-institutionalized (perhaps co-opted) unions and very militant (perhaps counterproductive) unions.
40. Agarwala 2006.
41. Frank 2004.
42. Jon Elster (1985) produced the most explicit attempt to meld these traditions.
43. Roy, Herring, and Geisler 2007; Herring 1985. With the divergences in local knowledge of agriculture in north India documented by Akhil Gupta (1998), one sees the complexity of farmers' dilemmas in sorting means to ends in agriculture.
44. Herring 2006.
45. Gadgil and Guha (1995) propose an alternative class system for ecology, based on relation to nature and consumption. For a more complicated look at the interests of their "eco-system people," see Baviskar 1995. On state property, see Herring 2002.
46. For a powerful case for the importance of narratives of environmental change and policy in differentiating interests of individuals, see Dryzek 1997. As evidentiary rules differ across paradigms, closure is cognitively difficult.
47. Peluso 1992, 235–36.
48. Agarwala 2006.
49. Guha 1983, 33; see also Baviskar 2005.
50. Scott 1985.
51. India's first Backward Classes Commission, appointed in 1953, offered empirical evidence of the well-understood social reality: inferior position in the caste hierarchy was the main determinant of social and economic backwardness.
52. Dirks 2001, esp. 43-60, on "the ethnographic state."
53. The text uses "caste," as is commonly done, to mean *jati*. All etymological derivations based on the *Oxford English Dictionary*.
54. For example, Saradamoni 1980. For a treatment of political implications in Palakkad District, see Herring 2001b; more broadly, Herring 1988.
55. Greenblatt 2004, chap. 2.
56. Krishna 2003, 1071; Chandra 2004.
57. One comparative study that presents the quantitative case carefully but goes beyond numbers to social relations and political history is the excellent work by Jean Drèze and Amartya Sen (1997).
58. Frankel and Rao 1989; Kohli 1987; Harriss 2003.
59. Ramachandran 1996; Heller 1999, 51–117; Herring 1988; Herring Forthcoming a.
60. Kohli 1987.

61. John Harriss (2003) finds that a decisive defeat of the dominant class/caste social coalition has occurred in Kerala, Tamil Nadu, and West Bengal. In these states, the umbrella accommodationist Congress Party lost its dominance early. Congress hegemony was replaced by anti-Brahmin populism in Tamil Nadu, and by aggressive Left coalitions in Kerala (first) and West Bengal (more enduringly). Despite the differing organizing principles used, namely, caste in Tamil Nadu and class in Kerala and West Bengal, all three state parties initiated successful redistributive policies. See also Frankel and Rao 1989.
62. Ramachandran 1996, 180–200; Herring 1988. Mass energy in social movements was organized as the Congress Socialist Party [Communist Party after 1942], which eclipsed conservative Congress elements by sheer weight of numbers and activity.
63. This understanding is not restricted to the subcontinent. If one were to ask, for example, why there is no working-class party in the United States, and thus no social democracy of the European variety (Sombart 1976), one would have to consider ethnic tensions generated from waves of immigration, which created intense competition for jobs and deflected anger to class-fellows of different ethnicity. These dynamics help explain the comparative absence of class consciousness or class formation that make the United States anomalous among industrialized societies.
64. In the *New York Times* series entitled "Class Matters," mobility is connected to cultural capital in the United States. See Correspondents 2005.
65. Karl Polanyi is perhaps the most noted theorist to insist on the unnatural nature of the process of commodification of human beings as labor. Responses to insecurities and indignities of commoditized labor in market society — child labor, for example, or discarding of the elderly when their labor has no market value — drive his vision of social policy that hems in the market. See Polanyi 1957.
66. Wright 1997a.
67. Grusky and Sorensen 1998.
68. Portes 2000; Wright 1997b.
69. Bardhan 1984.
70. Fernandes and Heller 2006; Harriss 2006a.
71. Bourdieu and Jean-Claude Passeron first used the term in *Cultural Reproduction and Social Reproduction* in 1973. On the concept and applications to India, see Fernandes and Heller 2006.
72. Sinha 2005.
73. See Woo 1999, chap. 1; Herring and Mohan 2001.
74. Herring 1999.
75. Chibber puts capital in a more active political role vis-à-vis the state in 2003, especially chaps. 5, 6, and 8.
76. This section owes much to John Harriss, who bears no responsibility for its flaws.
77. Wolf 1969; Paige 1975.
78. For an excellent treatment of the interaction of ideology and structure in reference to this line of reasoning, see Harriss 1982.
79. Contesting theorists launched what became known as the "mode of production debate," mainly but not entirely through the *Economic and Political Weekly*. See Harriss 1980; Thorner 1982; Mukhia 1999; and Herring 1985.
80. Rudolph and Rudolph 1987.
81. Byres 1981; Harriss 1994; Harriss-White and Janakarajan 2004.
82. Bhaduri 1986; Harriss-White and Janakarajan 2004.
83. Gaiha 1996; Herring and Edwards 1983; Harriss-White and Janakarajan 2004, 195–295.
84. Mayer 1996; Harriss 2006b on the former, and Gidwani 2000 on the latter.
85. Krishna 2002; 2003.
86. See Brass 1995; Lindberg 1995; Omvedt 1993; and Teitelbaum Forthcoming.
87. Zoya Hasan (1998) has suggested, with regard to Uttar Pradesh, that this form of mobilization of class interests has been eclipsed by the politics of Hindutva.
88. Omvedt 2005; Herring 2005.

89. For the analytical perspective of a farmer organization leader, see Joshi 2001; on the politics of the organization itself, see Omvedt 2005.
90. Frankel and Rao 1989, 2; see also Mendelsohn 1993.
91. Varshney 1998; see also, Lindberg 1995; and essays in Brass 1995.
92. Patrick Heller (1999, 237–48) rightly emphasizes the resultant pressure on the Kerala communists to make their own class compromises, and he thinks the class compromise may produce economic development.
93. Beyond the scope of this essay, it must be said that such generalizations are weak on evidence, and the connection to transgenic technology imaginary. See Herring 2006. For a broad overview of the crisis and farmer suicides, see Vaidyanathan 2006. Some sectors are doing better than others, some years are better than others: 2002–03 was a hard year for agriculture; 2003–04 was a banner year, with growth in excess of 9 percent; 2004–05 was a year of weaker performance.
94. GOI 2004.
95. Marmot summarizes findings from multiple studies. He notes: "When traveling along the distance of nearly twelve miles on the Washington, D.C., Metro from downtown to Montgomery County, Maryland, life expectancy of the local population segment rises about a year and a half for each mile traveled. Poor black men at one end of the journey have a life expectancy of 57 years, and rich white men at the other end have a life expectancy of 76.7 years." Marmot finds more generally that "In rich countries, such as the United States,...persistently, those at the bottom of the socioeconomic scale have worse health than those above them in the hierarchy" (Marmot 2006, 1304).
96. See, for example, Chakrabarty 2000; Chandravarkar 1994; Chibber 2003.
97. That neoliberal magic can work for the poor if they can only be em-propertied by legal changes is developed in Soto 2000. On pressures from multilateral agencies in the form of aid conditionality, see Herring and Esman 2001; Stiglitz 2002.
98. Tilly 1995; Western 1995.
99. Agarwala 2006.
100. Ibid.
101. Teitelbaum 2006.
102. Rueschemeyer, Stephens, and Stephens 1992.
103. Herring and Mohan 2001; Fernandes and Heller 2006.
104. Harriss 2006a.
105. Ibid.
106. Herring 2005.
107. Candland 2007.
108. Fernandes and Heller 2006.
109. For an explanation of cleavages without class politics before the resurgence of the left, see Roberts 2002.
110. States within India matter in differentiating the life-chances of citizens. Consider Drèze and Sen 1996; Harriss 2003; Heller 1999, 7–10, and Sinha 2005. Class interests may well be served by patronage systems in which carrots are plucked from a common patch but rewards sustain both local elites' political power and some floor guarantees for the poorest of the poor. See Herring and Edwards 1983.
111. Herring 1981.
112. Candland 2007.

## *Chapter 1 – Chibber*

1. The lineal relation between Marxism and postcolonial theory is a major theme of Robert Young's now-standard work, *Postcolonialism: A Historical Introduction* (2001).
2. Cohen 1993; Wald 1987.
3. *Statistical Abstract of the United States, 1949,* Table 142.
4. Denning 1996.
5. See Isserman 1994; Drucker 1994.
6. Anderson 1976, Chap. 2.

7. *Historical Statistics of the United States, Colonial Times to 1970,* Series H, 689–99, 382–83; *Statistical Abstract of the United States, 2004–2005,* Table 261.
8. See Berger 1997; Chilcote 1997, 73-77.
9. Among these, see Byres 2001, 210–44, and his perceptive essay on Charan Singh 1990, 139–89.
10. An excellent retrospective is provided by Byres himself in "The Peasants Seminar of the University of London, 1972–1989: A Memoir." See Byres 2001, 343–88.
11. Frankel 1979.
12. A quick search of the major database of American PhD dissertations reveals that political science was the only discipline among four — history, anthropology, sociology, and political science — in which dissertations on India actually *decreased* in number from the 1960s to the 1970s. The method used was to do a search using the Keyword "India" on the University Microfilms database for each decade.
13. It is not clear to me why this might have been. Some have ventured to guess that with the deterioration of relations between Indira Gandhi and the United States after 1970, it became harder for U.S. scholars to secure visas for field work in India, especially on political topics. Perhaps, but this remainS for someone else to check.
14. See, inter alia, Kochanek 1968; Weiner 1962; Weiner 1968; Brass 1965; Hanson 1966; and Austin 1966.
15. Rudolph and Rudolph 1987.
16. Terry Eagleton's opening chapter of *The Illusions of Postmodernism* (1992) captures this dynamic brilliantly.
17. This has been discussed well in Wood 1986 and Callinicos 1990.
18. See Sumit Sarkar 1994; Chakrabarty 2002, 16–17.
19. See Said's "Foreward" to *Selected Subaltern Studies,* Guha and Spivak, eds. 1988.
20. See Chatterjee 1984; Chatterjee 1986; and Guha 1983.
21. See the trenchant critique of the cultural studies appropriation of Gramscian concents in Panitch 1985.
22. See Przeworski 1985 and Przeworski and Sprague 1986.
23. Burawoy 1979; Burawoy 1985; Wright 1985; Femia 1990. Perry Anderson's well-known essay, in my view, offered an interpretation that is broadly consistent with this view. See Anderson 1977.
24. This is slightly misleading, since Althusser had a distinctly bimodal legacy in Anglo-American Marxism. The dominant trend was for his followers to veer toward some kind of post-structuralism, and this is conventionally taken as his legacy. Prominent examples are Stuart Hall, Ernesto Laclau, and Chantal Mouffe, the intellectuals around the journal *Rethinking Marxism*, and others. But a subordinate trend, which was nonetheless quite productive, led to a kind of materialist structuralism. This was exemplified in theorists such as Ted Benton, Erik Wright, Roy Bhaskar, and the Critical Realist school. The latter has not been as closely identified with an Althusserian legacy, largely, I think, because they don't advertise themselves as such.
25. A good sampling of the Birmingham school can be had in Hall 1980, and Laclau and Mouffe 1985.
26. Indeed, the fate of Gramsci in South Asian studies, particularly in the Subalternist variant, is worthy of study in its own right. His shadow looms over the entire *ouvre,* and not only in its early phase. But it has required a massive reconfiguration of the basic elements of his theory. And what is most ironic is that those parts of his thought that have been transplanted with some fidelity — like the notion of a passive revolution — are the ones least defensible. I hope to have an argument to this effect available soon.
27. Chatterjee 2003; Chakrabarty 2000.
28. Inden 1976.
29. Inden 1990.
30. Inden 1986, 445.
31. I am grateful to Atul Kohli for stressing this point in response to a presentation that I made at Princeton University in May 2006.

32. No doubt, for some intellectuals, especially younger ones, the open chauvinism of Hindutva, and the sheer mendacity with which so much of the middle class attacked the Mandal Commission, served as a source of some radicalization. Indeed, there was an influx of new, younger activists into civil liberties and democratic rights groups around the country, specifically in reaction to the social chauvinism rippling across the culture. But it should be conceded that political energy in the 1990s emanated from the Right. And what radicalization there was, was not in the direction of class politics per se, but a more diffuse disgust at the thin edge of fascism beginning to bare its teeth in Indian politics.
33. Relative, I should stress, not absolute.
34. My colleague Craig Calhoun informs me that, in his tenure as president of the Social Science Research Council, he tried to organize a systematic collection of data on trends in area studies hirings, but met with very limited success.
35. See Dezalay and Garth 2002; Babb 2001; Amsden 1994, 87–125.

## *Chapter 2 – Teitelbaum*

1. Luebbert 1991; Rueschemeyer et al. 1992.
2. Galenson 1959; de Schweinitz 1959.
3. O'Donnell 1978.
4. Pencavel 1997.
5. Labor economists commonly use "voice function" to refer to the ability of unions to voice the concerns of workers.
6. Freeman and Medoff 1984; Aidt and Tzannatos 2002.
7. Murillo 2001.
8. Heller 1999.
9. According to Agarwala (2006), the Indian government officially recognized the informal sector as the primary source of future employment of all Indians and has set up an official committee to give recommendations on improving productivity in the informal sector.
10. Frankel 2005, 610.
11. Heller 1999; Weiner 1991.
12. Drèze and Sen 1995, 39.
13. Ramaswamy 1977, 8. See the quote at the beginning of this article.
14. Ibid.
15. Chibber 2003, chap. 5.
16. Section 10 (1) of the Industrial Disputes Act reads as follows: "Where the appropriate Government is of the opinion that any industrial dispute exists or is apprehended, it may at any time, by order in writing — (a) refer the dispute to a Board for promoting a settlement thereof; or (b) refer any matter appearing to be connected with or relevant to the dispute to a court for inquiry; or (c) refer the dispute or any matter appearing to be connected with, or relevant to, the dispute, if it relates to any matter specified in the Second Schedule, to a Labour Court for adjudication; or (d) refer the dispute or any matter appearing to be connected with, or relevant to, the dispute, whether it relates to any matter specified in the Second Schedule or the Third Schedule, to a Tribunal for adjudication" (Malhotra, 2004).
17. Chibber 2003, 125.
18. Rudolph and Rudolph 1987, chap. 10.
19. Kennedy 1966, 192.
20. Raman 1967, 171.
21. Ramaswamy 1997, 71. It should be noted that Ramaswamy's arguments regarding the strength of the union movement are more nuanced than those of most authors writing on the subject. Ramaswamy acknowledges a period of union strength following Independence, but believes this strength was the product of a closed economy. Ramaswamy predicts that economic liberalization will result in the complete unraveling of India's unions.
22. *Trade Unions in India*, Ministry of Labour, Government of India, various years.

23. Trade union statistics based on the 1970 returns were published in the 1972 volume of the *Yearbook*. There is typically a two- to three-year delay between the time the returns are submitted and the time the trade union statistics based on the returns are published.
24. Bihar, Kerala, and Rajasthan.
25. Andhra Pradesh, Assam, Bihar, Kerala, Rajasthan, and West Bengal.
26. Andhra Pradesh, Assam, Bihar, Himachal Pradesh, Jammu and Kashmir, Karnataka, Kerala, Madhya Pradesh, Punjab, Rajasthan, Tripura, Uttar Pradesh, West Bengal, Chandigarh, and Dehli.
27. These 87 companies are the unionized subset of companies randomly selected for in-depth interviews from a pool of 294 companies that participated in a telephone survey in these three states. The original sample was drawn from manufacturer's directories such as those published by the Confederation of Indian Industry (CII) and the Bombay Chamber of Commerce (BCC). For more details on the sources and selection of this sample, please consult the online data appendix at http://home.gwu.edu/~ejt.
28. The ILO calculates union density by taking the number of union members reported by the government as a percentage of the number of paid employees. In its *Union Stats 2002* publication, the last year for which this calculation was available was 1997, when it stood at 26.2 percent.
29. For an in-depth discussion, see Ramaswamy 1997, 26–32.
30. Ibid., 100.
31. Rudolph and Rudolph 1987, 282.
32. Two partial exceptions include Kennedy (1966) and Crouch (1966). Both authors view unions as dominated by party interests, but note benefits associated with this dominance. Kennedy argues that politically affiliated union leaders are less short-sighted than independent leaders. Crouch argues that parties compensate for a supposed union weakness in collective bargaining by giving voice to worker concerns in the political arena (Crouch 1966, 279–81).
33. Raman 1967, 136.
34. Crouch 1966, 282.
35. Myers 1958, 323.
36. Ramaswamy 1984, 25.
37. Raman 1967, 166. Or, more dramatically: "[I]n the struggle for the control of labor, the outside leaders fitted with political boots have trampled the very bed of grass that they purportedly set out to develop into a Garden of Eden, filled with many a luscious fruit traditionally forbidden for labor to eat" (171).
38. Rudolph and Rudolph 1978, 278.
39. Chatterji 1980, 193; Chibber 2003, 121.
40. Assuming a labor-friendly government, it seems likely that if the Ministry of Labour were to be biased in any direction, it would be in favor of unions.
41. Chatterji 1980, 194–95.
42. The jurisdiction of labor courts is narrower than that of industrial tribunals. The jurisdiction of labor courts is spelled out in the second schedule of the Industrial Disputes Act and includes the following: (1) the legality of an order given to an employee under the Industrial Employment and Standing Orders Act; (2) the application and interpretation of standing orders; (3) issues pertaining to the discharge, dismissal and reinstatement of individual workers; (4) the legality of withdrawing customary concessions or privileges; (5) the legality of a strike or lockout; and (6) all matters not explicitly under the jurisdiction of Industrial Tribunals as listed in schedule three of the Industrial Disputes Act. The jurisdiction of industrial tribunals, as spelled out in schedule three of the act include these: (1) wages; (2) compensatory allowances; (3) hours of work and rest intervals; (4) leave with wages and holiday pay; (5) bonuses, profit sharing, provident fund and gratuity allowances; (6) the length of shifts; (7) the classification of workers by grades; (8) rules governing the discipline and behavior of workers; (9) the "rationaliza-

tion" of work; (10) retrenchment and closure of establishments; and (11) all matters falling under the jurisdiction of labor courts.

43. Andhra Pradesh, Assam, Bihar, Gujarat, Haryana, Karnataka, Kerala, Madhya Pradesh, Maharashtra, Orissa, Punjab, Rajasthan, Tamil Nadu, Uttar Pradesh, and West Bengal. Together, these states account for 90 percent of India's total population (as measured by the 2001 census) and 95 percent of its total industrial output (as calculated from the *Annual Survey of Industries*).
44. Dispute volume is typically calculated as the number of worker-days lost per one thousand *nonagricultural employees*. However, India's large informal sector makes this statistic problematic because (a) it is difficult to measure the number of nonagricultural employees and (b) the large informal sector would artificially deflate dispute volume and make the statistic less comparable to volume statistics in other countries.
45. Data for state-level volume calculations come from the same sources as the all-India aggregate calculation. See the notes in Figure 1 for details.
46. For data on strike volumes in European countries through 1970, see Hibbs 1987, 55–57.
47. One potential counterargument to my interpretation of these data is that strike activity is actually a sign of union weakness. Seeing that labor is bound to win, the argument might go, rational employers will give in to the union's demand to avoid a strike when labor is strong, so that high dispute volume is correlated with union weakness rather than strength. This argument assumes that unions will not strike when employers cave in. In fact, unions have incentives to strike even when they are sure to win their demand. Specifically, a union can attract more members and enhance its reputation for toughness by going on a short, victorious strike. In turn, an expanding membership and a reputation for toughness help a union to achieve its central goals, namely, to monopolize labor markets and to serve as an effective "distributional coalition." Thus, unless unions are provided a set of extra incentives by employers or the state in exchange for a reduction in militancy (as they are in corporatist countries like Norway or Sweden), we would expect unions to strike more when they are strong (as they did in Nordic countries before they were incorporated). For a more detailed treatment of this argument, see Teitelbaum 2007 (forthcoming).
48. World Bank 2000, chap. 6; Sachs et al. 1999; Stern 2001.
49. See Malik 2005.
50. Boilers Act, 1923 (Indian); Contract Labour (Regulation and Abolition) Act, 1970; Employees' Provident Funds and [Miscellaneous Provisions] Act, 1952; Employees' State Insurance Act, 1948; Employers' Liability Act, 1938; Equal Remuneration Act, 1976; Factories Act, 1948; Fatal Accidents Act, 1855; Industrial Disputes Act, 1947; Industrial Employment (Standing Orders) Act, 1946; Maternity Benefit Act, 1961; Minimum Wages Act, 1948; Payment of Bonus Act, 1965; Payment of Gratuity Act, 1962; Payment of Wages Act, 1936; Personal Injuries (Compensation Insurance) Act, 1963; Personal Injuries (Emergency Provisions) Act, 1962; Public Liability Insurance Act, 1991; Trade Unions Act, 1926; Weekly Holidays Act, 1942; Workmen's Compensation Act, 1923.
51. Coal Mines Provident Fund and Miscellaneous Provisions Act, 1948; Coir Industry Act, 1953; Dock Workers (Regulation of Employment Act, 1948; Dock Workers (Safety, Health and Welfare) Act, 1986; Dock Workers (Regulation of Employment) (Inapplicability to Major Ports) Act, 1997; Iron Ore Mines, Manganese Ore Mines and Chrome Ore Mines Labour Welfare Cess Act, 1976; Iron Ore Mines, Manganese Ore Mines and Chrome Ore Mines Labour Welfare Fund Act, 1976; Limestone and Dolomite Mines Labour Welfare Fund Act, 1972; Mica Mines Labour Welfare Fund Act, 1946; Mines Act, 1952; The Motor Transport Workers Act, 1961; Plantations Labour Act, 1951.
52. All information regarding amendments to the Industrial Disputes Act comes from Malik 2005.

53. Negative employer perception does not necessarily mean that the regulations are in fact bad for growth. My only point here is that if employers have such a strong distaste for the legislation, it is unlikely that the legislation is biased in their favor. Burgess and Besley (2004) attempt an econometric demonstration of the negative effects of labor regulation on Indian growth rates. Their analysis, however, is plagued by a grossly oversimplified method of coding the regulation.
54. World Bank 2000, 150.
55. World Bank 1995, 2005.
56. Candland 2001.
57. Ibid., 78.
58. Ramaswamy 1977, 7–8.
59. Ibid., 7.
60. Ibid., 8.
61. A number of sociological studies employ survey methods, but focus primarily on identifying the characteristics of trade union elites and issues pertaining to trade union governance. For representative examples, see Bhargava 1995; Bhatt 1993; Dayal and Sharma 1976; Devi 1991; Hiremath 1990; Masihi 1985; Metha 1991; and Punekar 1967.
62. Ramaswamy's most recent work, *A Question of Balance* (1997), is a compilation of opinion pieces written for *Business India*. These pieces tend to be reproachful toward unions and sympathetic toward management. See, for example, "A Chastened Trade Unionism."
63. Ibid.
64. Crouch 1966, 282–83.
65. Interview, 5 August 2003.
66. Interview, 6 August 2003.
67. Ibid.
68. Crouch 1966, 283.

## Chapter 3 – Candland

1. The only cabinets to include pro-working class politicians were the 1973–1975 cabinet, which included Tariq Aziz, Mubashir Hasan, Miraj Khalid, and Miraj Mohammad Khan, and the 1999–2002 cabinet, which included Omar Asgar Khan. These were not representatives of workers' organizations but did defend workers' rights.
2. The figure is calculated from data provided by the International Labour Office's online database of labor statistics (Laborsta) and is available online at http:// laborsta.ilo.org/ (accessed on 6 August 2006). The value reported is for 2002 and is derived from Government of Pakistan 2006.
3. The figure is reported by the ILO's Laborsta online database of labor statistics: http://laborsta.ilo.org/ (accessed on 6 August 2006). The value reported is for 2000 and is derived from Government of India 2001.
4. See Perveen and Ali 1993 on barriers to women's participation in unions.
5. Khaniz Fatma, a Karachi based labor leader, is a noteworthy exception. See Akhtar 1992 on women's participation in factory work and unions in Karachi.
6. See Hashmi 1992.
7. See Herring 1979, 520–25 and Herring 1983 for a discussion of the applicability of the concept and practice of "feudalism" to Pakistan.
8. I thank Karamat Ali for the points made in this paragraph. Interviews with Karamat Ali, Karachi, 25 December 1999 and 31 December 1999.
9. For excellent discussions of how the postcolonial state undermined working class formation in Pakistan see Alavi 1973, 1983, and 1989.
10. I want to acknowledge here the generosity and insights of Khurshid Ahmed, Nabi Ahmed, Humaira Akhtar, Karamat Ali, Zulfikar Ali, Charles Amjad Ali, Usman Baloch, Riffat Hussein, the late Omar Asghar Khan, the late Saeed Pasha Lodhi, Farhat Perveen, Gul Rahman, and Muhammad Yaqub. Many of these workers and organizers I first met when participating in a national effort in 1992 to establish a Workers' Education Foundation in Pakistan.

11. The interviews involved Nabi Ahmad, Mukhtar Ahmed, Imdad Ali, Choudhry Rehmattullah Aslam, Mohammad Aslam, Ibne Ayub, Zaheer Akhtar Beedri, Jamal Boota, Rehmatullah Choudhry, Abu Saeed Enver, Anis Hashni, Rifat Hussain, Saeed Pasha Lodhi, Attaullah Khan, Mehrab Khan, Mohammad Nizar Khan, Qazi Mohammad, Amanullah Khan Niazi, Saleh Mohammad Hayat Pasha, Niazi, S. Zafar Rizwi, Sobiha Shakil, Mohammad Sharif, Mohammad Sulaiman, Mohammad Tahir, Abdul Wahid, Khwaja Mohammad Wasim, Mohammad Yamin, Ismail Yousef, Riaz Haider Zaidi, and Syed Ayub Ali Zaidi. I copied the newspaper clippings kindly made available to me by the Dawn Newspaper Group. For elaboration on observations made in this essay and a fuller comparative discussion of Indian working class organizations, see Candland 2007.
12. For details on these estimates and their sources, see ILO 1998. The estimate for India is for 1991. The estimate for Pakistan is for 1994.
13. Candland 2007.
14. For a comparative study of labor institutions' impact on privatization patterns in Bangladesh, India, Pakistan, and Sri Lanka, see Candland 2002. I discuss the implications of the absence of a legal mechanism for recognizing unions as collective bargaining agents in Candland 2001, 2002, and 2007.
15. Samad 1995.
16. See Waseem 2002.
17. Ali 1983 66, citing Shaheed 1979; Addleton 1992, 33, citing Government of Pakistan 1951, 2–3.
18. See Ali 1983, 139.
19. Ibid., 119.
20. See Jalal 1985.
21. In addition to arms and ammunition, the Act prohibits unions in the production of cement, edible oils, electrical communication and broadcasting equipment, electricity, electrical equipment or appliances, glass and ceramics, chemicals, machines and precision tools, gauges, heavy engineering equipment, petroleum and mineral oils, minerals, non-ferrous metals, paper, cardboard and pulp, pharmaceuticals, industrial alcohol, preserved and prepared foods, rubber, scientific and mathematical instruments, seafood, ships, lighters, sugar, leather goods, textiles, and tobacco.
22. Economically active population is from the ILO's Laborsta online database of labor statistics: http://laborsta.ilo.org/ (accessed 4 June 2006). Claimed union members, for 1999 in India and for 2000 in Pakistan, are from the Government of India, *Manpower Profile* and from Government of Pakistan, *Pakistan Statistic Yearbook*, supplied by ILO on 4 June 2006. Note that the figures here include agricultural workers, unlike the union and union membership density figures cited above.
23. Ali 1983, 117.
24. Ibid.
25. Ali 1984, 116.
26. Waterston 1963.
27. Lewis 1954 and Lewis 1955.
28. Ibid.
29. Haq 1963, 1–3.
30. See Rosen 1985, 48 and 62–66.
31. APCOL had controlled the labor movement in the 1950s but was largely irrelevant in the 1960s.
32. Noor Khan, interview, Karachi, 28 and 29 March 1995. The conference Noor Khan organized did not, however, represent shop-floor labor or Left activists, those who helped force the government to address labor demands in the first place.
33. I thank Karamat Ali for the points made in this paragraph. Karamat Ali, interviews, Karachi, 26 December 1999 and 31 December 1999.
34. Bhutto 1972, 9–12. Cited in ibid., 118.
35. *Dawn* 1973.
36. Shaheed 1983, 282.

37. On the police killings, see ibid., 283–84.
38. The position on outside instigators was reaffirmed in an interview with Rahimdad Khan, provincial chief of the Pakistan Peoples Party, Peshawar, 11 August 2006.
39. See Shahid 1983, 280–87 and Ali 2005.
40. Interview with Gul Rahman, president, Pakistan Workers Confederation, Peshawar, 12 August 2006.
41. Machiavelli 1903, 49–50.
42. Trimberger 1979. I thank Lois Wasserspring for discussions about military governments and workers' organizations in Latin America.
43. Cohen 1984.
44. Marx 1852.
45. Gardezi 1998 discusses the origins of the weakness of social sciences in Pakistan. Also see Zaidi 2002.
46. Estimates of the periods over which the military controlled the government in Pakistan vary. Mohammad Waseem figures that the military controlled the government except for seven years, from 1973 to 1977 and from 1997 to 1999. See Waseem 2002 on elected governments' subordinate role to the military through Pakistan's history.

## *Chapter 4 – Agarwala*

1. Hart 1973.
2. Weeks 1975; Mazumdar 1976; Sethuraman 1976; Bromley and Gerry 1979; Moser 1978; Peattie 1987.
3. Portes, Castells, and Benton 1989.
4. NSSO 2001.
5. Ahluwalia 2002; Gupta 2002; NCL 2002.
6. Kulshreshtha and Singh 1999.
7. NCL 2002, 1969.
8. Kundu and Sharma 2001; NCL 2002.
9. Harris and Todaro 1970.
10. Luxemburg 1951; Lenin 1939.
11. Portes and Hoffman 2003.
12. The 7 percent figure was first asserted by informal workers' movements attempting to increase their salience and is now cited in numerous scholarly articles and government documents (see Kundu and Sharma 2001). The 18 percent figure is calculated by the author using the $55^{th}$ Round NSS.
13. Portes and Hoffman 2003, 45.
14. Punekar 1948.
15. Fisher 1961; Park 1949; Kennedy 1958.
16. Mehta 1957; Morris 1955, 1960; Weiner 1962.
17. Rudolph and Rudolph 1987; Omvedt 1993; Bardhan 2001.
18. Ray 2000; Basu 1992; Lind 1997; Kamat 2002; Katzenstein 1989.
19. Chandra Forthcoming; Varshney 2002; Katzenstein, Kothari, and Mehta 2001.
20. For differing views in the effectiveness debate on new mass politics in India, see Frankel and Rao 1989; Heller 2000; Migdal, Kohli, and Shue 1994; Weiner 2001.
21. Roberts 2002; Sandbrook 2006; Cross 1998; Fernandez-Kelly and Shefner 2006.
22. Other arguments made earlier are: (1) that opportunistic union leaders have made labor organizations into authoritarian spaces that fight for monetary benefits, rather than democratically driven spaces of class ideology (Ramaswamy 1988), and (2) that class politics has never been strong in India, because unions mirror the competitive pluralism of Anglo-American interest groups, rather than the Continent's corporatist structures of collective bargaining (Rudolph and Rudolph 1987).
23. Berger and Piore 1989; Gugler 1991; Chowdhury 2003; Harriss-White 2003; Hyman 1992.
24. Marx 1906.
25. Geertz 1963; Bairoch 1973; Harris and Todaro 1970; Lewis 1954; Marx 1906.

26. Herring and Hart 1977.
27. Kundu and Sharma 2001; Oberai and Chadha 2001; Mahadevia 1998; Sundaram 2001; Unni 1999, 2000; Kulshreshtha and Singh 1999; Joshi 2000; TISS and YUVA 1998.
28. Carr, Chen, and Jhabvala 1996; Sanyal 1991; Sharma and Antony 2001; Chowdhury 2003.
29. The author calculated these figures using the NSS. They include only regular workers (in the case of formal workers) and regular and casual workers (in the case of informal workers). These figures change only marginally when self-employed own-account workers and employers are included (along with regular and casual workers).
30. *Bidi* is a local Indian cigarette made of a rolled leaf and roasted tobacco.
31. Construction workers comprise 8 percent of India's labor force, and bidi workers comprise 2 percent. Although employment is growing rapidly in both industries, the bidi industry is under strong pressure from domestic and international campaigns against smoking. To reduce costs, most of the bidi production has shifted to rural areas (to avoid municipal taxes and fees). Urban bidi production may be considered a "sunset" industry, while urban construction work is a "sunrise" industry.
32. GOI 1929. For an in-depth account of employers' use of informal labor in the textile industry during India's early industrial history, see Chandravarkar 1994.
33. Although bidi manufacturing is not mechanized, the workshops in which workers sat to roll the bidis were referred to as "factories."
34. GOI 1960.
35. Interview with Ram Ratnagar, 1 July 2003. Similar sentiments were expressed in Girija, Ramakrishnan, and Ramakrishnan 1988, 94.
36. GOI 1970.
37. GOI 1952.
38. Isaac, Franke, and Raghavan 1998.
39. Each of the two primary left-wing political parties in India has its own federation of trade unions. The Communist Party of India (CPI)'s federation is called, All India Trade Union Congress (AITUC), and the Communist Party of India-Marxist (CPI-M)'s federation is called Center for Indian Trade Unions (CITU). While unions affiliated to right-wing and center parties also existed, their strategies were less revolutionary, and they did not make major gains in the bidi or construction industries.
40. Interview with Sundar Navelkar, 4 August 2003.
41. In 1970, the Minimum Wages Act of 1948 was extended to include the construction industry. In 1972, the Contract Labor Regulation and Abolition Act was passed to hold principal employers and contractors responsible for providing casual labor with minimum wages and decent working conditions; this Act was to be applied directly to construction workers. By the early 1970s, almost all states had passed the 1966 Bidi Act. Samant 1998.
42. Vaid 1999.
43. GOI 1990; 1952; 1960; 1970; 1980.
44. The parallels between these recent movements among informal workers and earlier peasant movements and the Employment Guarantee Scheme should be noted. For more, see Herring and Hart 1977.
45. Interview, 27 May 2003.
46. I have detailed elsewhere the historical development of the welfare boards, which first began in 1934 for dock workers. The earlier boards, however, were designed for formally employed workers.
47. Interview with Manohar Lal, director general of Labour Welfare Organisation, 2 June 2003.
48. GOI 2002; Government, Tamil Nadu 2006.
49. GOI 2002.
50. Singh 2004; Pandhe 2002.
51. Interview, 31 March 2003.
52. Interview with Geeta Ramakrishnan, head of TNCWU, 9 July 2004.

53. While the Tamil acronym for this union is TKTPS, I will use the English translation for the sake of clarity.
54. Reporter 1999; Manchanda 1993; Reporter 1994.
55. Interviews with M. Rajaram, labor commissioner, Tamil Nadu (12 June 2004); Ashok Khot, labor secretary, Maharashtra (25 March 2003); and Mohand Dhotre, national welfare commissioner (7 May 2003).
56. Note on the same day, the government also enacted the Building and Other Construction Workers' Regulation of Employment and Conditions of Service Act, which catered to the requests of the Builders Association to apply minimal protections on work conditions.
57. Gopinath 1997.
58. Similar struggles were pursued by workers in coal and mica mines, docks, railway loading, sugar, and tea plantations.
59. Unlike the construction boards, the Bidi Board is controlled by the Central government, under the Directorate General of Labor Welfare (DGLW) in the Ministry of Labor. In addition to the Bidi Fund, the DGLW overseas four additional welfare funds: Mica Mines Labour Welfare Fund Act (1946), Limestone and Dolomite Mines Labour Welfare Fund Act (1972), Iron Ore, Manganese Ore and Chrome Ore Mines Labour Welfare Fund Act (1976), and Cine Workers Welfare Fund Act (1981). State governments are responsible for implementing these Acts.
60. Interviews with Ram Ratnagar, general secretary of the All India Bidi and Cigar Workers Federation, and Rajangam, general secretary of CITU Bidi Federation for Tamil Nadu.
61. Staff 2002.
62. GOI 1990.
63. Although the welfare boards were designed to reach all workers (those in and not in an organization), the government has increasingly turned to organizations for assistance in finding and reaching workers. As a result almost all recipients of the board benefits are members of an organization.
64. Jyotsna used the English word "empower," although she does not speak English.
65. Interview, 16 December 2003.
66. Interview, 14 July 2003. Speaker's emphasis.

## *Chapter 5 – Harriss*

1. There is no means of determining the universe of associations in any city for sampling, and in these circumstances snowball sampling is widely considered to be the best means of proceeding.
2. By "civil organization" I mean those organizations that have professional staff, work to benefit others, and specialize on a particular set of issues, while by "social organization" I refer to those that represent their members or communities and mobilize for their own demands.
3. See Deshpande 2003, chap. 6.
4. Ibid., 141.
5. Harriss 1986, 232.
6. Gooptu 2001, 3.
7. O'Connor 2001, 15.
8. Nisbett 2004.
9. Verba, Schlozman, and Brady 1985, 8–9.
10. See Harriss 2005.
11. In São Paulo in 48 percent of problem-solving instances the person acted alone, and in 44 percent s/he drew on the support of acquaintances or family; in Mexico City the comparable figures are 28 percent and 76 percent; in Delhi they are 7 percent and 77 percent.
12. Comparative figures for São Paulo are 26 percent; and for Mexico City, 19 percent.
13. The terms employed here were first suggested by Peter Houtzager and Adrian Gurza Lavalle.
14. See, for example, Corbridge et al. 2005.

15. Manor 2004.
16. Chatterjee 2004, 38.
17. See Harriss 2005.
18. See Alam 2004.
19. Harriss 2005.
20. The text here draws extensively on work by Sudha Narayanan in Bangalore. My own research in Chennai was carried out with the able and genial assistance of C. Pritham.
21. Decentralization in urban government, under the 74th Amendment to the Indian Constitution has little if any real substance in either Bangalore or Chennai.
22. The fact that only one of my interviews took place almost entirely in Tamil is an indication of the extent of cultural capital disposed of by these social activists.
23. Nair 2005, 336.
24. Ibid., 336–37.
25. See reports in *The Hindu* of 15 March 2005 and 5 May 2005 on demonstrations on job security, wages, and pension guarantees for unorganized workers. A model bill has been drawn up, and a rally of about twenty thousand people from all over the country took place in New Delhi in May 2005, when a petition was presented to the Speaker of the Lok Sabha, "seeking inclusion of the right to employment, education and health security as fundamental rights."
26. Pushpa Arabindoo, personal communication. I have benefited considerably from reading parts of the draft of Pushpa Arabindoo's PhD dissertation (London School of Economics), and I am grateful to her for this opportunity.
27. One factor here may be the neglect by men of their family responsibilities and the problem of drunkenness amongst them.
28. Appadurai 2004.
29. Nair 2005.
30. I owe my recognition of the possible significance of the uses of the word "activist" in Chennai, and the arguments of this paragraph, entirely to Venkatesh Chakravarthy.
31. Rueschmeyer et al. 1992.
32. Pavan Varma 1998.
33. Watt 2005.
34. World Bank 1997, 113. Emphasis added.
35. Watt 2005.
36. Chandhoke 2002, 47.
37. Ibid., 46.
38. Agarwala 2006.

## Chapter 6 – Herring

1. Bharathan 2000; Bunsha 2001; Jayaraman 2001; Parmer and Visvanathan 2003; Herring 2005; Herring In press a; Scoones 2005, chap. 7.
2. Omvedt 2005.
3. Madsen 2001.
4. Herring 2005.
5. McHughen 2000.
6. Qayum and Sakkhari 2005, 31; on broader alliances and actors, see Scoones 2005, 315–27.
7. James 2002.
8. Data here and below from ISAAA New Delhi, courtesy Baghirath Choudhary. Official data from Ministry of Agriculture. *Press Trust of India*, 10 February 2004, reported that "an illegal variety of Bt cotton covers nearly 90 per cent of the cotton area in Gujarat." Estimates are inconsistent but all move in the same direction: rapid expansion of Bt acreage. On stealth seeds as a general phenomenon, see Herring In press a.
9. Gupta and Chandak 2005; Roy, Herring, and Geisler 2007.
10. Jayaraman 2004.

11. Personal communication. October 2005.
12. In June of 2005, I found that locally hybridized transgenic cotton cultivars in Gujarat sold for Rs. 250–700 per packet (roughly enough to plant one acre) — or 15 to 40 percent of the local official seed price; F2 transgenic seeds were selling for Rs. 10 for the same weight packet, so cheap as to be worrisome to some farmers, but much appreciated by others.
13. Data in this section from Bhagirath Choudhary, personal communication, and *ISAAA: Fact Sheet on Approved Bt Cotton Hybrids in India* 2006.
14. Gupta and Chandak 2005; Jayaraman 2004; Roy, Herring, and Geisler 2007.
15. Shiva and Jafri 2004.
16. Shiva 1997, 91.
17. Qayum and Sakkhari 2005, 38.
18. URL: http://www.navdanya.org/events/06bija_yatra.htm. Accessed 6 October 2006. See Shiva 1999 for analogies between corporate "manipulation and monopoly" and colonial rule.
19. URL: http://www.navdanya.org/about/practice_earth_dem.htm. Accessed 6 October 2006.
20. www.navdanya.org/articles/ge_trials.htm. Accessed 6 October 2006.
21. Herring 2005, 209–10.
22. Gupta, personal communication 2004; Gupta and Chandak 2005.
23. *The Economist* 2006, 63.
24. Pray and Naseem In press.
25. Herring In press a.
26. RAFI International, "Terminator 2 Years Later: Suicide Seeds on the Fast Track." RAFI International Office, Winnipeg, Manitoba, Canada. Website no longer active. There is no space here to describe the various ways that terminator technology might someday work; the suicide-seed formulation is only one possibility. Delta and Pine Land Co. holds the patent, in collaboration with the U.S. Department of Agriculture's Agricultural Research Service: U.S. Patent 5,723,765, granted 3 March 1998.
27. On the construction, see Gold 2003; on the science, see Ramanjaneyula and Ravindra 1999; and Jha 2001. In an interview, Devinder Sharma is quoted as saying "Bt cotton will kill farmers, financially and literally." http://us.rediff.com/money/2001/dec/12inter.htm. Accessed 6 October 2006.
28. Press release, Asian Social Forum [Hyderabad] Seminar, 2003.
29. Gosh 2001, 11.
30. Paarlberg 2001, 99–100; Bharathan 2000. On the debt nexus as a cause of suicides, see Centre for Environmental Studies 1998; Department of Agriculture and Cooperation 1998; Stone 2002; and Shiva et al. 2000, 64–110. There are elements of crisis in Indian agriculture, and many tragic outcomes, but no evidence whatsoever that Bt has made things worse. For a sensible analysis of the real factors in rural India's difficulties, see Vaidyanathan 2006.
31. Mistry 1998.
32. Stone 2001, 1.
33. Consider the novel *All Over Creation*, by Ruth Ozeki. I have seldom given a lecture on this subject, especially outside the United States, without someone commenting that suicide seeds are killing farmers in India.
34. Shiva et al. 2000, 98; Sahai 1999, 84; Assayag 2005, 70–71.
35. Though with emancipatory potential as well. See Prakash 1999; see also Nandy 1990.
36. Nanda 2002.
37. P.V. Sateesh posted this response to Shantharam 2005 on 3 May 2005 at http://www.gmwatch.org/archive2.asp?arcid=5194.
38. Sharma 2006.
39. Press release, 20 June 2003, New Delhi.
40. Sanat Mehta, ed. 2005, 60–76; interviews with Dr. D.B. Desai and the breeder of Navbharat 151, Dr. N.P. Mehta, in Ahmedabad, June 2005.

41. See James 2002 for comparative data; on India, the only carefully controlled study is Bambawale et al. 2005; see also Roy, Herring, and Geisler 2007; Morse et al. (2005) explain why varietal difference is consistent with success of Bt technology.
42. See discussion in Roy, Herring, and Geisler 2007.
43. See the account of a leader of a local farmer organization in Joshi 2001; see also Visvanathan and Parmer 2002; Shaik 2001.
44. CII 2001.
45. Department of Biotechnology 2001; 2002.
46. See, for example, Scoones 2005, 326. Ajit Singh, minister of agriculture during the discovery of underground Bt plants, believes pesticide firms fund the opposition, along with European NGOs (interview, New Delhi, 22 June 2005).
47. *The Hindu* Business Line, 14 November 2003.
48. An exception is Qayum and Sakkhari 2005; see also, Shantharam 2005.
49. For an analysis of cotton farmers' reasoning, based on extensive interviews, see Roy 2006; Roy, Herring, and Geisler 2007.
50. Stone 2007.
51. Naik et al. 2005.
52. Bambawale et al. 2004, 1633.
53. McAdam et al. 1996.
54. Edelman 1962.
55. Unlike the African cases, the India shipments were directly from the United States, not the United Nations, and were part of a continuous program for improving health in areas of high malnutrition.
56. Tarrow 2005.
57. Social movement "organizations" reflects self-representation rather than empirical coding: many "organizations" are thin on the ground but have a substantial web presence. See Bob 2005 on the importance of publicity and the representation of social movements.
58. Piven and Cloward 1977; Herring 2005, 213–22.
59. Professor Nanjundaswamy's Inter-Continental Caravan of Indian farmers to Europe caused one participant to complain of the *neta-chamcha* [leader-sycophant] character of relations in the movement. [*Chamcha*, literally "spoon," carries an even more derogatory connotation than "sycophant."] See Madsen 2001. Farmers also criticized the use of English by the leaders as exclusionary.
60. On "scale shift," see Tarrow 2005, 120–40.
61. Wright 1997; on India, see Fernandes and Heller 2006; Harriss 2006.
62. See, for example, Assayag and Fuller 2005.
63. Chibber 2006.
64. This essay was reprinted as Guha 2003.
65. For example, "1600 sheep die after grazing in Bt cotton field 30 April 2006" sify.com/news/fullstory.php?id=14194773. For full details of the sheep study, see www.gmwatch.org/archive2.asp?arcid=6494. For a scientific response, see Shanthu Shantaram, www.biospectrumindia.com/content/columns/106061 51.asp.
66. See www.ipsnews.net/africa/print.asp?idnews=32438. Accessed March 2006. Presumably because the article is for sale, it is marked NOT FOR PUBLICATION IN CANADA, AUSTRALIA, BRAZIL, CANADA, NEW ZEALAND, CZECH REPUBLIC, IRELAND, POLAND, THE UNITED STATES, AND THE UNITED KINGDOM. See also Shiva 2006 for similar statements.
67. In one month of campaigning, the organization got 504 organizations to sign the petition: "We oppose all forms of Terminator technology (Genetic Use Restriction Technologies or GURTs). We ask all national governments and international bodies to ban Terminator in order to ensure that the technology is never field tested or commercialized." See www.banterminator.org/endorsements.
68. NGOs such as the Foundation for Biotechnology and Awareness consistently present alternative views, based in science (see Rao 2004, for example), but the center stage has been dominated by oppositional NGOs. Interests supporting biotechnology largely remained above the fray, knowing they had the support of farmers and

the government and were unwilling to draw more attention to the sensationalist claims of opponents. Interviews, CII, DBT Delhi 2002.

69. Herring and Esman 2001, 11, passim.
70. For example, Department of Agriculture and Cooperation 1998; Centre for Environmental Studies Warangal 1998.
71. Pinstrup-Andersen and Schiøler 2000, xi.
72. Stig Toft Madsen (2000) describes these effects on the KRRS after its emergence on the global stage as representative of India's farmers. The Intercontinental Caravan of Indian farmers to Vevey was significant in the dissolution of the KRRS, the farmers' organization that launched Operation Cremate Monsanto, in part for reasons given in the text. Ironically, Europeans doubted the authenticity of such farmers from India as the farmers were able to afford transcontinental commercial airline fares. These large expenditures fed internal dissension and rumors of funding from pesticide firms with an interest in stopping Bt.
73. Jung 2006, 3.
74. For example, Assayag 2005.

## *Chapter 7 – Fernandes and Heller*

1. See for example Rudolph and Rudolph 1987.
2. Reuschemeyer, Stephens, and Stephens 1992; Luebbert 1991.
3. We use hegemony in the traditional Gramscian sense to refer to a specific type of class domination that relies on eliciting consent from subordinate groups (more so than on coercion) through a "political-ethical" project that is effective because it resonates ideologically with the "common sense" of the masses and because it is materially grounded, and specifically that the interests of the dominant group or bloc are "concretely coordinated" with "the general interests of subordinate groups." Gramsci explicitly contrasts the material interests of a hegemonic class (or bloc) with dominant classes that act in accordance with their "narrowly corporate economic interest." See Gramsci 1972, 182.
4. Social science analyses have tended to neglect the role of the middle classes and have focused primarily on state-capital-bourgeoisie relations. See Chibber 2003; Kohli 2004. Exceptions to this include Bardhan 1984 and 1993 and Deshpande 2003.
5. For a useful critical discussion of attempts at measuring the middle classes, see Deshpande 2003.
6. The contrast between the bourgeoisie and the middle class is worth emphasizing. The bourgeoisie has structural power that translates into political power in ways that make it less necessary for this class to mobilize visibly and politically in order to reproduce itself. Its strategy of reproduction is driven by the systemic logic of capital accumulation. The middle class is characterized by a higher degree of structural complexity and uncertainty and exists through itself, that is, through the practices through which it reproduces itself.
7. For culturalist approaches, see Mankekar 1999; Rajagopal 2001b; for economistic approaches at measuring the middle class, see Sridharan 2004.
8. Yadav 2000.
9. The Congress has adopted what analysts have called a soft Hindutva approach in recent electoral campaigns. The Congress has also tried to use appeasement and a management of competing religious nationalist groups: see, for example, Rajiv Gandhi's attempt to manage the Ayodhya movement by granting permission to build the temple near the site and his well-publicized mismanagement in the Shah Bano case.
10. Our discussion of Hindu nationalism focuses on the Hindu middle classes because we are concerned with dominant segments of the middle classes that are attempting to draw the ideological and material boundaries of a hegemonic project; for historical discussions of the Muslim middle class, see Hasan 1997.
11. Such a comparative perspective is especially important in order to avoid the exceptionalist tendency to view Hindutva as a phenomena particular to India. In

fact this politics of middle class illiberalism does not have to take a religious nationalist form and can take the form of a secular illiberalism. This is true both in the Indian context as well as in comparative contexts where middle class illiberalism has centered around political reactions based on race, ethnicity, and nationality (as seen in contemporary middle-class responses to immigration in the United States).

12. Wright 1985.
13. Bourdieu 1984.
14. See Varma 1998.
15. Corbridge and Harris 2000.
16. Chatterjee 1993.
17. Kaviraj 1988 and Bardhan 1998.
18. Gramsci 1972, 260.
19. Bardhan 1984.
20. Chatterjee 1993, 214.
21. See Frankel 1979; Corbridge and Harriss 2000.
22. See Hasan, 1998.
23. Vanaik, 2002. Opposition to the Emergency from segments of the middle class was, of course, strong. The point however, is that aspects of the Emergency, particularly developmental aspects such as slum demolition and family planning, invoked middle-class models of developmentalism and civic order.
24. Khilnani 1997; Deshpande 2003.
25. Deshpande 2003, 139.
26. Kohli 2006.
27. Vanaik 2002, 231.
28. In Kerala with its long history of Communist Party mobilization or Tamil Nadu with its anti-Brahminical movements the BJP has made limited inroads. And while the Communist Party of India-Marxist (CPIM) hierarchy in West Bengal has reproduced upper caste dominance, the party has built linkages between middle-class, working-class, and rural interests. Clearly, varying regional class configurations have produced alternative political trajectories that coexist with the broad national patterns analyzed in this article. In Kerala and to a lesser extent West Bengal and Tamil Nadu, redistributive class coalitions, born to varying degrees of social movements, have effectively linked lower-class demands to state policies. It remains to be seen how and to what extent liberalization will change such processes. In Kerala, the CPIM has promoted democratic decentralization as a specific response to liberalization. See Heller 2005.
29. Yadav 1999.
30. Hansen 1999; Corbridge and Harriss 2000; Jaffrelot 1996.
31. Luebbert 1991.
32. Rueschemeyer, Stephens, and Stephens 1992.
33. Davis 2004.
34. Linz and Stepan 1996.
35. Hansen 1999.
36. Sridharan 2004; Fernandes 2000.
37. See Katzenstein 1979.
38. Sridharan 2004, 423.
39. Scholars of popular culture have analyzed the ways in which advertising images and television programming encode representations of middle-class identity with symbols that invoke idealized representations of family order and Hindu identity. Rajagopal 2001b.
40. The middle class presents itself in universalistic terms even as its own practices reproduce various social hierarchies. When middle class discourses (in the media, for instance) specifically speak of caste or religion they do so by naming subordinated social groups as "special interest." Caste, for instance, only becomes visible when the term is invoked by subordinate social groups making demands through reified bureaucratic categories such as SC and OBC. It is rendered invisible or misrecognized in the politics of the middle classes.

41. Hansen 1999.
42. Ibid.
43. Bourdieu 1984, 77.
44. See Rajagopal 2001a.
45. Polanyi 1944, 35.
46. Rudolph and Rudolph 2001.
47. Bourdieu 2001, 11–12.
48. See Rudolph and Rudolph 1987.
49. The figure is for 1998/99. Gragnolati et al. 2005, 1.
50. See Basu 2001.
51. *The Hindu,* AE-2, 20 May 2004.
52. Ibid.
53. Bourdieu 1984.
54. Cited in World Bank 2006, 8.
55. Tilly 1998.
56. Deshpande 2003, 115.
57. Chopra 2003, 434.
58. Kapur, citing Rosenthal 2006, 12.
59. Weiner 1991.
60. Chopra 2003, 438. Emphasis in original.
61. Bourdieu has made precisely this argument about class and the recalibration of academic credentials in France.
62. Chopra 2003, 439.
63. Cited in ibid., 437.
64. Kapur 2006.
65. Ibid.
66. Castells 2004.
67. Harvey 1990.
68. Sheth, 1999a and 1999b.
69. Sheth 1999a.
70. Jaffrelot 2000.
71. Hasan 1998.
72. On Calcutta, see Roy 2003; on Delhi, see Harriss 2005 and this volume; on Bangalore, see Heitzman 1999; on Mumbai, see Fernandes 2004.
73. Bhowmick 2002.
74. Note that this type of exclusionary middle-class claim on democratic process can also be seen more broadly in public interest litigation. This form of litigation has been a preserve of NMC politics because it requires knowledge of courts, legal connections, English skills (laws are often not published in the vernacular), and technical skills — the kinds of social and cultural capital we have argued is central to middle-class formation and politics. Thanks to Ron Herring for pointing this out.
75. Kapur 2006, Table 1a.
76. Solomon and Bhuvaneshari 2001, 108.
77. See Mehta 2006 and Yadav and Deshpande 2006.

# References


Addleton, John. 1992. *Undermining the centre: The Gulf migration and Pakistan*. Karachi: Oxford University Press.

Agarwala, Rina. 2006. From work to welfare: A new class movement in India. *Critical Asian Studies* 38 (4): 419–44.

Ahluwalia, Montek S. 2002. *Report of the Task Force on Employment Opportunities*. New Delhi: Planning Commission.

Ahmad, Aijaz. 2000. *Lineages of the present: Ideological and politics in contemporary South Asia*. London and New York: Verso.

Aidt, T., and Z. Tzannatos. 2002. *Unions and collective bargaining: Economic effects in a global environment*. Washington, D.C.: The World Bank.

Akhtar, Humaira. 1992. Female factory workers' survey report. Mimeographed paper.

Alam, J. 2004. *Who wants democracy?* Hyderabad: Orient Longman.

Alavi, Hamza. 1973. The state in postcolonial societies: Pakistan and Bangladesh. In Kathleen Gough and Hari Sharma, eds. *Imperialism and revolution in South Asia*. New York: Monthly Review Press.

———. 1983. Class and state. In Hassan Gardezi and Jamal Rashid, eds. *Pakistan: The roots of dictatorship*. London: Zed Books.

———. 1989. Formation of the social structure of South Asian under the impact of colonial rule. In Hamza Alavi and John Harriss, eds. *Sociology of developing societies*. London: Macmillan.

Ali, Kamran Asdar. 2005. The strength of the street meets the strength of the state: The 1972 labor struggle in Karachi. *International Journal of Middle Eastern Studies* 37 (1): 83–107.

Ali, Karamat. 1983. *The state, industrialization, and class formation in a multi-national state*. Unpublished MA thesis (Institute of Social Studies, The Hague).

Ali, Tariq. 2003. The colour khaki. *New Left Review* 19. January-February.

Amsden, Alice. 1994. The spectre of Anglo-Saxonization is haunting South Korea. In Lee Jay Cho and Yoon Hyung Kim eds. *Korea's political economy: An institutional perspective*. Boulder: Westview Press.

Anderson, Perry. 1977. The antinomies of Antonio Gramsci. *New Left Review* 100.

———. 1978. *Considerations on Western Marxism*. London: Verso.

Assayag, Jackie. 2005. Seeds of wrath: Agriculture, biotechnology and globalization. In Assayag and Fuller, eds. 2005.

Assayag, Jackie, and C.J. Fuller, eds. 2005. *Globalizing India: Perspectives from below*. London: Anthem Press.

Austin, Granville. 1966. *The Indian constitution: Cornerstone of a nation*. Oxford: Clarendon Press.

Babb, Sarah. 2001. *Managing Mexico: Economists from nationalism to neoliberalism*. Princeton, N.J.: Princeton University Press.

Bairoch, Paul. 1973. *Urban unemployment in developing countries: The nature of the problem and proposals for its solution*. Geneva: ILO.

Bambawale, O.M., et al. 2004. Performance of Bt cotton (MECH-162) under integrated pest management in farmers' participatory field trial in Nanded district, Central India. *Current Science* 86 (12): 25 June.

Bardhan, Pranab K. 1984. *The political economy of development in India*. Oxford: Blackwell.

———. 1998 (1984). Rev. ed. *The political economy of development in India*. London: Oxford University Press.

———. 2001. Sharing the spoils: Group equity, development and democracy. In A. Kohli, ed. *The success of India's democracy*. Cambridge: Cambridge University Press. 226–41.

Bardhan, Pranab K., and Ashok Rudra. 2003. Thinking left: Totems and taboos of left mythology. In Pranab K. Bardhan, ed. *Poverty, agrarian structure, and political economy in India: Selected essays*. New Delhi: Oxford University Press.

Basu, Amrita. 1992. *Two faces of protest: Contrasting modes of women's activism in India*. Berkeley and Los Angeles: University of California Press.

———. 2001. The dialectics of Hindu nationalism. In Atul Kohli, ed. *The success of India's democracy*. Cambridge: Cambridge University Press.

Basu, Amrita, and Atul Kohli, eds. 1998. *Community conflicts and the state in India*. Delhi: Oxford University Press.

Baviskar, Amita. 1995. *In the belly of the river: Tribal conflicts over development in the Narmada Valley*. Delhi: Oxford University Press.

———. 2005. Red in tooth and claw? Looking for class in struggles over nature. In R. Ray and M. Katzenstein, eds. *Social movements in India: Poverty, power, and politics*. Lanham, Md.: Rowman and Littlefield.

Becker, Gary. 1976. *Economic approach to human behavior*. Chicago: University of Chicago Press.

Berger, Mark. 1995. *Under northern eyes: Latin American studies and U.S. hegemony in the Americas, 1898–1990*. Bloomington: Indiana University Press.

Berger, Suzanne, and Michael Piore. 1989. *Dualism and discontinuity in industrial societies*. Cambridge: Cambridge University Press.

Berman, Sheri. 1997. Civil society and the collapse of the Weimar Republic. *World Politics* 49: 401–29.

Besley, T., and R. Burgess. 2004. Can labor regulation hinder economic performance? Evidence from India. *Quarterly Journal of Economics* 19 (1): 91–134.

Bhaduri, A., et al. 1986. Persistence and polarization: A study in the dynamics of agrarian contradiction. *Journal of Peasant Studies* 13 (3): 82–89.

Bharathan, Geeta. 2000. Bt-Cotton in India: Anatomy of a controversy. *Current Science* 79 (8): 1067–75 (25 October).

Bhargava, P.P. 1995. *Trade union dynamism*. Jaipur: Printwell.

Bhatt, S. 1993. *Democracy in trade unions*. New Delhi: Uppal Publishing House.

Bhowmick, Sharit. 2005. Street vendors in Asia: A review. *Economic and Political Weekly*. 28 May–June 4: 2256–64.

Bhutto, Zulfikar Ali. 1972. *Speeches and statements: December 20, 1971–* March 31, 1972. Karachi: Government of Pakistan, Dept. of Films and Publications.

———. 1973. Bhutto's speech at labour moot: Text. *Dawn*. 22 November.

Bob, Clifford. 2005. *The marketing of rebellion.* New York: Cambridge University Press.

Bourdieu, Pierre. 1984. *Distinction: A social critique of the judgment of taste.* Trans. Richard Nice. Cambridge: Harvard University Press.

———. 2001. *Firing back: Against the tyranny of the market 2.* New York: The New Press.

Brass, Paul. 1965. *Factional politics in an Indian state: The Congress Party in Uttar Pradesh.* Los Angeles and Berkeley, University of California Press.

Brass, Tom. ed. 1995. *New farmers movements in India*, London: Frank Cass.

Bromley, Ray, and Chris Gerry. 1979. Who are the casual poor? In R. Bromley and C. Gerry, eds. *Casual work and poverty in third world cities.* New York: Wiley.

Bunsha, Dionne. 2001. A can of bollworms. *Frontline* 18 (24): 24 November–7 December.

Burawoy, Michael. 1979. *Manufacturing consent.* Chicago: University of Chicago Press.

———. 1985. *The politics of production.* London: Verso.

Byres, Terry J. 1979. Of neo-populist pipe dreams: Daedalus in the third world and the myth of urban bias. *Journal of Peasant Studies* 6 (2): 210–44.

———. 1981. The new technology, class formation and class action in the Indian countryside. *Journal of Peasant Studies* 8 (4): 405–54.

———. 1990. Charan Singh (1902–87): An assessment. *Journal of Peasant Studies* 15 (2): 139–89.

———. 2001. The peasants seminar of the University of London, 1972–1989: A memoir. *Journal of Agrarian Change* 1 (3): July. 343–88.

Callinicos, Alex. 1990. *Against postmodernism.* London: Blackwell.

Candland, Christopher. 2001. The cost of incorporation: Labor institutions, industrial restructuring, and new trade union strategies in India and Pakistan. In Candland and Sil 2001: 69–94.

———. 2002. The political element in economic reform: Labor institutions and privatization patterns in South Asia. In Linda Cook and Marsha Pripstein Posusney, eds. *Labor and privatization: Responses and consequences in global perspective.* Brookfield: Edward Elgar.

———. 2007. *Organized labor, democracy, and development in India and Pakistan.* Abingdon: Routledge.

———. 2007 (forthcoming). Working class solidarity in Pakistan. *Critical Asian Studies* 39 (1): March.

Candland, Christopher, and R. Sil., eds. 2001. *The politics of labor in a global age: Continuity and change in late-industrializing and post-socialist economies.* Oxford: Oxford University Press.

Carr, M., M. Chen, and R. Jhabvala, eds. 1996. *Speaking out.* New Delhi: Vistaar Publications.

Centre for Environmental Studies Warangal. 1998. *Citizens' report: Gathering agrarian crisis—farmers' suicides in Warangal District (A.P.) India.* Kishanpura: Centre for Environmental Studies Warangal.

Chakrabarty, Dipesh. 1989. *Rethinking working class history: Bengal 1890–1940.* New Delhi: Oxford University Press.

———. 2000a. *Provincializing Europe: Postcolonial Thought and Historical Difference.* Princeton, N.J.: Princeton University Press.

———. 2000b. *Rethinking working-class history.* Princeton, N.J.: Princeton University Press.

———. 2002. A small history of Subaltern studies. In *Habitations of modernity: Essays in the wake of* Subaltern Studies. Chicago: University of Chicago Press. 3–19.

Chandhoke, N. 2002. The limits of global civil society. In Marlies Glasius, Mary Kaldor, and Helmut Anheier, eds. *Global civil society 2002*. Oxford: Oxford University Press.

Chandra, Kanchan. 2004. *Why ethnic parties succeed: Patronage and ethnic head counts in India*. New York: Cambridge University Press.

———. Forthcoming. Ethnic parties and democratic stability. *Perspectives on Politics*.

Chandravarkar, Rajnarayan. 1994. *The origins of industrial capitalism in India: Business strategies and the working classes in Bombay, 1900–1940.* Cambridge: Cambridge University Press.

Chatterjee, Partha. 1984. Gandhi and the critique of civil society. In Ranajit Guha, ed. *Subaltern Studies III.* Delhi: Oxford University Press.

———. 1986. *Nationalist thought and the colonial world: A derivative discourse?* London: Zed Press.

———. 1993. *The nation and its fragments: Colonial and postcolonial histories*. Princeton, N.J.: Princeton University Press.

———. 2003. *The nation and its fragments.* Princeton, N.J.: Princeton University Press.

———. 2004. *The politics of the governed: Reflections on popular politics in most of the world*. New York: Columbia University Press.

Chatterji, R. 1980. *Unions, politics and the state*. New Delhi: South Asian Publishers.

Chibber, Vivek. 2003. *Locked in place: State-building and late industrialization in India.* Princeton, N.J.: Princeton University Press.

———. 2006. On the decline of class analysis in South Asian studies. *Critical Asian Studies* 38 (4): 357–87.

Chilcote, Ronald. 1997. U.S. hegemony and academics in the Americas. *Latin American Perspectives* 24 (1): 73–77.

Chopra, Rohit. 2003. Neoliberalism as doxa: Bourdieu's theory of the state and the contemporary Indian discourse on globalizaiton and liberalization. *Cultural Studies* 17: 419–44.

Chowdhury, Supriya Roy. 2003. Old classes and new spaces: Urban poverty, unorganised labour and new unions. *Economic and Political Weekly* 38 (58): 13 December.

Cohen, Robert. 1993. *When the old left was young: Student radicals and America's first mass student movement, 1929–1941.* New York: Oxford University Press.

Cohen, Stephen. 1984. *The Pakistan army.* Berkeley and Los Angeles: University of California.

Confederation of Indian Industry [CII]. 2001. Biotechnology on the fast track. Unpublished conference proceedings. New Delhi.

Corbridge, Stuart, and John Harriss. 2000. *Reinventing India: Liberalization, Hindu nationalism and popular democracy.* Cambridge: Polity Press.

Corbridge, S., G. Williams, R.Veron, and M. Srivastava, 2005. *Seeing the state*. Cambridge: Cambridge University Press.

Correspondents. 2005. *Class matters*. New York: Henry Holt.

Cross, John. 1998. *Informal politics: Street vendors and the state in Mexico City*. Stanford: Stanford University Press.

Crouch, H. 1966. *Trade unions and politics in India*. Bombay: Mankatala.

Davis, Diane. 2004. *Discipline and development: Middle classes and prosperity in East Asia and Latin America*. New York: Cambridge University Press.

Dawn 1973. Bhutto's speech at labour moot: Text. *Dawn*. 22 November.

Dayal, I., and B. Sharma. 1976. *Management of trade unions*. New Delhi: Shri Ram Centre for Industrial Relations and Human Resources.

Deaton, Angus, and Jean Drèze. 2002. Poverty and inequality in India: A re-examination. *Economic and Political Weekly*. 7 September: 3729–48.

Denning, Michael. 1996. *The cultural front: The laboring of American culture in the twentieth century*. London: Verso.

Department of Agriculture and Cooperation, Ministry of Agriculture, Government of India. 1998. *Report of the Study Group on Distress Caused by Indebtedness of Farmers in Andhra Pradesh*. New Delhi. September.

Department of Biotechnology, Ministry of Science and Technology, Government of India. 2001. *Biotechnology: A vision*. New Delhi.

———. 2002. *Annual report 2001–2002*. New Delhi.

Deshpande, Satish. 2003. *Contemporary India: A sociological view*. New Delhi: Penguin Books.

Devi, D.P. 1991. *Leadership and democracy among the trade unions*. New Delhi: Mittal.

Dezalay, Yves, and Bryant G. Garth. 2002. *The internationalization of palace wars: Lawyers, economists, and the contest to transform Latin American states*. Chicago: University of Chicago Press.

Dirks, N.B. 2001. *Castes of mind: Colonialism and the making of modern India*. Princeton, N.J.: Princeton University Press.

Drèze, Jean, and Amartya Sen. 1995. *India: Economic development and social opportunity*. Oxford: Oxford University Press.

———. 1997. *Indian development: Selected regional perspectives*. Delhi: Oxford University Press.

Drucker, Peter. 1994. *Max Shachtman and his left: A socialist's odyssey through the "American century."* Atlantic Highlands, N.J.: Humanities Press.

Dryzek, John. 1997. *The politics of the earth*. New York: Oxford University Press.

Eagleton, Terry. 1992. *The illusions of postmodernism*. London: Verso.

Eaton, Richard M. 2000. *Essays on Islam and Indian history*. New Delhi: Oxford University Press.

*The Economist*. 2006. *World in figures*. London.

Edelman, Murray. 1962. *The symbolic uses of politics*. Champagne/Urbana: University of Illinois Press.

Edwards, S., and N.C. Lustig. 1997. *Labor markets in Latin America: Combining social protection with market flexibility*. Washington, D.C.: Brookings Institution Press.

Elster, Jon. 1985. *Making sense of Marx*. Cambridge: Cambridge University Press.

Femia, Joseph. 1990. *Gramsci's political theory*. Oxford: Oxford University Press.

Fernandes, Leela. 2000. Restructuring the new middle class in liberalizing India. *Comparative Studies of South Asia, Africa and the Middle East* 20 (1 and 2): 88–104.

Fernandes, Leela. 2004. The politics of forgetting: Class politics, state power and the restructuring of urban space in India. *Urban Studies* 41 (12): 2415–30.

———. 2006. *India's new middle class: Democratic politics in an era of economic reform*. Minneapolis: University of Minnesota Press.

Fernandes, Leela, and Patrick Heller. 2006. Hegemonic aspirations: New middle class politics and India's democracy in comparative perspective. *Critical Asian Studies* 38 (4): 495–522.

Fernandez-Kelly, Patricia, and Jon Shefner. 2006. *Out of the shadows: Political action and the informal economy in Latin America*. University Park: Pennsylvania State University Press.

Fisher, Paul. 1961. The economic role of unions in less developed areas. *Monthly Labor Review* 84 (9): 951–56.

Frank, Thomas. 2004. *What's the matter with Kansas? How conservatives won the heart of America*. New York: Metropolitan Books.

Frankel, Francine R. 1979. *India's political economy, 1947–1977: The gradual revolution*. Princeton, N.J.: Princeton University Press.

———. 2005. *India's political economy, 1947–2004: The gradual revolution*. New Delhi: Oxford University Press.

Frankel, Francine R., and M.S.A. Rao, eds. 1989. Vols. 1 and 2. *Dominance and state power in modern India: Decline of a social order*. Delhi and New York: Oxford University Press.

Freeman, R., and J. Medoff. 1984. *What do unions do?* New York: Basic Books.

Gadgil, Madhav, and Ramachandra Guha. 1995. *Ecology and equity: The use and abuse of nature in contemporary India*. New Delhi: Penguin.

Gaiha, R. 1996. How dependent are the rural poor on the employment guarantee scheme in India? *Journal of Development Studies*. 32 (5): 669ff.

Galenson, W., ed. 1959. *Labor and economic development*. New York: John Wiley and Sons.

Gardezi, Hassan. 1973. Neocolonial alliances and the crisis of Pakistan. In Kathleen Gough and Hari Sharma, eds. *Imperialism and revolution in South Asia*. New York: Monthly Review Press.

———. 1998. Sociology: Inception of a social science in Pakistan. In Hassan Gardezi, *A reexamination of the socio-political history of Pakistan: Reproduction of class relations and ideology*. Lewiston, Me.: Edwin Mellen.

Geertz, Clifford. 1963. *Peddlers and princes: Social change and economic modernization in two Indonesian towns*. Chicago: University of Chicago Press.

Ghosh, P.K. 2001. Genetically engineered crops in India with special reference to Bt cotton. *IPM Mitr.* 1. December.

Gidwani, V. 2000. Laboured landscapes: Agroecological change in central Gujarat, India. In A. Agrawal and K. Sivaramakrishnan, eds. *Agrarian environments: Resources, representations and rule in India*. Durham, N.C.: Duke University Press.

Girija, P.L.T., Geetha Ramakrishnan, and Shyamala Ramakrishnan. 1988. *A Study of chitals: Women construction labour in the city of Madras*. Madras: Institute for the Study of Women.

GOI (Government of India). 1929. *Royal Commission report on the labour of India.*

———. 1952. *Indian labour year book.* New Delhi: Ministry of Labour and Rehabilitation.

———. 1960. *Indian labour year book.* Ministry of Labour and Rehabilitation.

———. 1970. *Indian labour year book.* Ministry of Labour and Rehabilitation.

———. 1980. *Indian labour year book.* Ministry of Labour and Rehabilitation.

———. 1990. *Indian labour year book.* Ministry of Labour and Rehabilitation.

———. 2001. National Sample Survey Organization, 2001. *Employment and unemployment survey.*

———. 2002. *Directorate General labor welfare report.*

———. 2006. Prime Minister Manmohan Singh address. Ed. P.M.O. Press Information Bureau. 13 April.

GOI, Registrar General of India. 2004. *Census 2004.* Ed. D.O.E. Statistics.

Gold, Ann Grodzins. 2003. Vanishing: Seeds' cyclicality. *Journal of Material Culture* 8 (3): 255–72.

Gooptu, N. 2001. *The politics of the urban poor in early twentieth-century India.* Cambridge: Cambridge University Press.

Gopinath. 1997. Welfare of construction workers: Legal measures. *Hindu.* 3 February: H51.

Government of Pakistan. 1951. Vol. 1. *Census of Pakistan, 1951.* Karachi: Manager of Publications.

———. 2006. Federal Bureau of Statistics. *Labour force survey.* Available online at http://www.statpak.gov.pk/depts/fbs/publications/lfs0506_q3/lfs0506_q3. html.

Government, Tamil Nadu. 2006. Labor and employment department policy note 2005–2006.

Gragnolati, Michele, Meera Shekar, Monica Das Gupta, Caryn Brendenkamp, and Yi-Kyoung Lee. 2005. India's undernourished children. *HNP Discussion Paper.* Washington, D.C.: World Bank.

Gramsci, Antonio,1971. Trans. and ed. Quintin Hoare and Geoffrey Nowell-Smith. *Selections from the Prison Notebooks of Antonio Gramsci.* New York: International Publishers.

Greenblatt, Stephen. 2004. *Will in the world.* New York: W.W. Norton.

Grusky, David B., and Jesper B. Sorensen. 1998. Can class analysis be salvaged? *American Journal of Sociology* 103: 1187–234.

Gugler, Josef. 1991. Political responses to poverty. In A. Gilbert and J. Gugler, eds. *Cities, poverty, and development: Urbanization in the third world.* Oxford: Oxford University Press.

Guha, Ramachandra. 2001. *An anthropologist among the Marxists.* New Delhi: Permanent Black.

———. 2003. The ones who stayed behind. In Jackie Assayag and Veronique Benei, eds. *At home in diaspora: South Asian scholars and the West.* Delhi: Permanent Black.

Guha, Ranajit. 1983a. *Elementary aspects of peasant insurgency.* Durham, N.C.: Duke University Press.

———. 1983b. *The prose of counterinsurgency. Subaltern studies II.* Delhi: Oxford University Press.

Guha, Ranajit, and Gayatry Chakravorty Spivak, eds. 1988. *Selected subaltern studies.* Oxford: Oxford University Press.

Gupta, Akhil. 1998. *Postcolonial developments: Agriculture in the making of modern India.* Durham, N.C.: Duke University Press.

Gupta, Anil K., and Vikas Chandak. 2005. Agricultural biotechnology in India: Ethics, business and politics. *International Journal of Biotechnology* 7 (1/2/3).

Gupta, Ranjit Kumar. 2004. *The crimson agenda: Maoist protest and terror.* Delhi: Wordsworth.

Gupta, S.P. 2002. Report of the Special Group on Targeting Ten Million Employment Opportunities Per Year over the 10th Plan Period. New Delhi: Planning Commission.

Hall, Stuart, ed. 1980. *Culture, media, language: Working papers in cultural studies, 1972–79.* London: Hutchinson, Centre for Contemporary Cultural Studies, University of Birmingham.

Hansen, Thomas Blom. 1999. *The saffron wave: Democracy and Hindu nationalism in modern India.* Princeton, N.J.: Princeton University Press.

Hanson, A.H. 1966. *The process of planning: A study of India's five-year plans, 1950–1964.* London: Oxford University Press.

ul Haq, Mahbub. 1963. *The strategy of economic planning.* New York: Oxford University Press.

Harriss, John. 1980. Contemporary Marxist analysis of the agrarian question in India. *Discussion Paper.* Madras: Madras Institute of Development Studies.

———. 1982. *Capitalism and peasant farming: Agrarian structure and ideology in Northern Tamil Nadu.* New Delhi: Oxford University Press.

———. 1986. The working poor and the labour aristocracy in a South Indian city: A descriptive and analytical account. *Modern Asian Studies* 20 (2): 231–84.

———. 1994. Between economism and post-modernism: Reflection on research on "agrarian change" in India. In David Booth, ed. *Rethinking social development: Theory, research and practice.* Harlow: Longman.

———. 2001. *Depoliticizing development: The World Bank and social capital.* New Delhi: Leftword.

———. 2003. Do political regimes matter? Poverty reduction and regime differences across India. In P. Houtzager and M. Moore, eds. *Changing paths: The new politics of inclusion.* Ann Arbor: University of Michigan Press.

———. 2005. Middle-class activism and poor people's politics: Citizen-state relations in Delhi and the role of civil and political organizations. Unpublished paper.

———. 2005. Political participation, representation and the urban poor: Findings from Delhi. *Economic and Political Weekly* XL (11): 1041–54. 12 March.

———. 2006a. Middle-class activism and the politics of the informal working class: A perspective on class relations and civil society in Indian cities. *Critical Asian Studies* 38 (4): 445–65.

———. 2006b. Postscript to the North Arcot Papers. In J. Harriss, ed. *Power matters: Essays on institutions, politics and society.* Delhi: Oxford University Press.

Harriss, John, and M. Todaro. 1970. Migration, unemployment and development: A two sector analysis. *American Economic Review* 40: 126–42.

Harriss-White, Barbara. 2003. *India working: Essays on society and economy.* New York: Cambridge University Press.

Harriss-White, Barbara, and S. Janakarajan. 2004. *Rural India facing the twenty-first century: Essays on long-term village change and recent development policy*. London: Anthem Press.

Hart, Keith. 1973. Informal income opportunities and urban employment in Ghana. *Journal of Modern African Studies* 11: 61–89.

Harvey, David. 1990. *The condition of post-modernity*. Cambridge: Blackwell.

———. 2001. *Spaces of capital: Towards a critical geography*. New York: Routledge.

Hasan, Mushirul. 1997. *Legacy of a divided nation: India's Muslims since independence*. Boulder, Colo.: Westview Press.

Hasan, Zoya. 1998. *Quest for power: Oppositional movements and post-Congress politics in Uttar Pradesh*. New Delhi: Oxford University Press.

Hashmi, Taj-ul Islam. 1992. *Pakistan as a peasant utopia: The communalization of class politics in East Bengal, 1920–1947*. Boulder: Westview Press.

Heitzman, James. 1999. Corporate strategy and planning in Science City: Bangalore as "Silicon Valley." *Economic and Political Weekly*. 30 January: PE 2–11.

Heller, Patrick. 1999. *The labor of development: Workers and the transformation of capitalism in Kerala, India*. Ithaca: Cornell University Press.

———. 2000. Degrees of democracy: Some comparative lessons from India. *World Politics* 52: 484–519.

———. 2005. Reinventing public power in the age of globalization: The transformation of movement politics in Kerala. In R. Ray and M. Katzenstein, eds. *Social movements in India: Poverty, power and politics*. New York: Rowman and Littlefield.

Herring, Ronald J. 1979. Zulfikar Ali Bhutto and the "eradication of feudalism" in Pakistan. *Comparative Studies in Society and History* 21 (4): 519–57. (October).

———. 1983. *Land to the tiller: The political economy of agrarian reform in South Asia*. New Haven: Yale University Press.

———. 1985. Economic consequences of local power configurations in South Asia. In M. Desai, S. Rudolph, and A. Rudra, eds. *Agrarian power and agricultural productivity*. Berkeley and Los Angeles: University of California Press.

———. 1988. Stealing Congress thunder: The rise to power of a communist movement in South India. In Peter Merkl and Kay Lawson, eds. *When parties fail*. Princeton, N.J.: Princeton University Press.

———. 1999. Embedded particularism: India's failed developmental state. In Meredith Woo-Cumings, ed. *The developmental state*. Ithaca, N.Y.: Cornell University Press.

———. 2001a. Making ethnic conflict: The civil war in Sri Lanka. In M. J. Esman and R. J. Herring, eds. *Carrots, sticks and ethnic conflict: Rethinking development assistance*. Ann Arbor: University of Michigan Press.

———. 2001b. Contesting the "great transformation": Local struggles with the market in South India. In J.C. Scott and N. Bhatt, eds. *Agrarian studies: Synthetic work at the cutting edge*. New Haven: Yale University Press.

———. 2002. State property rights in nature (with special reference to India). In J.F. Richards, ed. *Land, property and the environment*. Oakland: Institute of Contemporary Studies.

———. 2003a. The political impossibility theorem of agrarian reform: Path dependence and terms of inclusion. In Peter Houtzager and Mick Moore, eds.

*Changing paths: The new politics of inclusion*. Ann Arbor: University of Michigan Press.

———. 2003b. Data as social product. In Ravi Kanbur, ed. *Q-squared: Combining Qualitative and quantitative methods in poverty appraisal.* New Delhi: Permanent Black.

———. 2005. Miracle seeds, suicide seeds and the poor: GMOs, NGOs, farmers and the state in social movements. In Raka Ray and Mary Fainsod Katzenstein, eds. *India: Poverty, power, and politics*. New Delhi: Oxford University Press.

———. 2006. Why did "Operation Cremate Monsanto" fail? Science and class in India's great terminator-technology hoax. *Critical Asian Studies* 38 (4): 467–93.

———. Forthcoming a. From "fanaticism" to power: Deep roots of Kerala's agrarian exceptionalism. In William Pinch, ed. *Speaking of peasants: Essays on Indian history and politics in honor of Walter Hauser*. New Delhi: Manohar.

———. Forthcoming b. Agrarian reform for a liberal pattern of society? Karnataka's land policy and poverty alleviation. In G. Kadekodi, R. Kanbur, and V. Rao, eds. *Development in Karnataka: Challenges of governance, equity and empowerment*. New Delhi: Academic Foundation.

———. Forthcoming c. Political ecology from landscapes to genomes: Science and interests. In J.E.A. Pretty, ed. *Sage Handbook on Environment and Society*. London: Sage Publications.

———. In press a. Stealth seeds: Biosafety, bioproperty, biopolitics. *Journal of Development Studies* 43 (1).

———. In press b. The genomics revolution and development studies: Science, politics and poverty. *Journal of Development Studies* 43 (1).

———. In press c. Genetically modified crops. In Kaushik Basu, ed. *The Oxford companion to economics in India*. New Delhi: Oxford University Press.

Herring, Ronald J., and Ann Grodzins Gold. 2005. Indian cotton: Biology and utility, meanings and histories. *Economic and Political Weekly*. 17 September.

Herring, Ronald J. and Milton J. Esman. 2001. Projects and policies, politics and ethnicities. In Ronald J. Herring and Milton J. Esman, eds. *Carrots, sticks and ethnic conflict: Rethinking development assistance*. Ann Arbor: University of Michigan Press.

Herring, Ronald J., and Rex M. Edwards. 1983. Guaranteeing employment to the rural poor: Social functions and class interests in the employment guarantee scheme in Western India. *World Development* 11 (7).

Herring, Ronald J., and Henry C. Hart. 1977. Political conditions of land reform: Kerala and Maharashtra. In R.E. Frykenberg, ed. *Land tenure and peasant in South Asia*. New Delhi: Orient Longman.

Herring, Ronald J., and Chardra N. Mohan. 2001. Economic crisis, momentary autonomy and policy reform: Liberalization in India, 1991–1995. In A. Shastri and A.J. Wilson, eds. *The post-colonial states of South Asia: Democracy, development and identity*. London: Curzon Press.

Hibbs, D. 1987. *The political economy of industrial democracies*. Cambridge: Harvard University Press.

Hiremath, S.L. 1990. *Trade union leadership: An industrial relations approach*. Jaipur: Arihant Publishers.

*Historical Statistics of the United States, Colonial Times to 1970*, Series H 689-699. 382–83. Washington, D.C.: U.S. Census Bureau.

Hutnyk, John. 2003. The chapatti story: How hybridity as theory displaced Maoism as politics in subaltern studies. *Contemporary South Asia* 12 (4).

Hyman, Richard. 1992. Trade unions and the disaggregation of the working class. In M. Regini, ed. *The future of labour movements*. Newbury Park: Sage.

Inden, Ronald B. 1976. Marriage and rank in Bengali culture: A history of caste and clan in middle period Bengal. Los Angeles and Berkeley: University of California Press.

———. 1986. Orientalist constructions of India. *Modern Asian Studies* 20 (3): 401–46.

———. 1990. *Imagining India*. London: Blackwell.

International Labour Organization. 1998. *World labour report 1997–1998: Industrial relations, democracy, and social stability*. Geneva: International Labour Organization.

Isaac, T.M. Thomas, Richard W. Franke, and Pyaralal Raghavan. 1998. *Democracy at work in an Indian industrial cooperative*. Ithaca, N.Y.: Cornell University Press.

Isserman, Maurice. 1994. *If I had a hammer: The death of the old left and the birth of the new left*. New York: Basis Books.

Jaffrelot, C. 1996. *The Hindu nationalist movement and Indian politics: 1925 to the 1990s*. New Delhi: Viking Press.

———. 2000. Hindu nationalism and democracy. In Francine Frankel, Zoya Hasan, Rajeev Bhargava, and Balveer Arora, eds. *Transforming India: Social and political dynamics of democracy*. New Delhi: Oxford University Press. 353–78.

Jalal, Ayesha. 1985. *The sole spokesman: Jinnah, the Muslim League, and the demand for Pakistan*. Cambridge: Cambridge University Press.

———. 1990. *The state of martial law: Pakistan's political economy of defence*. Cambridge: Cambridge University Press.

James, Clive. 2002. Global review of transgenic crops. 2001 feature: Bt cotton. *ISAAA Briefs* 26. Ithaca, N.Y.: ISAAA.

Jayaraman, K.S. 2001. Illegal Bt cotton in India haunts regulators. *Nature Biotechnology* 19 (12): 1090 (December).

———. 2004. India produces homegrown GM cotton. *Nature Biotechnology* 22 (3): 255–56 (March).

Jha, Srinand. 2001. Seeds of death, GMO cotton, India. www.tompaine.com. 30 May.

John, Mary. 2005. Feminism, poverty and the emergent social order. In R. Ray and M. Katzenstein, eds. *Social movements in India: Poverty, power, and politics*. Lanham, Md.: Rowman and Littlefield.

Joshi, Sharad. 2001. Unquiet on the western front. *The Hindu*, Business Line. 19 December.

Joshi, Vasudha. 2000. Informal sector: A review. *Labour and Development* 6 (1 and 2).

Jung, Jai Kwan. 2006. Disentangling protest cycles: An event history analysis of new social movements in Western Europe, 1975–1989. Paper presented to the Mini-APSA Conference, Cornell University, 29 April.

Kalyvas, Stathis N. 2006. *The logic of violence in civil war*. Cambridge: Cambridge University Press.

Kamat, Sangeeta. 2002. *Development hegemony: NGOs and the state in India*. New York: Oxford University Press.

Kanbur, Ravi. 2003. *Q-squared: Combining qualitative and quantitative methods in poverty appraisal.* New Delhi: Permanent Black.

Kapur, Devesh. 2004. Ideas and economic reforms in India: The role of international migration and the Indian diaspora. *India Review* 3 (4): 364–84.

———. 2006. Globalization and the paradox of Indian democracy. *World Politics.* Forthcoming. Department of Political Science at the University of Pennsylvania.

Kapur, Devesh, and Pratap Mehta. 2004. Indian higher education reform: From half-baked socialism to half-baked capitalism. Center for International Development Harvard University. *Working Paper* 108: 1–49 (September).

Katzenstein, Mary. 1979. *Ethnicity and equality: The Shiv Sena Party and preferential policies in Bombay*. Ithaca, N.Y.: Cornell University Press.

———. 1989. Organizing against violence: Strategies of the feminist movement in India. *Pacific Affairs* 62 (1).

Katzenstein, Mary, Smitu Kothari, and Uday Mehta. 2001. Social movement politics in India: Institutions, interests, and identities In A. Kohli, ed. *The success of India's democracy.* Cambridge: Cambridge University Press.

Kaviraj, S. 1998. A critique of the passive revolution. In Partha Chaterjee, ed. *State and politics in India.* Delhi: Oxford University Press.

Kennedy, Van D. 1958. The conceptual and legislative framework of labor relations in India. *Industrial and Labor Relations Review* 11 (4): 487–505.

———. 1966. *Unions, employers and government*. Bombay: P.C. Manaktala and Sons.

Khilnani, Sunil. 1997. *The idea of India*. New York: Farrar, Straus and Giroux.

Kochanek, Stanley. 1968. *The Congress Party of India: The dynamics of one-party democracy.* Princeton, N.J.: Princeton University Press.

Kohli, Atul. 1987. *The state and poverty in India: The politics of reform*. Cambridge; New York: Cambridge University Press.

———. 2006. Politics of economic growth in India, 1980–2005. *Economic and Political Weekly.* 1 April: 1251–59, and 8 April: 1361–70.

Krishna, Anirudh. 2002. *Active social capital: Tracing the roots of development and democracy*. New York: Columbia University Press.

———. 2003. What is happening to caste? A view from some North Indian villages. *Journal of Asian Studies* 62 (4): 1171–94.

Krugman, Paul. 2006. Class war politics. *New York Times*. 19 June: A19.

Kulshreshtha, A.C., and Gulab Singh. 1999. Gross domestic product and employment in the informal sector of the Indian economy. *Indian Journal of Labour Economics* 42 (2).

Kundu, Amitabh, and Alakh N. Sharma, eds. 2001. *Informal sector in India: Perspectives and policies*. New Delhi: Institute for Human Development and Institute of Applied Manpower Research.

Laclau, Ernesto, and Chantal Mouffe. 1985. *Hegemony and socialist strategy*. London: Verso.

Lenin, V.I. 1939. *Imperialism, the highest stage of capitalism*. New York: International Publishers.

Lewis, W. Arthur. 1954. Economic development with unlimited supplies of labour. *Manchester School of Economic and Social Studies* 22 (2): 139–91.

———. 1955. *The theory of economic growth*. London: Allen and Unwin.

Lind, Amy. 1997. Gender, development and urban social change: Women's community action in global cities. *World Development* 25 (8): 1205–23.

Lindberg, Staffan. 1995. Farmers' movements and cultural nationalism in India: An ambiguous relationship. *Theory and Society* 24 (6 December).

Linz, Juan J., and Alfred C. Stepan. 1996. *Problems of democratic transition and consolidation: Southern Europe, South America, and post-communist Europe*. Baltimore, Md.: Johns Hopkins University Press.

Luebbert, Gregory M. 1991. *Liberalism, fascism, or social democracy: Social classes and the political origins of regimes in interwar Europe*. New York: Oxford University Press.

Luxemburg, Rosa. 1951. *The accumulation of capital*. Trans. A. Schwarzschild. London: Routledge and Kegan Paul.

Machiavelli, Nicolo. 1952. (1903). *The prince*. New York: New American Library.

Madsen, Stig Toft. 2000. Post festum: The lotus and the mud in an Indo-global context. Paper presented at the Conference on Globalization and Democratic Developments in Asia, Lund University, 18–20 May.

———. 2001. The view from Vevey. *Economic and Political Weekly*. 29 September: 3733–42.

Mahadevia, Darshini. 1998. Informalisation of employment and incidence of poverty in Ahmedabad. *Indian Journal of Labour Economics* 41 (3).

Malhotra, O.P. 2004. *The law of industrial disputes*. New Delhi: LexisNexis.

Malik, P.L. 2005. *Industrial law*. Lucknow: Eastern Book Company.

Manchanda, Rita. 1993. Building the builder's movement. *Telegraph*. November: H51.

Mankekar, Purnima. 1999. *Screening culture, viewing politics: An ethnography of television*. Durham, N.C.: Duke University Press.

Manor, J. 2004. "Towel over armpit": Small-time political "fixers" in India's states. In Ashutosh Varshney, ed. *India and the politics of developing countries: Essays in memory of Myron Weiner*. Delhi: Sage Publications.

Marmot, Michael G. 2006. Status syncrome. *Journal of the American Medical Association* 295: 1304–7.

Marx, Karl. 1852. *The eighteenth brumaire of Louis Bonaparte*. London: Allen and Unwin (1926).

———. 1906. *Capital: A critique of political economy*. Chicago: C.H. Kerr.

Masihi, E. 1985. *Trade union leadership in India: A sociological perspective*. Delhi: Ajanta Publications.

Mayer, Adrian. 1996. At the threshold of untouchability: Pallars and valaiyars in a Tamil village. In C.J. Fuller, ed. *Caste today*. Delhi and New York: Oxford University Press.

Mazumdar, Dipak. 1976. The urban informal sector. *World Development* 4 (8): 655–79.

McAdam, Doug, John D. McCarthy, and Mayer N. Zald, eds. 1996. *Comparative perspectives on social movements: Political opportunities, mobilizing structures, and cultural framings*. New York: Cambridge University Press.

McHughen, Alan. 2000. *Pandora's picnic basket: The potential and hazards of genetically modified foods*. Oxford: Oxford University Press.

Mehta, Asoka. 1957. The mediating role of the trade union in underdeveloped countries. *Economic Development and Cultural Change* 5 (3): 16–23.

Mehta, B.L. 1991. *Trade union movement in India*. Delhi: Kanishka Publishing House.

Mehta, Pratap. 2006. Being middle class is OK. *The Indian Express*. 7 June.

Mehta, Sanat, ed. 2005. *Bt cotton: A painful episode*. Vadodara, Gujarat: Gujarat Kapas Utpadak Hitrakshak Sangh.

Mendelsohn, O. 1993. The transformation of *authority* in rural India. *Modern Asian Studies* 27: 805–42.

Migdal, Joel, Atul Kohli, and Vivienne Shue, eds. 1994. *State power and social forces*. New York: Cambridge University Press.

Mistry, Sharad. 1998. Terminator gene a figment of imagination: Monsanto chief. *Indian Express*. 4 December.

Morris, David. 1955. Labor discipline, trade-unions, and the state in India. *Journal of Political Economy* 63 (4): 293–308.

———. 1960. The recruitment of an industrial labor force in India, with British and American comparisons. *Comparative Studies in Society and History* 2 (3): 305–28.

Moser, Caroline. 1978. Informal sector or petty commodity production: Dualism or dependence in urban development? *World Development* 6 (9/10): 1041–64.

Mukhia, Harbans, ed. 1999. *The feudalism debate*. New Delhi: Manohar.

Murillo, V. 2001. *Labor unions, partisan coalitions, and market reforms in Latin America*. Cambridge: Cambridge University Press.

Myers, C. 1958. *Industrial relations in India*. Cambridge: Harvard University Press.

Naik, Gopal, et al. 2005. Bt cotton controversy: Some paradoxes explained. *Economic and Political Weekly*. 9 April: 1514–17.

Naim, Moises. 2005. *Illicit: How smugglers, traffickers and copycats are hijacking the global economy*. New York: Doubleday.

Nair, J. 2005. *The promise of the metropolis: Bangalore's twentieth century*. Delhi: Oxford University Press.

Nanda, Meera. 2003. *Prophets facing backward*. Delhi: Permanent Black.

Nandy, Ashis. 1990. *Science, hegemony, and violence*. New Delhi: Oxford University Press.

NCL (National Commission on Labour). 1969. *Report of the National Commission on Labour (NCL) employment and rehabilitation*. Delhi: Ministry of Labour, Government of India.

———. 2002. Report of the second National Commission on Labour. New Delhi: Ministry of Labour, Government of India.

Nisbett, N. 2004. *Knowledge, identity, place and (cyber) space: Growing up male and middle class in Bangalore*. PhD diss. (University of Sussex).

NSSO (National Sample Survey Organisation). 2001. Employment and unemployment situation in India, 1999–2000. Calcutta: NSSO, Government of India.

O'Connor, A. 2001. *Poverty knowledge: Social science, social policy, and the poor in twentieth-century US history*. Princeton, N.J., and Oxford: Princeton University Press.

O'Donnell, G. 1978. Reflections on the patterns of change in the bureaucratic-authoritarian state. *Latin American Research Review* 13 (1): 3-38.

Oberai, A.S., and G.K. Chadha, eds. 2001. *Job creation in urban informal sector in India: Issues and policy options*. New Delhi: International Labour Organisation (ILO).

Omvedt, Gail. 1993. *Reinventing revolution: New social movements and the socialist tradition in India*. Armonk, N.Y.: M.E. Sharpe.

———. 2005. Farmers' movements and the debate on poverty and economic reforms in India. In R. Ray and M.F. Katzenstein, eds. *Social movements in India: Poverty, power, and politics*. New Delhi: Oxford University Press.

Ost, David. 2005. *The defeat of solidarity: Anger and politics in postcommunist Europe*. Ithaca: Cornell University Press.

Paarlberg, Robert L. 2001. *The politics of precaution: Genetically modified crops in developing countries*. Baltimore, Md.: Johns Hopkins University Press.

Paige, J.M. 1975. *Agrarian revolution: Social movements and export agriculture in the underdeveloped world*. New York: Free Press.

Pandhe, Anil. 2002. Ed. M.E.D. Corporation. Mass housing scheme for bidi workers: The Sholapur experience — The first of its kind in Asia. Maharashtra Infrastructure Summit, 2002.

Park, Richard L. 1949. Labor and politics in India. *Far Eastern Survey* 18 (16): 181–87.

Parmar, Chandrika, and Shiv Visvanathan. 2003. Hybrid, hyphen, history, hysteria: The making of the Bt cotton controversy. Paper presented at the IDS Seminar on Agriculture Biotechnology and the Developing World, Sussex, UK. 1-3 October.

Parveen, Farhat, and Karamat Ali. 1993. Research in action: Organizing women factory workers in Pakistan. *Al-Mushir* [The Counsellor] 35: 1.

Peattie, Lisa R. 1987. An idea in good currency and how it grew: The informal sector. *World Development* 15 (7): 851–58.

Peluso, N.L. 1994. *Rich forests, poor people: Resource control and resistance in Java*. Berkeley and Los Angeles: University of California Press.

Pencavel, J. 1997. The legal framework for collective bargaining in developing economies. In Edwards and Lustig 1997: 27-61.

Phillips, Kevin. 1990. *The politics of rich and poor: Wealth and the American electorate in the Reagan aftermath*. New York: Random House.

Pinstrup-Anderson, Per, and Ebbe Schiøler. 2000. *Seeds of contention: World hunger and the global controversy over GM crops*. Baltimore, Md.: Johns Hopkins University Press.

Piven, Frances Fox, and Richard Cloward. 1977. *Poor people's movements: Why they succeed, how they fail*. New York: Vintage Books.

Polanyi, Karl. 1944. *The great transformation*. New York and Toronto: Farrar and Rinehart.

———. 1957 (1944). *The great transformation*. Boston: Beacon Press.

Portes, Alejandro. 2000. The resilient importance of class: A nominalist interpretation. *Political Power and Social Theory* 14: 333–45.

———, and John Walton. 1981. *Labor, class and the international system*. New York: Academic Press.

———, Manuel Castells, and Lauren A. Benton. 1989. *The informal economy: Studies in advanced and less developed countries*. Baltimore, Md.: Johns Hopkins University Press.

———, and Kelly Hoffman. 2003. Latin American class structures: Their composition and change during the neoliberal era. *Latin American Research Review* 38 (1): 41-82.

Prakash, Gyan. 1999. *Another reason: Science and the imagination of modern India*. Princeton, N.J.: Princeton University Press.

Pray, Carl E., and Anwar Naseem. In press. Supplying crop biotechnology to the poor: Opportunities and constraints. *Journal of Development Studies* 43 (1).

Press release, Asian Social Forum [Hyderabad] Seminar. 2003. Beyond Bhopal and Bt.: Taking on the biotech giants. Research Foundation for Science, Technology and Ecology. Delhi. 4 January.

Przeworski, Adam. 1985. The material basis of consent. In *Capitalism and social democracy*. Cambridge: Cambridge University Press. Chap. 4.

Przeworski, Adam, and Joey Sprague. 1997. The material basis of consent. In *Paper stones: A history of electoral socialism*. Chicago: University of Chicago Press.

Punekar, S.D. 1948. *Trade unionism in India*. Bombay: New Book Company.

Punekar, S.D., and S. Madhuri. 1967. *Trade union leadership in India: A survey*. Bombay: Lalvani Publishing House.

Qayum, Abdul, and Kiran Sakkhari. 2005. *Bt cotton in Andhra Pradesh*. Hyderabad: Deccan Development Society.

Rajagopal, Arvind. 2001a. *Politics after television: Religious nationalism and the making of a Hindu public*. Cambridge: Cambridge University Press.

———. 2001b. Thinking about the new middle class: Gender, advertising and politics in an age of globalization. In Rajeswari Sunder Rajan, ed. *Signposts: Gender issues in post-independence India*. New Brunswick, N.J.: Rutgers University Press.

Ramachandran, V.K. 1996. On Kerala's development achievements. In Drèze and Sen, eds. 1997.

Raman, N.P. 1967. *Political involvement of India's trade unions*. Bombay: Asia Publishing House.

Ramanjaneyula, G.V., and A. Ravindra. 1999. *Terminator logic: Monsanto, genetic engineering and the future of agriculture*. New Delhi: Science for People/Research Foundation for Science, Technology and Ecology. January.

Ramaswamy, E.A. 1977. *The worker and his union: A study in south India*. Bombay: Allied Publishers.

———. 1983. The Indian management dilemma: Economic vs. political unions. *Asian Survey* 23 (8): 976–90.

———. 1984. *Power and justice: The state in industrial relations*. Oxford: Oxford University Press.

———. 1988. *Worker consciousness and trade union response*. New Delhi: Oxford University Press.

———. 1997. *A question of balance: Labour, management and society*. Oxford: Oxford University Press.

Rao, C. Kameswara. 2004. *Frontline mischief*. Bangalore: Foundation for Biotechnology Awareness and Education. 18 May.

Ray, Raka. 2000. *Fields of protest*. New Delhi: Kali for Women.

Rediff.com. 2001. Bt cotton will kill farmers, financially and literally. An interview with Devinder Sharma. 12 December. http://us.rediff.com/money/2001/dec/12inter.htm.

Roberts, Kenneth. 2002. Social inequalities without class cleavages in Latin America's neoliberal era. *Studies in Comparative International Development* 36 (4): 3–33.

Rosen, George. 1985. *Western economists and eastern societies: Agents of change in South Asia, 1950–1970*. Baltimore, Md.: Johns Hopkins University Press; New Delhi: Oxford University Press.

Roy, Ananya. 2003. *City requiem, Calcutta: Gender and the politics of poverty*. Minneapolis: University of Minnesota Press.

Roy, Devparna. 2006. *Adoption paradox of Bt cotton in Gujarat, India*. PhD diss. (Cornell University, Dept. of Development Sociology).

Roy, Devparna, Ronald J. Herring, and Charles C. Geisler. 2007. Naturalizing transgenics: Loose seeds, official seeds, and risk in the decision matrix of Gujarati cotton farmers. *Journal of Development Studies* 43 (1): January.

Rudolph, Lloyd I., and Susanne Hoeber Rudolph. 1987. *In pursuit of Lakshmi: The political economy of the Indian state*. Chicago: University of Chicago Press.

———. 2001. The iconization of Chandrababu: Sharing sovereignty in India's federal market economy. *Economic and Political Weekly* 36: 1546–60 (5-11 May).

Rueschemeyer, Dietrich, Evelyne Huber Stephens, and John D. Stephens. 1992. *Capitalist development and democracy*. Chicago: University of Chicago Press.

Sachs, J., et al., eds. 1999. *India in the era of economic reforms*. New Delhi: Oxford University Press.

Sahai, Suman. 2002. Bt cotton: Confusion prevails. EPW commentary. *Economic and Political Weekly*. 25 May. Posted also on AgBioIndia List, 19 June 2002. http://www.agbioworld.org/.

Samad, Yunas. 1995. *A nation in turmoil: Nationalism and ethnicity in Pakistan, 1937–1958*. Karachi: Oxford University Press.

Samant, S.R. 1998. *Employer's guide to labour laws*. Mumbai: Labour Law Agency.

Sandbrook, Richard, et al. 2006. *Social democracy in the global periphery: Origins, challenges, and prospects*. Cambridge: Cambridge University Press.

Sanyal, Bishwapriya. 1991. Organizing the self-employed: The politics of the urban informal sector. *International Labour Review* 130 (1): 39–56.

Saradamoni, K. 1980. *Emergence of a slave caste*. New Delhi: People's Publishing House.

Sarkar, Sumit. 1997. The decline of the subaltern in Subaltern studies. In Sumit Sarkar, *Writing social history*. Delhi: Oxford University Press.

de Schweinitz, K. 1959. Industrialization, labor controls, and democracy. *Economic Development and Cultural Change* 7 (4): 385–404.

Scoones, Ian. 2005. *Science, agriculture and the politics of policy: The case of biotechnology in India*. Hyderabad: Orient Longman.

———. 2006. *Science, agriculture and the politics of policy*. Hyderabad: Orient Longman.

Scott, James. 1985. *Weapons of the weak: Everyday forms of peasant resistance*. New Haven: Yale University Press.

Sethuraman, S.V. 1976. The urban informal sector: Concepts, measurement and policy. *International Labor Review* 114 (1): 69–81.

Shaheed, Zafar. 1977. *The organisation and leadership of industrial labour in Pakistan (Karachi)*. Unpublished PhD diss. (University of Leeds, Dept. of Politics).

———. 1979. Union leaders, work organization and strikes: Karachi, 1969–72. *Development and Change* 10: 181–204.

———. 1983. Role of government in the development of the labour movement. In Hassan Gardezi and Jamal Rashid, eds. *Pakistan: The roots of dictatorship*. London: Zed Books. 270–90.

Shaik, Sajid. 2001. Farmers decide to defend their Bt gene cotton crops. *The Times of India*. 31 October.

Shantharam, Shanthu. 2005. The brouhaha about Bt-cotton in India. *AgBioView*. 2 May. www.agbioworld.org.

Sharma, Alakh N., and Piush Antony. 2001. *Women workers in the unorganised* sector: The more the merrier? New Delhi: Institute for Human Development.

Sharma, Devinder. 2001. The introduction of transgenic cotton in India. *Biotechnology and Development Monitor* 44: 10–13 (March).

———. 2006. Risks covered up. *The Deccan Herald*. July 31.

Sheth, D.L. 1999a. Secularisation of caste and making of new middle class. *Economic and Political Weekly*. 21–28 August: 2502–10.

———. 1999b. Caste and class: Social reality and political representations. In V.A. Pai Panandiker and Ashis Nandy, eds. *Contemporary India*. New Delhi: Tata McGraw Hill. 337–63.

Shiva, Vandana. 1997. *Biopiracy: The plunder of nature and knowledge*. Boston: South End Press.

———. 1999. Ecological balance in an era of globalization. In Nicholas Low, ed. *Global ethics and environment*. London: Routledge. 47–69.

———. 2006. Resources, rights and regulatory reform. *Context* 3 (1): 85–91 (spring/summer).

Shiva, Vandana, Ashok Emani, Afsar H. Jafri. 1999. Globalization and threat to seed security: Case of transgenic cotton trials in India. *Economic and Political Weekly*. 6-12 and 13-19 March.

Shiva, Vandana, et al. 2000. *Seeds of suicide: The ecological and human costs of globalization of agriculture*. Delhi: Research Foundation for Science, Technology and Ecology.

Shiva, Vandana, and Afsar H. Jafri. 2004. Failure of GMOs in India. *Synthesis/Regeneration* 33 (winter). New Delhi, India: Research Foundation for Science, Technology and Ecology.

Singh, Anil. 2004. Solapur housing project was a big challenge. *Times News Network*, 9 January.

Sinha, Aseema. 2005. *The regional roots of developmental politics in India: A divided leviathan*. Bloomington: Indiana University Press.

Sombart, W. 1976. *Why is there no socialism in the United States?* London: Macmillan.

de Soto, Hernando. 2000. *The mystery of capital: Why capitalism triumphs in the West and fails everywhere else*. New York: Basic Books.

Sridharan, E. 1999. Role of the state and the market in the Indian economy. In V.A. Pai Panandiker and Ashis Nandy, eds. *Contemporary India*. New Delhi: Tata McGraw Hill. 107–36.

———. 2004. The growth and sectoral composition of India's middle classes: Its impact on the politics of liberalization in India. *India Review* 1 (4): 405–28.

Staff Reporter. 1994. Representation for workers in new board sought. *The Hindu*. 16 May: H51.

Staff Reporter. 1999. A better deal for construction workers. *The Hindu*. 27 March: H51.

Staff Reporter. 2002. Construction workers welfare board constituted. *The Hindu*. 25 October.

*Statistical Abstract of the United States, 1949*. Washington, D.C.: U.S. Census Bureau.

Statistical Abstract of the United States, 2004–2005. Washington, D.C.: U.S. Census Bureau.

Stern, N. 2001. *A strategy for development*. Washington, D.C.: The World Bank.

Stiglitz, Joseph E. 2002. *Globalization and its discontents*. New York: W.W. Norton.

Stone, Glenn Davis. 2002. Biotechnology and suicide in India. *Anthropology News*. May.

———. 2007. Agricultural deskilling and the spread of genetically modified cotton in Warangal. *Current Anthropology* 48 (February).

Sundaram, K. 2001. The employment-unemployment situation in India in the 1990s: Some results from the NSS 55th round survey (July 99–June 2000). *Economic and Political Weekly* 34 (11): 931–40.

Tarlo, Emma. 2003. *Unsettling memories: Narratives of the Emergency in India*. Berkeley and Los Angeles: University of California Press.

Tarrow, Sidney. 1998. *Power in movement*. Cambridge: Cambridge University Press.

———. 2005. *The new transnational activism*. Cambridge: Cambridge University Press.

Teitelbaum, Emmanuel. 2006. Was the Indian labor movement ever co-opted? Evaluating standard accounts. *Critical Asian Studies* 38 (4): 389–417.

———. 2007. In the grip of a green giant: How the rural sector defeated organized labor in India. *Comparative Political Studies* 40 (6).

Thorner, Alice. 1982. Semi-feudalism or capitalism? *Economic and Political Weekly* 17 (4): 1961–68.

Tilly, Charles. 1995. Globalisation threatens labor's rights. *International Labor and Working-Class History* 47: 1–23.

———. 1998. *Durable inequality*. Berkeley and Los Angeles: University of California Press.

Tilly, Charles, and Sidney Tarrow. 2006. *Contentious politics*. Boulder, Colo.: Paradigm.

TISS, and YUVA. 1998. Census survey of hawkers on BMC lands. Mumbai: Brihanmumbai Municipal Corporation (BMC).

Trimberger, Ellen Kay. 1979. *Revolution from above: Military bureaucrats and development in Japan, Turkey, Egypt, and Peru*. New Brunswick, N.J.: Transaction.

Unni, Jeemol. 1999. *Urban informal sector: Size and income generation processes in Gujarat*. Ahmedabad: Gujarat Institute of Development Research and Self-Employed Women's Association.

———. 2000. *Gender and informality in the labour market in South Asia*. Ahmedabad: Gujarat Institute of Development Research.

Vaid, K.N., ed. 1999. *Women in construction*. Mumbai: NICMAR Publications Bureau.

Vaidyanathan, A. 2006. Farmers' suicides and the agrarian crisis. *Economic and Political Weekly*. 23 September: 4009.

Vanaik, Achin. 2002. Consumerism and new classes in India. In Sujata Patel, Jasodhara Bagchi, and Krishna Raj, eds. *Thinking social science in India: Essays in honour of Alice Thorner.* New Delhi and Thousand Oaks, Calif.: Sage Publications.

Varma, Pavan. 1998. *The great Indian middle class*. New Delhi: Viking.

Varshney, Ashutosh. 1998. *Democracy, development, and the countryside: Urban-rural struggles in India.* Cambridge: Cambridge University Press.

———. 2002. *Ethnic conflict and civic life: Hindus and Muslims in India*. New Haven: Yale University Press.

Verba, S., K.L. Schlozman, and H. Brady. 1985. *Voice and equality: Civic voluntarism in American politics.* Cambridge: Harvard University Press.

Visvanathan, Shiv, and Chandrika Parmer. 2002. A biotechnology story: Notes from India. *Economic and Political Weekly.* 6 July: 2714–24.

Wade, Robert. 1988. *Village republics: Economic conditions for collective action in South India.* Cambridge: Cambridge University Press.

Wald, Alan. 1987. *The New York intellectuals: The rise and decline of the anti-Stalinist left from the 1930s to the 1980s.* Chapel Hill: University of North Carolina Press.

Waseem, Mohammad. 2002. Causes of democratic downslide. *Economic and Political Weekly* 41 (48): 2–9 November.

Waterston, Albert. 1963. *Planning in Pakistan.* Baltimore, Md.: The Johns Hopkins University Press.

Watt, C.A. 2005. *Serving the nation: Cultures of service, association and citizenship in colonial India.* Delhi: Oxford University Press.

Weeks, John. 1975. Policies for expanding employment in the informal sector of developing countries. *International Labour Review* 111 (1): 1–13.

Weiner, Myron. 1962. *The politics of scarcity: Public pressure and political response in India.* Chicago: University of Chicago Press.

———. 1968. *State politics in India.* Princeton, N.J., Princeton University Press.

———. 1991. *The child and the state in India: Child labor and education policy in comparative perspective.* Princeton, N.J.: Princeton University Press.

———. 2001. The struggle for equality: Caste in Indian politics. In A. Kohli, ed. *The success of India's democracy.* Cambridge: Cambridge University Press.

Western, Bruce. 1995. A comparative study of working-class disorganization: Union decline in eighteen advanced capitalist countries. *American Sociological Review* 60 (2): 179–201.

Wolf, Eric. 1969. *Peasant wars of the twentieth century*. New York: Harper and Row.

Woo-Cumings, Meredith, ed. 1999. *The developmental state*. Ithaca: Cornell University Press.

Wood, Ellen Meiksins. 1986. *The retreat from class.* London: Verso.

Workers Education Research and Welfare Society. 2002. Nijkari ke sub Pakhtunkhwa aur mazdooron par asrat [The privatization of the entire Pakhtun nation and its effect on workers]. Peshawar: WERWS.

World Bank. 1995. *World development report, 1995: Workers in an integrating world*. Washington, D.C.: The World Bank.

———. 2000. *India: Reducing poverty, accelerating development*. New Delhi: Oxford University Press.

———. 2005. *World development report, 2005: A better investment climate for everyone*. Washington, D.C.: The World Bank.

———. 2006. *World Bank development report: Equity and development.* Washington, D.C.: The World Bank and Oxford University Press.

Wright, Erik Olin. 1985. *Classes*. London: Verso.

———. 1997a. *Class counts: Comparative studies in class analysis.* Cambridge: Cambridge University Press.

———. 1997b. Rethinking once again the concept of class structure. In Patrick Joyce and J.R. Hall, eds. *Reworking class.* Ithaca: Cornell University Press.

Yadav, Yogendra. 1999. The BJP's new social bloc: Analysis by CSDS based on the electoral outcome and findings of a nationwide post-election survey. *Frontline.* 19 November.

———. 2000. Understanding the second democratic upsurge. In Francine Frankel, Zoya Hasan, Rajeev Bhargava, and Balveer Arora, eds. *Transforming India.* New Delhi: Oxford.

———. 2004. The elusive mandate of 2004. *Economic and Political Weekly.* 18 December: 5383–95.

Yadav, Yogendra, and Satish Deshpande 2006. Wrong route, right direction. *Times of India.* 31 May.

Young, Robert. 2001. *Postcolonialism: A historical introduction.* Basil Blackwell.

Zaidi, S. Akbar. 2002. The dismal state of social science in Pakistan. *Economic and Political Weekly* 41 (49): 31 August.

❑

# Contributors

**Rina Agarwala** is an assistant professor in the Department of Sociology at Johns Hopkins University. She holds a Ph.D. in sociology and demography from Princeton University, a Masters in Public Policy (M.P.P.) in political and economic development from Harvard University, and a Bachelor of Arts (B.A.) in economics and government from Cornell University. Agarwala has worked at the United Nations Development Program (UNDP) in China, the Self-Employed Women's Association (SEWA) in India, and Women's World Banking (WWB) in New York. Email: agarwala@jhu.edu.

**Christopher Candland,** an assistant professor in the Department of Political Science, Wellesley College (Wellesley, Mass.), received his doctorate from Columbia University and has had research appointments in Indonesia, Pakistan, and India, in addition to the East-West Center (Honolulu) and UC Berkeley. His publications include "The political element in economic reform: Labor institutions and privatization patterns in South Asia," in Linda Cook and Marsha Pripstein Posusney, eds., *Labor and Privatization: Responses and Consequences in Global Perspective* (Edward Elgar, 2004), and *Organized Labor, Democracy, and Development in India and Pakistan* (Routledge, 2006). Email: ccandlan@wellesley.edu.

**Vivek Chibber** is Associate Professor in Sociology at New York University. He is the author of *Locked in Place: State-building and Late Industrialization in India* (Princeton, 2003), which received the American Sociological Association's Barrington Moore Award in 2005. He is working on a project comparing the political economy of development in the nineteenth and twentieth centuries. Email: vivek.chibber@nyu.edu.

**Leela Fernandes** is Associate Professor of Political Science at Rutgers University-New Brunswick. Her most recent book is entitled *India's New Middle Class: Democratic Politics in an Era of Economic Reform* (University of Minnesota Press, 2006). She is also the author of *Producing Workers: The Politics of Gender, Class and Culture in the Calcutta Jute Mills* (University of Pennsylvania Press, 1997) and Transforming Feminist Practice (A. Lute Books, 2003). Email: lfernand@rci.rutgers.edu.

**John Harriss** is an anthropologist, who has researched a wide range of questions bearing on politics and society in India. He is the author, with Stuart Corbridge, of *Reinventing India* (Polity, 2000). For many years a member of the

Development Studies Institute at the London School of Economics he is now director of the School for International Studies at Simon Fraser University, Vancouver. Email: jharriss@sfu.ca.

**Patrick Heller** is Associate Professor of Sociology at Brown University. He is the author of *The Labor of Development* (Cornell University Press, 1999), which explores the role of workers and peasants in the development of the state of Kerala (India), and *Social Democracy in the Global Periphery: Origins and Prospects* (Cambridge University Press, forthcoming), coauthored with Richard Sandbrook, Marc Edelman, and Judith Teichman. His current research explores processes of democratic deepening in South Africa, Brazil, and India. Email: Patrick_Heller@brown.edu.

**Ronald J. Herring** teaches political economy and political ecology at Cornell University, where he has held the John S. Knight Chair of International Relations and served as director of the Mario Einaudi Center for International Studies, chair of the Department of Government, and acting director of the Title VI National Resource Center for South Asia. His earliest academic interests were with land relations: *Land to the Tiller: The Political Economy of Agrarian Reform in South Asia* (Yale and Oxford University, 1983). Current work includes state property in nature, politics of genetically engineered organisms, and connections between economic development and ethnicity. See, for example, *Carrots, Sticks and Ethnic Conflict: Rethinking Development Assistance*, edited with Milton Esman (University of Michigan Press, 2001). Email: rjh5@cornell.edu.

**Emmanuel Teitelbaum** is Assistant Professor of Political Science and International Affairs at the George Washington University in Washington, D.C. His research has been supported by grants from the National Science Foundation, the Fulbright Foundation, and the Social Science Research Council. He is currently writing a series of articles and a book on the political economy of labor in South Asia. Email: ejt@gwu.edu.

# Index

Abdul Kalam, A.P.J. (Former president of India) 103
activists 136, 140
*adivasis* ("tribals") 6
Africa 24
African socialism 31
African studies 30
Agarwala, R. 1–24, 50, 91, 91–108, 126
agrarian question 16–19
agrarian studies 31
Ahmedabad 131
air pollution 113
Algerian F.L.N. 30
Ali, K. 83
All India Bidi and Cigar Workers Federation 99—100
All India Trade Union Congress (AITUC) 53; affiliated to Communist Party of India (CPI) 60
All Pakistan Confederation of Labor (APCOL) 83
All-India Democratic Women's Association (AIDWA) 122
Allende, S. 30, 32
Alliance for Restoration of Democracy 90
Althusser, L. 40
Ambedkar, B.R. 3
Anderson, P. 28
Andhra Pradesh 138
Andhra Pradesh Coalition in Defence of Diversity 128
Anglo-American scholarship; Gramsci's influence 40
Anglo-American universities 34
anti-biotechnology movement 143
anticommunist alliances 82
Appadurai, A. 122
Argentina 133
Azad Mazdoor Federation 86
Backward Castes 18
Bahujan Samaj Party (BSP) 164
*bandh* ("strike") 63
Bangalore 117, 120, 123, 164
Bangalore Agenda Task Force 118, 120
Bangalore's Public-Private Partnerships (PPPs) 118
Bangladesh (creation of) 78
Baran, P. 28
Bardham, P.K. 14, 15, 150
Basic Democrats under Field Marshal Ayub Khan 75
basic needs, access to 113
Benton, L. 92
Bhagidari Scheme of the Delhi Government 118, 124
Bharat 130–3
Bharatiya Janata Party (BJP) 4
Bharatiya Kamgar Sena (BKS) affiliated to Shi Sena 60
Bharatiya Mazdoor Sangh (BMS) affiliated to Bharatiya Janata Party (BJP) 60
Bhopal 133
Bhutto, Z.A. 85, 87; government 78
Bidi and Cigar Workers Conditions of Employment Act 100
Bidi industry 99–100
Bidi Welfare Board 105; housing project 101
Bidi Worker's Welfare Cess and Fund Act 105
*bija yatra* (seed march ) 130
biological pollution 128, 139
*Biopiracy: The Plunder of Nature and Knowledge* (Shiva, V.) 135
biotechnology, horrors of 142
Birmingham University's Centre for Cultural Studies 40
Bogotá 6

Bollgard hybrids 129
bollworms 144; management of, 136; "bollworm rampage" of 2001 in Gujarat 137
Bombay 6
Bourdieu, P. 149, 157, 160, 164; analysis of class structures 159; habitus 161
bourgeoise 149
Brady, H. 113
Brahmin dominance 119
Brass, P. 32
Brazil 45, 133
British colonialism in Africa 31
brokerage; cultural capital and authenticity rents 140–2
Bt cotton 127, 136; seeds 7; banning of 17; hybrids 129; in Andhra Pradesh 137
Building and Other Construction Workers' Welfare Cess Act 105
*Bulletin of Concerned Asian Scholars* 30
"Bullock capitalists" (Rudolph, L.and S.) 17
Burawoy, M. 40
bureaucratic-managerial-intellectual elite 150
Byers, T. 17, 31

Calcutta 164
Campaign for the Right to Education 125
Campaign for the Right to Information 125
campus radicalism 35–8
"Can Class Analysis Be Salvaged?" (Grusky and Sorensen) 14
Candland, C. 21, 68, 73–90
capitalism 44
capitalist class 110
Cartagena Protocol on Biosafety 127
caste 11–14; in South India 11
caste theory 13
Castells, M. 92
Castro, F. 32
Center for Indian Trade Unions (CITU) affiliation with Communist Party of India-Marxist (CPI-M) 60
Center for the Study of Developing Societies (CSDS) 158
Chandhoke, N. 125
Chatterjee, P. 40, 116
Chayanov, A.V.; Russian economist 16
Chayanovian self-exploitation 17
Chennai 98, 117, 119, 123
Chennai's Bidi Union 106
Chibber, V. 5, 24–49, 53
Chile 30
China 13, 51, 129, 132, 133, 136
Chinese version of BT cotton 133
Chopra, R. 161
Christian mobilizational movements 119
Chundra, K.; castes in Uttar Pradesh 12
citizens' rights 101
citizens and the state 113
citizenship 20, 117, 124
CITU Mumbai Bidi Union 103
CIVIC (Citizens Voluntary Initiative for the City) 117
civil society 123; analyzing 109; in Bangalore and Chennai 109; and class relations 113; participation 117–22; and political society 116
class analysis 3, 19, 43, 91; decline 24, 42; displacement of 26; New Left 36; of Indian agriculture 31; in South Asian Studies 24–49; in U.S. Academy 27–9
class analytics 1, 2, 146; bias in interview data 68; and caste 111; decline 1, 47; differences 1; mobilization 6; politics 95; strategy 18; structure 9; struggle 97
caste everyday practices of 160
class formation; Jerala and West Bengal 22
class inequality absence (Guha) 10
class interests in genetic engineering 136–40
class in practice 161–3
class relations and civil society in Indian Cities 109–26
class relationships and the city 110–13
class-in-itself; Marx 8
class-of-itself (Marx) 23
Orientalism 32
cold war 82
colonial institutions of government 81
colonial and postcolonial literature study 35
Communist Party of India (CPI) 102
Communist Party of India-Marxist (CPI-M) 6, 60
Communist Party of India-Marxist-Leninist (CPI-ML) 100
Communist Party of Pakistan 83
Congress Party 5, 152; hegemony of 13; motivations of 63
construction workers' union 100
contemporary Indian politics 146
Convention of Biological Diversity at UN 142
Corbridge, S. 150

core cultural values 157
cotton hybrids 129
Crouch, H. 69
Cry1Ac gene 139
Cry1Ac transgene 135
Cuban Revolution 30
cultivars and traits 138
cultural capital 110, 111

Dalits 6, 119
Darwin, C. 11
Deccan Development Society 13, 138, 142; study of Bt cotton 130
Defence of Pakistan Rules 84
definitions "to think with" 110, 111
Delhi 102, 109, 113, 114, 123, 136, 164
Delhi's biosafety regulations 134
Delhi's economic interventionist policies 15
depressed classes 124
Desai, Dr. D.B.; CEO of Navbharat Seeds 135
Deshpande, S. 152; analytical procedure 110
Deve Gowda , H.D.; prime minister 104
developmental-state theory; Japan (Chalmers Johnson's work) 15
*dharmic* law 12
dominant proprietary classes (Bardhan) 14
Dow Chemical 133
Dréze, J. 51
Dumont 42
Durkheimian framework 42

East Bengal riots 83
Eastern Europe (Ost) 4
*Economic Approach to Human Behavior* (Becker); Nobel Prize 7
education access to 162
education level and employment 96
educational field in India 161
Egypt 87
elections in India (2004) 4, 158
electoral democracy 155
Elster, J. 2; class location 2; Orientalist assumptions 7
England 26
Enterprise unions 60
epistemological relativism 4
epistemology 8
Essential Services Maintenance Act 82
ethnic mobilization and working class organization 79
Europe 5, 154
European discourse on transgenics 131
Exnora International 120
exploitation 3
exploitation defined (Wright) 3

Factory Act (1926) 98
Faislabad 80
family peasantry 154
family welfare 105
farmer organizations (Nanjundaswamy's KRRS) 18
farmers' movements 9
Femia, J. 40
Fernandes, L. 9, 146–65
food aid from United States 143
Forum for Biotechnology and Food Security 28
Frank, T. 9
Frankel, F.R. 51; book on post-independence politics 31
free-market fundamentalism 25
free-market ideology 24
Freedom of Association and Protection of the Right to Organize Convention 82
Frelimo in Mozambique 30
*Frontier* 44
fundamentalist organizations 6
fusion genes 129

Gandhi, I. 43
Gandhi, M. 3
Gandhinagar 15
Gene Campaign leader Sahai, S. 134
gene use restriction technology (GURT) 133
genetic engineering 127; in agriculture 13
Genetic Engineering Approval Committee in Delhi 129
genetically modified organism (GMO) 127
genocidal seeds 21
global culture 157
Global South 34
globalization 18, 91, 140, 144; and transgenics 130
Golden Rice 133
Gooptu, N.; work on North Indian Cities 111
Gopalan, A.K. 100
governance via circuits 164
government aids 16
Government of India Act (1935) 81
government statistics on unions 55

Gramsci, A. 27, 151; concepts 39; influence in Anglo-American scholarship 40
Great Britain 24
Great Terminator-Technology Hoax (India) science 133–6; science and class 127–45
Green Revolution 16
Greenpeace 128, 140
Griffin, K. 31
Gross Domestic Product (GDP) 5
Gross National Product (GNP) 5
growth obstacles 65
Grusky, D. 14
Guevara, C. 32
Guha, R. 40; absence of class inequality 10
Gujarat 5, 13, 129, 131, 134
Gujranwala 80
Gupta, A. 131
Gupta, R.K. 1

habitus 159
Hansen, A. 32
Harriss, J. 7, 13, 15, 31, 109–26, 150
Harriss-White, B. 31
*hartal* 63
Haryana 102
Haveri 131
hawker menace 164
health care access 113
hegemonic aspirations 146–65
hegemonic bourgeoise 146
hegemony 40
*Hegemony and Socialist Strategy* (Laclau and Mouffe) 40
Heller, P. 9, 146–65
Herring, R.J. 1–24, 7, 21, 31, 127–45
higher education; United States 27
Hindu ideology's focus 11
Hindu nationalism 148, 153
Hinduism Great Tradition of 157
Hindutva 147, 153, 155; cultural politics of 155; hegemonic project limits 158; ideology 153; and liberalization 156 as a mass strategy 45; movement 159; politics 157; rise and limits 165
Hoffman, K.; informal worker 93
hostility to science 143
human capital 161
human rights 124
human and women's rights activists 88
humanities; postmodernist theory 8
Hyderabad 80

identity politics 6, 37
ideological or cultural indoctrination 40
ideology: old-style 33; in Pakistan 89
*Illicit: How Smugglers, Traffickers and Copycats Are Hijacking the Global Economy* (Naim) 132
*Imagining India* (Inden) 42
imperialist science 4
Inden, R. 42
India 24; economic reforms 92; genetic engineering 128; new class movement 91–108; transgenic grains 140
India and Pakistan union strength 76
India as satellite 42–7
India Shining 4, 157
Indian Administrative Service (IAS) 162
Indian agriculture; class analysis 31
Indian cities 109
Indian class literature 95
Indian exceptionalism in social science 12
Indian farmers 127
Indian government 1, 56
Indian Independence 53
Indian labor movement 50–72
Indian labor studies 52, 68
*Indian Labour Yearbook* 57
Indian Marxism 44
Indian National Congress 53
Indian National Trade Union Congress (INTUC) 53; affiliated to Congress Party 6
Indian National Trinamool Trade Union Congress (INTTUC) affiliated to Trinamool Congress 60
Indian scholarship in Anglo-American universities 38
India's bidi and construction industries 101
India's industrialization strategy compared with China's 51
India's informal workers and class structure 94
India's liberal democracy 154
India's middle class 161
India's New Middle Class (NMC) democracy 146; durability of caste 154–60; perspective 146–55
India's NMC politics 150
India's political and economic development 50
India's political mobilization literature class 95–7
indigenous Bt 131
Indira Gandhi's Emergency 152

Indonesia 132
Industrial Conflict trends 65–7
Industrial disputes, volume in India 66
Industrial Disputes Act (1947) 53, 63, 64, 67
Industrial Disputes Act (1959) 82
industrial protest in India 52
industrial relations 63, 64
Industrial Relations Ordinance 78, 84–5
informal labor 91
informal laborers 9
informal proletariat 94
informal sector 92
informal sector industries (bidi and construction) 98
informal workers: as a class 93–5, 98–107; and class structure in India 94; defined 92; identity 105
Informal Workers' Welfare Boards 102
informal workers' movement 108
informal workers' organizations 101
informal working class 110, 111, 125
intellectual property 136
interference by political parties 63
International Confederation for Free Trade Unions (ICFTU) 79, 83
INTUC (Indian National Trade Union Congress) 53, 70
ISAAA (International Service for the Acquisition of Agri-biotech Applications) 138, 179
Islamic state 89
IT sector 112

Jafri, A.H. 130
Janaagraha 117
Japan 87
Jawaharlal Nehru University (JNU) 43
Jinnah, M.A. 81, 82
JK Seeds 129
Joshi, S. 135
*Journal of Peasant Studies* 31

Kapur, D. 162
Karachi 80
Karnataka 13, 76, 127; decentralization of urban governance in 119
Karnataka and Bengal (Kohli) 13
Karnataka Rajya Raitha Sangha (Karnataka State Farmers' Organization, KRRS) 128
Kaviraj, S. 150
Kenya debate 31
Kerala 13, 58, 66, 102
Kerala and West Bengal class formation 22
Kerala's Communist-Marxist Party 100
Khan, A.; declaration of martial law 82
Khan, Field Marshal M.A. 77, 83, 84, 86
Khan, General Y.84
Khan, N. (deputy marshal law administrator) 84
Khobragade , U. 103
Kisan (peasant) Co-ordinating Committee 128
KKNSS (Karnataka Kolageri Nivasigala Samyuktha Sanghatana ) 118
Kochanek, S. 32
Kohli, A.; work on Karnataka and Bengal 13
Kolkatta Communist Construction Union 106
Kolkatta/West Bengal 98
Kothari 150
Krishna, A.; survey on North Indian villages 12

labor 110; permanent co-optation 53–65
labor movement fragmented 55
labor movement model alternative; informal workers 107
labor organizers in Pakistan 75
labor repression 85
Laclau, E. 40
Ladies' Clubs 122
Lahore 80
land reforms 84
landless workers 137
landlordism; semi-feudal 16
Latin America 24, 32, 109, 154
*Latin American Perspectives* 30
Latin American studies 30, 33
Latin America's dominant classes 93
Lenin, V.I. 27, 93
Lewis, W.A. 83
liberal hegemony 154
liberalization 91, 157; benefits and virtues of 150
life chances 1
Linz, J.J. 155
Llyalpur 80
local influentials; *pradhans* 117
local politics of democracy 163–4
Luebbert, G. 154
Luxemburg, R. 27, 93

McCarthyism 28
Machiavelli, N. 86
Madhya Pradesh 102

Mahalingappa, S. 11
Maharashtra 13, 58, 67, 100, 134, 156
Maharashtra State Housing and Area Development Authority 103
Mahila Milan; women's organization 122
Mahyco-Monsanto Biotech (MMB) 129
Mahyco-Monsanto Bollgard MECH–162 controlled study 139
Mahyco-Monsanto hybrids 128; price reductions for technology fees 132; seeds 139
*Mainstream* 44
Malaysia 10
Malik, A.; Minister of Labour 83
Mandal Commission 45
Maoist rebels; Nepal 1
Maoist-influenced Naxalite movement 16
market triumphalism 4
Marx; class-in-itself 8
Marx, K. 4, 8, 10
Marxian analysis 4
Marxian and Weberian class analysis 2
Marxism's decline 24, 27, 45
Marxist historian school and political economists in India 38–9
Marxist theory 27, 36
Marxists in South Asian studies 26
methodological positivism 7
Mexico City 109, 113, 114
middle class 20, 110, 117; activism 109–26, 123–6; defined 110; growing 1; illiberalism 147; liberalism 165; politics 154; reaction 154
migrant labor force 80
military and elections 84
military and workers organizations 86
Ministry of Labor 56
Mirza, I. (first president of Pakistan) 77
modern stratification theory 14
Moore, B. 12
Mouffe, C. 40
Mozambique 30
*muhajir* 79
multiplicity myth 54–61
Mumbai 100, 122, 164
Mumbai bidi union 102
Mumbai/Maharashtra 98
Muslim League 79
Muttahida Labour Federation 86
Myers, C. 62

Nadu Slum Dwellers' Rights Movement 120
Nair, J. 120, 122
Nanjundaswamy; Professor 144; and KRRS 18
Nath seeds 129
National Contract Labor Act 100
National Sample Survey Organisation of India 92
nativism; social basis 33–8
Navbharat (151) 134
Navbharat seeds 129, 131, 135
Navelkar, S.; lawyer 100
Naxalbari 44
Naxalism 18
Naxalite movement 1
Nehruvian ideology of developmentalism 152
Nehruvian modernist project 150
Nehruvian period, middle classes 155
Nehruvian project 155
Nehruvian state 152
neoclassical development strategies 83
neoliberal reforms 20
neoliberalism 25; as *doxa* 157; as political project 24
Nepal; Maoist rebels 1
New Left 28, 29, 31, 36
New Left intelligentsia 48
New Middle Class. *See* India's New Middle Class.
new social movements 144
New York City 6
next generation 47
Nirman Mazdoor Panchayat Sangh (construction workers' union) 120
Nisbett, N.; employment in IT industry 112
Non-Resident Indians (NRI) 117
nonagricultural labor force 73
nongovernmental organizations (NGOs) 6, 7, 21, 98, 114, 124
North Chennai Christian network 120
North Indian villages survey (Krishna) 12
Nyerere, J. 31

OBCS (Other Backward Castes) 153, 163
O'Connor, A.; working poor 111
O'Donnell, G. 31
Omvedt, G. 31
Operation Cremate Monsanto 7, 127–45
opportunity and mobility 150
organized labor in political arena 67–8
organization of poor women 120
Orientalism 23, 32
Orissa 76
Ost, D.; writing on Eastern Europe 4

Pakistan 5, 21; elite class 89; ideology 89; and India union strength 76; labor organizers 75; Ministry of Labour; Manpower and Overseas Pakistanis 76; Peoples Party 85; Rules Defence 84; working class power 22; working class solidarity 74; workers' organizations 73–90
Pakistani and Indian Union Growth 77
Pakistan's female workers 74
Pakistan's Movement for Restoration of Democracy 90
Parivar, S. 153, 157
partition: of British India 79; and migration 79
partnerships between residents'welfare associations and government 8
Pathan workers 80
Patkar, R.; CITU Mumbai Bidi Union 103
peasant economy (Chayanov) 16
Penn Uramai Iyyakkam 120, 122
Peoples' Health Movement 125
*Perspectives from Below* (Assayag) 134
*Persuit of Lakshmi* (Rudolph) 33
Peru 87
Pinstrup-Anderson, P. 144
piracy of computer software 132
Polanyi, K. 154
political dynamics 1
Political illiberalism and New Middle Class 156–9
political interference 61–5
politically engineered strikes 62
politics accommodation in Maharashtra and Karnataka 13; informal working class 109
Ponticherry 102
Portes, A. 92; informal worker 93
postcolonial theory 24
postcolonial Pakistan 81
post-fordist era 4
postindependence ideal 1
postindependence incorporation of labor 53–65
post-Marxist theorizing 40
postmodernist theory; humanities 8
post-structuralism 5; and postcolonial theory (PSPC) 24
poverty reduction 1
*Practicing Earth Democracy* (Shiva) 130
privatization of services 113
proletariat and bourgeoisie (Marx) 14
property; patents; and power 130–3
protest movements, failure of 127
Przeworski, A. 40
PSPC 25, 33, 41, 3739; Marxism's decline 43; onslaught 29; phenomenon 24; theorists 47
public authority hallowing 164
public tribunals (*bij panchayat*) 128
Public Affairs Centre (PAC) 117
Punjab; United Province 79

Rahman, G. (president of Pakistan Workers' Confederation) 86
Rajasthan 67
Ramaswamy, E.A. 52, 54, 61, 62, 68
Rashtriya Swayamsevak Sangh (RSS) family organizations 156
Ratnagar, R. 99
recovering class 19–24
redistribution 25
reserve army of labor (Marx) 97
responsible unionism (Crouch) 69
restoring agency to class 1–24
*Review of African Political Economy* 30
revolutions from above (Trimberger) 87
right to employment 125
right to food 125
Right to Organize and Collective Bargaining Convention 82
rights representation and the poor 109
Roman Catholic Church 154
Roy, M.N. 83
Rudolph, L.I., and Rudolph, S.H. 17, 54, 58, 61–3
Rural Advancement Foundation International (RAFI) of Canada 133
rural mobilization 16
Russia 132

Sahai, S.; Gene Campaign leader 134
Said, E. 39
Samad, Y. 78
Sangh Parivar 45, 158
Sanjy Gandhi's use of authoritarian state practices 152
São Paulo 109, 114
Satheesh, P.V. 135
Schlozman, K.L. 113
Scott, J. *Weapons of the Weak* 10
SEATO 73; Pakistan's membership in 79
*Seeds of Suicide* (Shiva et al.) 130, 134
semi-feudal landlordism 16
Sen, A. 51
Sena, S. 156
Shakespeare, W. 11
Sharma, D. 135; New Delhi 128

Shetkari Sanghatana (Agriculturalist Association) 128, 135
Shiva, V. 7, 128, 130, 142
Sindh Industrial and Trading Estates protest 85
Singh, M.; prime minister 1
Sinha, A. 15
slum areas (*jhuggi jhopris*) 114
slum dwellers 116
social capital 7; accumulation 162
*Social Origins of Dictatorship and Democracy* (Moore) 12
socialist ideology 30
Sons of Soil movements 156
Sorensen, J. 14
South Africa 45
South Asia scholarship 24, 34
South Asian studies 1; peculiarity 30–3
South Chennai advocacy associations 121
South Korea 45
Southeast Asian Treaty Organization. *See* SEATO.
Southern Telengana 137
Sri Lanka 5
Sridharan, E. 156
state intervention 64
state legislatures (Sabhas) 67
Stepan, A.G. 155
Stone, G. 134, 138
strategy of maximum profits (Lewis) 83
stratification of organizations 117
struggle against the state 101
subaltern 111
Subaltern Studies 24, 38–42
subcontinent 1
suicide seed 21; coalition 128, 132
Swat textile mill 86
Syaloinism 28

Tamil Nadu 13, 102, 121; state government 103Tamil Nadu Construction Board 102
Tamil Nadu Construction Workers Union (TNCWU) 104
Tamil Nadu Slum Dwellers' Rights Movement 119
Tanzanian experiment 31
Teitelbaum, E. 50–72
terminator gene 133
Thatcher's assault on higher education 46
*The Development of Capitalism in Russia* (Lenin) 16
*The Economist* 132
*The Great Indian Middle Class* (Varma) 123
*The Ones Who Stayed Behind* (Guha) 141
*The Worker and His Union* (Ramaswamy) 50
Tilly, C. 160
trade unions 97, 111. *See also* unions
Trade Unions Act 98
Trade Unions Act (1926) 55
Trade-Related Intellectual Property Rights (TRIPs) 9
transformation of area studies 29–30
transgenic cottons India and China 130
transgenic hybrid (NB151) 135
Trimberger, E.K. 87
Trotsky, L. 27
Trust and Societies Act 99
Turkey 87

Ukraine 132
ul Haq, M. 84
ul Haq, General Z. 78, 86–7
Union Councilors under General Pervez Musharraf 75
unions: categorized 59; government statistics 55; membership in India 55, 76; structure 58
United States 5, 24, 26, 111, 113; Communist Party 28; elections 4; Federation of Labor-Confederation of Industrial Organizations (AFL-CIO) 79; food aid 143; foreign policy 90; higher education 27; increases in higher education 34; withdrawal from Vietnam 44
Unorganised Workers' Federation 120
untouchable (*avarna*) status 11
urban bias 130–3
urban poor and working class 111
urban services, access to 113
Uttar Pradesh castes (Chundra) 12
Uttarakhand forest mobilization 10

Verba, S. 113
Via Campesina 128
Vietnam 30, 132, 133; U.S. withdrawal 44
violence and crime 113
Vishva Hindu Parishad (VHP) 153

Washington consensus 5
Washington, D.C. 136
Watt, C.A. 123
*Weapons of the Weak* (Scott) 10
Weber, M. 8
Weberian and Marxian class analysis 2

Weiner, M. 32, 161
West Bengal 5, 6, 58, 66, 67, 76; and Kerala class formation 22
Western science 4
*What's the Matter With Kansas?* (Frank) 10
Women's micro-finance organizations 6
women's movements 122
Women's Voice 118
worker identity card 106
workers' organizations in Pakistan 73–90
workers' struggle 98
workers and workers' organizations 73
working class 110; political and economic development 50; solidarity in Pakistan 74
working class organizations 36; suppression 87
working poor 111; politics 123–6
Workmen's Compensation Act (1923) 98
World Bank 158; survey 67
*World Development Report* (World Bank) 124
World Trade Organisation (WTO) rulings 9
Wright, E.O. 8, 40, 154; defines exploitation 3

Yadev, Y. 147; analysis of poll data 153

Zakat Committees under General Zia ul Haq 75
Zambia 140
Zimbabwe 140